D0062502

DEVELOPED AT THE
UNIVERSITY OF WASHINGTON
SCHOOL OF MEDICINE

EDITED BY
DAVID W. SMITH, M.D.
Professor of Pediatrics
University of Washington School of Medicine

EDWIN L. BIERMAN, M.D.
Professor in Internal Medicine
University of Washington School of Medicine

THE
BIOLOGIC
AGES
OF MAN

from
conception
through old age

1973

W. B. SAUNDERS COMPANY

PHILADELPHIA • LONDON • TORONTO

W. B. Saunders Company: West Washington Square
                           Philadelphia, Pa.   19105

                           12 Dyott Street
                           London, WC1A   1DB

                           833 Oxford Street
                           Toronto 18, Ontario

THE BIOLOGIC AGES OF MAN   ISBN 0-7216-8423-8

Print No: 9   8   7   6   5   4   3   2   1

*To students: may they enhance
the quality of life
for their patients.*

CONTRIBUTORS

EDWIN L. BIERMAN, M.D., Professor of Medicine, University of Washington School of Medicine; Head, Division of Metabolism and Gerontology, University Hospital and Veterans Administration Hospital; Attending Physician, Harborview Medical Center and Veterans Administration Hospital, Seattle.

DOUGLAS DER YUEN, M.D., Instructor, Department of Obstetrics & Gynecology, University of Washington; Attending Physician, University Hospital, Seattle.

SHERREL L. HAMMAR, M.D., Chairman and Professor, Department of Pediatrics, University of Hawaii School of Medicine; Chief of Pediatrics, Kauikeolani Children's Hospital, Honolulu.

WILLIAM R. HAZZARD, M.D., Associate Professor of Medicine, University of Washington School of Medicine; Attending Physician, Harborview Medical Center, University Hospital, Seattle.

ALAN W. HODSON, M.D., Associate Professor, Department of Pediatrics; Head, Division of Neonatal Biology, University of Washington, Seattle.

VANJA A. HOLM, M.D., Assistant Professor, Department of Pediatrics, University of Washington School of Medicine; Attending Physician, University Hospital, Children's Orthopedic Hospital and Medical Center, Harborview Medical Center, Seattle.

JAMES W. M. OWENS, M.D., Clinical Associate Professor, University of Washington School of Medicine; Attending Physician, Children's Orthopedic Hospital, University of Washington Hospital, Seattle.

DAVID W. SMITH, M.D., Professor, Department of Pediatrics, Head, Dysmorphology Unit, University of Washington School of Medicine, Seattle.

KENT UELAND, M.D., Associate Professor, Department of Obstetrics & Gynecology, University of Washington School of Medicine; Director of Obstetrics, University Hospital; Attending Obstetrician-Gynecologist, Harborview Medical Center, U.S. Public Health Service Hospital, Seattle.

BEVERLY VANDER VEER, Ph.D., Associate, Department of Pediatrics, University of Washington School of Medicine; Staff Psychologist, Clinical Training Unit, Child Development Mental Retardation Center, University of Washington, Seattle.

RICHARD P. WENNBERG, M.D., Assistant Professor, Department of Pediatrics, Division of Neonatal Biology, University of Washington School of Medicine, Seattle.

WALDEMAR H. WENNER, M.D., Assistant Professor, Department of Pediatrics, University of Washington School of Medicine; University of Washington Hospital, Children's Orthopedic Hospital, Seattle.

NICHOLAS ANTHONY WILTZ, Jr., Ph.D., Instructor, and Psychologist, Department of Pediatrics, University of Washington School of Medicine, Seattle.

DAVID E. WOODRUM, M.D., Assistant Professor, Department of Pediatrics, Division of Neonatal Biology, University of Washington School of Medicine, Seattle.

PREFACE

The purpose of this text is to provide an integrated portrayal of human life from conception through old age. The changing nature of the life situation, the common disorders, and the needs for health maintenance are considered for each of the seven biologic ages of man. Initial presentations on the biology of growth, the biology of aging, and preparation for new life, in addition to a concluding consideration of death and dying are presented to provide an even more comprehensive view of life. The appendix contains graphs and charts on some of the data that are pertinent to more than one of the seven life stages.

This primary book was designed to offer a basic framework of knowledge about the whole human being at all ages. The student should be able to interweave into this framework the in-depth knowledge on particular organ systems, diseases, and disorders. Beyond being of value in the basic learning process, this approach may enhance the likelihood that the health professional will view any health disorder in the total context of the life stage of the patient.

DAVID W. SMITH, M.D.

EDWIN L. BIERMAN, M.D.

ACKNOWLEDGMENTS

We wish to acknowledge the following colleagues who contributed toward Chapter Ten, Old Age: Carl Eisdorfer, M.D., Professor of Psychiatry, Caroline E. Preston, M.D., Associate Professor of Psychiatry, and Nathaniel N. Wagner, Ph.D., Professor of Psychology.

Mrs. Phyllis Wood of the University of Washington Department of Medical Illustration drew the illustration on the cover, as well as many of those, including charts, within the text. The assistance of the University of Washington Medical Photography group is also acknowledged.

The secretarial and editorial assistance of Mrs. Diane Frankel is most gratefully appreciated.

The library research of Mrs. Lyle Harrah is greatly appreciated, particularly with regard to Chapters One, Three, and Four.

CONTENTS

CHAPTER ONE

GROWTH 1

David W. Smith

CHAPTER TWO

BIOLOGY OF AGING 17

Edwin L. Bierman and William R. Hazzard

CHAPTER THREE

PREPARATION FOR NEW LIFE 26

David W. Smith

CHAPTER FOUR

PRENATAL LIFE AND THE PREGNANT WOMAN 32

David W. Smith and Douglas Der Yuen

CHAPTER FIVE

PERINATAL LIFE FOR THE MOTHER AND BABY 62

Labor and Delivery 62

Kent Ueland

The Perinate 70

Richard P. Wennberg, David E. Woodrum and W. Alan Hodson

CHAPTER SIX

INFANCY: THE FIRST TWO YEARS 85

Waldemar H. Wenner and Beverly Vander Veer

CHAPTER SEVEN

CHILDHOOD 105

Vanja A. Holm and Nicholas A. Wiltz

CHAPTER EIGHT

ADOLESCENCE 139

S. L. Hammar and J. W. M. Owens

CHAPTER NINE

ADULTHOOD, ESPECIALLY THE MIDDLE YEARS 154

Edwin L. Bierman and William R. Hazzard

CHAPTER TEN

OLD AGE, INCLUDING DEATH AND DYING.................. 171

Edwin L. Bierman and William R. Hazzard

APPENDIX 191

INDEX 203

INTRODUCTION

Life is an ever-changing process, a moving picture rather than a series of snapshots. Projection of each frame of a motion picture may be useful in analyzing details of the whole film. In this volume we have attempted such a sequential analysis, beginning with the origin of life, conception, and ending with the final event, death. The most meaningful interpretation of these chapters will be made by the reader who resynthesizes the contents into the continuum of events which is life. And the optimal application of this knowledge by the thoughtful health professional will require a comparison between the general characterization of life sketched in this volume and the particular patient whose life is under examination. For the individual human being with a unique set of internal and external environmental circumstances is still the central figure in the effective delivery of health care.

WILLIAM R. HAZZARD

The Biologic Ages—A Pictorial Overview

The ten photographs which follow present a brief over-view of the life stages of one individual, Mrs. Myrtle Larson, from early childhood to her present age of 77 years. Mrs. Larson (a very healthy individual) is the mother of Mrs. Phyllis Wood, the illustrator of this book. The photographs and the accompanying text were most graciously supplied by Mrs. Larson. It is hoped that this pictorial biography, with its revealing age-related changes, will provide the reader with a more human perspective toward *The Biologic Ages of Man.*

Age 2 years.

I was born in 1896 in Juneau, Alaska. We moved to Skagway, where my father died when I was four years old. He died of a ruptured appendix. My mother left me with some friends when she went to the hos-pital and I can still remember how hard I cried and could not be consoled. His obitu-ary said he was a loving and indulgent father.

We had been to Europe for six months the year before he died and my parents had gone to a fortuneteller—maybe on a lark (they were good church people)—and my father was told he would be killed the next year by a gray-haired man with a knife. Al-though he may not have believed it, he bought more life insurance.

He was in agony with the ruptured appendix and was operated on in the middle of the night by a gray-haired doctor; his own doc-tor was out of town. There was no penicillin in 1901.

Age 6 years.

My mother's first interest was always my sister and myself. After my father's death we moved to Seattle, where we lived on a lake. We had a rowboat and would row all around the lake. I later was on the women's crew at the Uni-versity of Washington.

Age 11 years.

My mother married again when I was eleven. We were always good friends, but my stepfather never had anything to say about my upbringing. My mother never forgot her great love for my father.

At this age I fell from a teeter-totter at school and dislocated my left shoulder, and a doctor pulled it back in place.

Age 14 years.

My adolescence was quite normal with lots of activity, including tennis. I began to think I was smarter than my mother, which, of course, I wasn't. She was kind and gentle.

I had my teeth straightened when I was in High School. I also had my tonsils removed, after having them clipped twice at 5 and 10 years of age, in the old-fashioned way.

Age 21 years.

This was taken on board a cruise ship to Juneau, where I visited friends and climbed to the top of Mount Juneau with young friends.

On the way back to Seattle my fiancé met the boat in Vancouver. He soon left for overseas, World War I. He returned a second lieutenant. Half of his machine-gun battalion had been killed. We were married March 10, 1920.

Age 30 years.

We always wanted children, and our first child, a daughter, was born a year and three months after we were married; another daughter, Phyllis, two years and four months later, and then a son, four years and two months later.

We always enjoyed our children.

Age 44 years.

I was busy—golf at the Country Club, president of our Orthopedic Guild for the Children's Orthopedic Hospital, Ladies of Kiwanis, et cetera.

Age 49 years.

Our 25th wedding anniversary. My husband always encouraged me in everything I did—generous in every way.

One Christmas I had pleurisy.

Age 69 years.

We moved to California in 1960. My husband died in 1967. He was in the hospital a year and three months. I visited him every day.

My throat had bothered me off and on since our move to California, apparently related to some nodules of tonsil which were left over when my tonsils were removed. There was some concern as to whether these nodules were a tumorous growth. I had x-rays taken and never did find out if my nodules looked O.K. or not. My internal medicine doctor wanted me to have my throat operated on by the same surgeon who had performed a gastric resection and also a hernia operation on my husband. I said, "Shouldn't I see a throat specialist?" He said, "What did you come to me for?" Needless to say, I didn't have the operation. This was ten years ago. I knew what he was going to say afterwards if I'd had it done—"Aren't we lucky it wasn't malignant?"

Age 76 years.

In 1972, all of a sudden, my back acted up—it killed me to get up or sit down. I finally got a doctor (most doctors here won't take a new patient). He took several x-rays, gave me some medicine, and the next day I was fine again. Did he help me or did it run its course?

One thing we don't like is when the first thing a doctor says is, "How old are you?" He might as well say, "Don't you know you have to start having something that's going to kill you?"

We have to keep our sense of humor and enough money so we can be independent.

We know death is a part of living, or rather the end of living, and I try to keep it that way—and live while I live.

I have just returned from three days at Disneyland with my son and grandchildren.

I swim half an hour every day in the large heated pool here at the apartment and end up with five minutes in the 108° whirlpool. I golf one day a week and enjoy an occasional trip to Las Vegas and the horse races.

CHAPTER ONE

GROWTH

DAVID W. SMITH

The unicellular organism is able to utilize its entire genome, and multiplies immortally at a rate which is dependent upon the environment. The multicellular organism evolves from a single cell with a programmed system of constraints on development and growth. Constraints are placed on the portion of the genome which will be active in a particular cell type, thus accounting for differentiation. There are also constraints on the rate of cell division of specific cells, thereby regulating cell number and growth. These control mechanisms normally carry the organism through a harmoniously channeled sequence of development. The rate of this process and thereby the time required to achieve the mature adult form is variable. The stage an individual is in at a particular time may be referred to as "biologic age."

BASICS OF GROWTH

Control over Mitotic Rate. Though cell size plays a role, the rate of growth of the whole individual or of a given organ tissue is most fundamentally determined by mitotic rate, and thereby cell number. Studies of strains of large versus small rabbits demonstrated a higher mitotic rate and thereby a greater cell number in the large rabbit. This was evident from the 48-hour blastula stage of development onward, as is shown in Figure 1–1. Breeding studies with these strains of large and small rabbits indicated that the difference in mitotic rate and thereby size was the effect of many genes, or polygenic. Thus there may be some general control over mitotic rate that is operative even before implantation. Beyond this there appear to be specific factors which affect the mitotic rate and thereby cell number and size of particular organ tissues. One such factor is implied for the liver. Removal of part of the liver will result in an increased mitotic rate of the remaining liver cells, with a return toward the usual liver size within a few weeks. Studies indicate this effect is mediated by a humor-

1

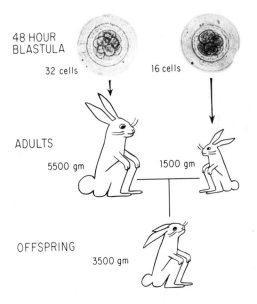

48 HOUR
BLASTULA

32 cells   16 cells

ADULTS

5500 gm   1500 gm

OFFSPRING

3500 gm

Figure 1-1 Size difference in large versus small rabbits was interpreted as due to a difference in mitotic rate and thereby cell number, evident from the 48-hour blastula stage onward. The inheritance of this difference in mitotic rate was considered polygenic, the offspring of the large and small rabbits being intermediary in size. (Adapted from Castle, W. E., and Gregory, P. W.: The embryonic basis of size inheritance in the rabbit. J. Morph. Physiol. 48:81, 1929.)

al protein factor. The hypothesis is that individual liver cells produce and project a particular protein into the circulation which, when accumulated in adequate amount from enough liver cells, has an antimitotic effect on the liver cells in general. This type of humoral negative feedback mechanism would also tend to keep the liver size proportionate to the whole individual during growth, since it would require more of the factor to maintain the same plasma level as the circulation expands. A similar negative feedback of a tissue-specific antimitotic factor has been implied for growth control of the kidney and spleen. The question has been raised whether these factors might not be the same which confer organ tissue antigen specificity. On the other hand, there have been indications of tissue-specific factors which enhance growth. One example is the nerve growth factor which specifically stimulates growth in sympathetic ganglia.

In summary, the control over growth is most fundamentally a control over mitosis and thereby cell number. It would appear that there are general factors relating to total body mitotic rate and size, and specific humorally transmitted factors which affect mitotic rate and thereby size in particular tissues. The precise nature of this feedback and the growth capacity of a given organ probably vary in timing and for each tissue. For example, neuronal cells seem to be incapable of mitosis, certainly beyond the time of early infancy at the latest. This is an exciting area in which new knowledge may be not only of basic interest relative to normal growth but also relative to problems of deficient as well as uncontrolled growth.

Critical Periods in Growth and Development. The most critical period in the development of the whole individual or in the growth of a particular organ tissue is during the time of the most rapid cell

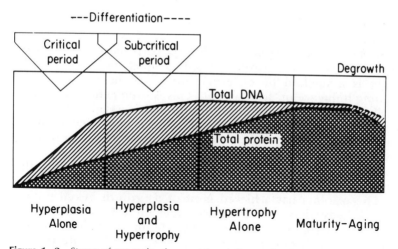

Figure 1-2 Stages of organ development in relation to the DNA and protein content. The earlier stages are the more critical ones in terms of permanent residua arising from problems during that period. (Adapted from Winick, M.: Fetal nutrition and growth processes. Hosp. Pract. 34:33, May, 1970.)

divisions. Most organ tissues go through the developmental stages shown in Figure 1-2 and are most susceptible to permanent residual alterations in growth during the period of rapidly increasing cell numbers. The critical period will thereby vary in different organs in accordance with the timing and duration of increasing cell numbers for that tissue. Figure 1-3 depicts the critical periods for some tissues.

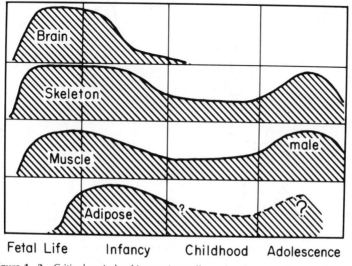

Figure 1-3 Critical periods of increasing cell number for several organ tissues.

GROWTH AND DEVELOPMENT

General. Each biologic age has its particular growth characteristics. Fetal growth is heavily dependent upon the mother, and birth weight is influenced by maternal size, since the uterus has a constraining influence on fetal weight. This is exemplified in Figure 1–4. Ideally, birth weight should be interpreted in relation to the size of the mother, as shown in Figure 1–5. This is also evident for human twins, who grow at a normal pace until about 30 weeks of gestation and thereafter tend to grow at a slower than usual pace. Once the combined weight of fetal twins exceeds about seven pounds, there is a restraint on further growth.

The placenta has achieved most of its growth in cell number by 30 weeks' gestation, and its enlargement thereafter is mainly due to cellular hypertrophy. In time the placenta may become a constraining influence. This is evident in a slight deceleration in late fetal life of the previously rapid linear growth, which tends to pick up again after birth. Following the advent of adipose tissue at 7 to 8 fetal months there is a doubling of weight in the last 2 months of fetal life.

Infancy is a period of continued rapid linear growth, with a 50 per cent increase of length in the first year. During this time the individual is moderately obese and triples in weight at a consistent, almost linear rate. Between 1 and 2 years there is a relatively abrupt shift downward in growth rate, and some children, especially those whose parents are small, will drop to a lower percentile in the growth grids,

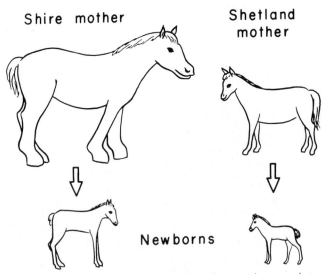

Figure 1–4 Influence of maternal size on the offspring of a cross between a small Shetland stallion and a large Shire mare (left) and a Shire stallion with a Shetland mare (right). Though the genetic situation is the same, the offspring of the larger mother is distinctly bigger. (Adapted from Hammond, J.: Growth in size and body proportions in farm animals. In Zarrow, M. X.: Growth in Living Systems. New York, Basic Books, Inc., 1961, p. 321.)

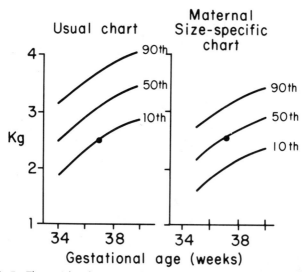

Figure 1–5 The weight of a 5 pound newborn baby, born of a 4-foot, 11-inch, 88-pound mother, plotted on a usual growth grid to the left and on one which is specific for the maternal size on the right. (Adapted from Winick, M.: Biological correlations. Am. J. Dis. Child. *120*:416, 1970. The standards on the right are from Thomson, A. M. *et al.*: The assessment of fetal growth. J. Obstet. Gynec. Brit. Comm. *75*:903, 1968.)

such as those shown in the Appendix. The rate slows to 2 to 3 inches and 2 to 3 pounds per year during childhood, accompanied by a relative decrease in adiposity and a mild increase in muscle mass. With the sex hormone induced changes of adolescence there is an appreciable growth spurt.

Growth of Specific Tissues and Their Assessment. Following are some pertinent comments on the development of particular tissues and the means of assessing their growth. There is one critical point relative to growth assessment: *Always* compare the individual to the immediate background (the *parents and siblings*) *first,* before comparing the individual to general population standards. The general standards are helpful in providing a range of normal, and in some growth grids these are broken down into percentiles for each age (see Appendix). However, there is individual variability in each aspect of growth and development, and this can be best understood by looking to the immediate genetic background, certainly before any interpretation is made relative to potential disease. This applies to growth, maturational rate, developmental progress, adolescence, and behavior. For example, Figure 1–6 shows the variant growth curves of two normal girls in relation to the variant mean stature of their parents. Growth charts are being developed which are specific for the mean size of the parents and these will be most helpful.

Skeleton. The skeletal system has a prolonged critical period during which cell numbers are increasing at the epiphyseal plate and in the subperiosteal areas. Skeletal growth is reflected in stature,

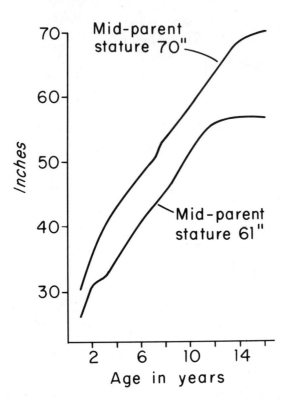

Figure 1-6 The growth of two normal girls, one from tall parents, the other from short parents. This dramatically illustrates the need to relate the growth of each child to the projected expectancy based on parental size. (Adapted from Garn, S. M., and Rohman, C. G.: Interaction of nutrition and genetics in the timing of growth and development. Pediat. Clin. N. Amer. *13*:353, 1966.)

measured as length during infancy, and standing height thereafter. Length should be obtained with the knees straight, and height should be taken with the heels and head against a wall and a right-angle device placed on top of the head to ensure accurate reading of the measurement. The pace of linear growth is an excellent feature to follow in order to detect any change in *growth rate,* which may signify a problem. This can be done on the usual Stuart growth grids (see Appendix), which have the age-appropriate percentiles for growth. However, ideally, it is best to plot the growth on a chart giving normal values for the children of the same mean parental height as the patient.

It is always well to think in terms of growth *rate* in increments per year. Figure 1-7 shows the growth and increments per year for one child. Obviously, the rapid periods of growth during infancy and adolescence are the most critical times.

Skeletal tissues not only provide the best gauge of general growth progress through stature, but they also give us our best approximation of biologic age. This can be crudely assessed by facial bone development, utilizing height of the nasal bridge, prominence of the malar eminences, and relative size of the mandible for an overall indication of how old the child looks. When indicated, skeletal roentgenograms can be utilized to assess "bone age" by contrasting the findings for mineralization of secondary centers of ossification and advancing bony form to age-related standards. Prior to 3 months, views of the knee and foot are most helpful. Thereafter, a roentgenogram of the hand and wrist is the single most helpful area for evaluation, though some clinicians prefer to obtain roentgenograms of additional centers. Figure 1–8 shows the changes in the hand and wrist at 4 and 6 years, as an example. Bone age is a crude assessment; at 2 years of age there is a normal range of variability of 1 year and at 10 years of age the variability is 2 years. However, it is still the best indicator of biologic age which we have at the present time, as indicated by the fact that bone age correlates more closely with the advent of adolescence than does chronologic age or height age. (Height age is the age for which the individual's height represents the 50th percentile.) Thus a 13-year-old with a bone age of 8 years would not be expected to reach the advent of adolescence for several years at least. Bone age determination may be helpful as an index of biologic age in growth problems and in determining whether an older child with no signs of adolescence has reached the *biologic age* of adolescence or not. During infancy, a lag in osseous maturation may be evident in the calvarium by unusually large fontanels for age, in the absence of increased intracranial pressure.

The skeleton does not grow in a thoroughly proportionate man-

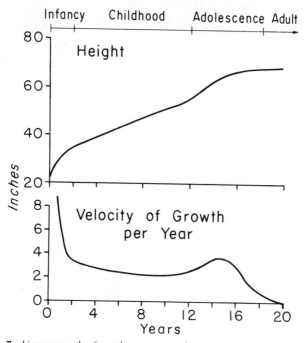

Figure 1–7 Linear growth of one boy, expressed as increments per year (below). Note the rapid rate in infancy and adolescence with rather consistent rates in between. (Adapted from Falkner, F.: The Physical Development of Children. Pediatrics 29:448, 1962, reproduced with permission.)

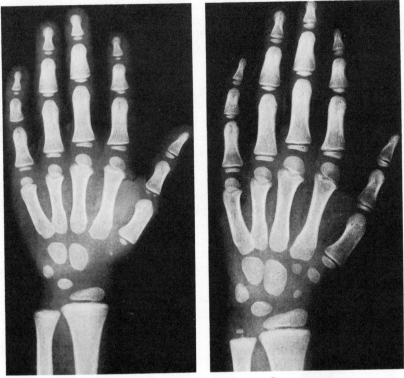

4 years   6 years

Figure 1–8 Roentgenograms of the hand and wrist at the 4- and 6-year age in males. The advancement in mineralization of secondary centers of ossification and in bony form during this biologic age allows for some discrimination of "bone age," crude though it may be. (Adapted from Greulich, W. W., and Pyle, S. I.: Radiographic Atlas of Skeletal Development of the Hand and Wrist. 2nd ed. Stanford, Calif., Stanford University Press, 1959.)

ner. At birth the upper to lower (the pubis being the intermediary point of assessment) ratio is 1.7, and as the legs grow out it is 1.0 by 10 years. Relative to adult size, growth rate is more precocious in the distal leg than in the proximal leg. The foot is half adult size in the 18-month-old boy whereas the femur is not half adult size until 4 years of age. Accelerated growth of the feet is one of the earliest and most sensitive indicators of the advent of adolescence, and usually precedes and predicts the general adolescent growth spurt. The feet also reach final growth 1 to 2 years before the remaining leg bones have stopped growing. Thus the feet mature more rapidly than the long bones of the legs. Even after the major growth spurt is over there may be a little further linear growth in the third decade, mainly from continued growth in the trunk.

Skeletal measurements other than height need only be obtained on indication. There is little value in routine measurement of arm span, chest circumference, and upper-to-lower-segment ratio. There is probably little value in routine foot measurement, although this has not been evaluated carefully in health and disease.

Brain. The critical period for brain growth and development extends into infancy, as shown in Figure 1–9. The brain is growing at a very rapid pace at the time of birth and on through the first year, and increases threefold in weight during infancy. Although most of the neurones are present at birth, a major addition of glial cells occurs at 1 to 3 months. Most of the myelination process, the responsibility of the glial cells, occurs during the first year. Axone networks, critical to function, are also developing. The functional consequences of this rapid brain growth are reflected in the orderly progression of advancing performance during this time. Brain growth is almost complete by 2 years, the organ being about 80 per cent of adult size by that age.

The best present assessment of brain size is head circumference, which correlates well with DNA content of the brain and thereby with cell number in the brain. The measurement is taken as the widest occipital-frontal circumference. Head circumference should be followed serially as a gauge of the rate of brain development, and plotted on normal head-size charts such as those in the Appendix. An unusually rapid rate of gain may raise concern of increased intracranial pressure, and a slow rate should raise concern about a problem in brain development. Again, it is important first to compare the child's head size to that of the parents before further evaluating a child with an unusual head size. You may find that the head size of one of the parents is similarly unusual. In general, the smaller the size of the head, the lower the intelligence. This is especially true when the head

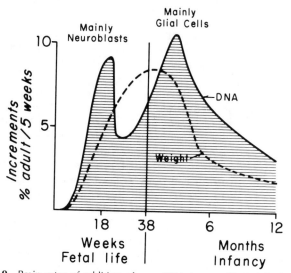

Figure 1–9 Brain rates of addition of new DNA (new cells) and fresh weight during the critical period of brain growth and development. (Adapted from Dobbing, J.: Undernutrition and the developing brain. Am. J. Dis. Child. *120*:411, 1970.)

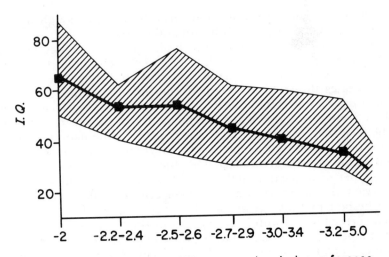

Figure 1–10 Relationship between the smallness of the head (microcephaly) by head circumference and IQ values, showing means and interquartile range. The correlation coefficient was 0.51, showing a high degree of correlation. (Adapted from Pryor, H. B., and Thelander, H.: Abnormally small head size and intellect in children. J. Pediat. *73*:593, 1968.)

circumference is more than 2 standard deviations below the normal, as shown in Figure 1–10. Another indirect method for assessing brain development is in terms of performance, both with respect to neurologic function for age and developmental capabilities. The infant's capabilities can be compared to age standards such as those set in the Denver Developmental Screening Test (see Chapter Six, Infancy, the First Two Years, and Appendix). However, it is important to realize that all developmental lag is not due to problems of brain *development*.

Lymphoid Tissue. The amount of lymphoid tissue is proportionately greatest in childhood and decreases with adolescence. Thus the tonsils which look relatively large at 6 years of age may not appear so at 14 years.

Dentition. Teeth are developing from 5 months of fetal age. Deciduous teeth begin erupting at about 5 to 8 months, and all 20 are usually erupted by 2 years. The relative "underbite" may change in time as the mandible "catches up" to the maxilla in growth. The permanent dentition begins erupting around 6 to 7 years. The teeth most commonly missing are the third molars and the upper lateral incisors. Dental maturation is a poor index of biologic age.

Adipose Tissue. The fetus is 0.5 per cent fat in the first half of gestation. At around 7 months of fetal life adipose tissue begins to develop and the fetus progresses from 3.5 per cent fat at that age to 16 per cent fat by birth. The child continues to be obese through infancy, then tends to slim out until the preadolescent age, when some children again become mildly obese. With adolescence, girls maintain a mild obesity and boys tend to lose it under the effects of androgen. As regards cell number, fat cells continue to be added during infancy and childhood. It has now been shown that most obese individuals have excess fat cells and the question is being raised as to whether hyperalimentation during early life can increase the number of fat cells and thereby the liability towards obesity at a later age.

Muscle. Muscle cells are multinucleate, and the number of nuclei continues to increase throughout childhood, being slightly higher in boys than in girls. Under the effects of androgen the adolescent male doubles the number of nuclei, and his muscle cells also hypertrophy. As a consequence, strength almost doubles, and coordination usually improves. Athletic prowess in teenagers relates better to bone age than to chronological age, again reflecting the correlation between bone age and biologic age of adolescence.

Endocrine. The major endocrine developmental change which occurs during childhood is related to hypothalamic function in terms of gonadotrophin production. The present hypothesis is that a change in the hypothalamic threshold increases the level of estrogen or androgen required to suppress gonadotrophin; hence higher levels of gonadotrophin and thereby sex hormones are produced, introducing the biologic age of adolescence. The values for estrogen and testosterone are low during childhood, as are those for gonadotrophin. There *are* childhood sex hormone differences and it is not yet possible to state how much of a role they play in normal growth and developmental differences between boys and girls. The slow advent of adolescence is a consequence of the gradual increase in gonadotrophin, which results in an insidious rise in the relative amounts of estrogen in the girl and testosterone in the boy. There follows a more rapid rise toward adult levels of sex hormones, which is associated with the major growth spurt and changes of adolescence. The gonadotrophin and sex hormone values through childhood are summarized in Figure 1–11.

The effects of gonadotrophin can be assessed in the male by measuring testicular length. Length gradually increases from about 1.5 to 2.0 cm at the biologic age of 8 to 9 years, with a major spurt in size at the biologic age of 13 to 14 years; this correlates with the testosterone-induced major growth spurt at that age. The early effects of estrogen can best be appreciated by breast and nipple enlargement, and labia minora and vaginal mucosal hypertrophy. The early effects of testosterone in the male can best be appreciated by accelerated growth (feet first!), enlargement of the penis, and secretion from apocrine sweat glands. Both testosterone and estrogen accelerate the pace of osseous maturation, bringing the individual to final height attainment sooner than without such hormones. The concomitant growth spurt is less with estrogen than testosterone, partially explaining the shorter stature in women. It is difficult to name a tissue which is not affected by the sex hormones at adolescence and these changes are more completely delineated in Chapter 8, Adolescence.

Sex Differences in Growth and Development. There are major differences in growth and development between boys and girls, necessitating separate growth charts for virtually every parameter in growth and development.

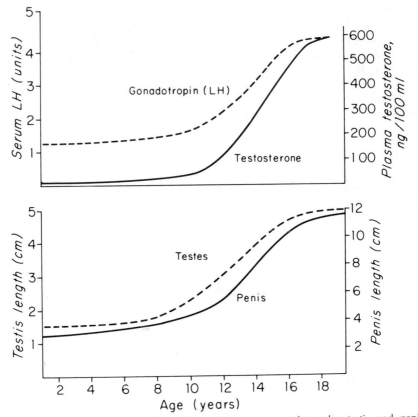

Figure 1–11 Serum gonadotrophin and testosterone values plus testis and penis measurements through childhood and adolescence. As the gonadotrophin level rises, the testes enlarge and produce more testosterone, which, in turn, enlarges the size of the penis. (Adapted from Winter, J. S. D., and Faiman, C.: Pituitary-gonadal relationships in male children and adolescents. Pediat. Res. 6:126, 1972.)

Studies indicate that genes on the X and Y chromosomes are some of the many genes which play a role in the determination of size and pace of maturation. One striking difference is that girls mature more rapidly. At time of birth they are already 4 weeks ahead of boys, and at adolescence they are 2 years ahead. Because they mature more rapidly, they reach the advent of adolescence at an earlier age, and full sexual maturity and final height are attained sooner. Girls are also more precocious in language development and early school performance. For example, early reading failures are one-third to one-sixth as common in girls as compared to boys. Whether this is a direct consequence of the precocious maturation affecting brain development as well as skeletal maturation remains to be determined. Boys have better perceptual motor performance than girls and are taller at a given biologic age (bone age).

Secular Changes in Growth and Maturation. In 1876, an astute older English physician noted that "the factory child of 9 years weighs as much as one did at 10 years in 1833—each age has gained one year in 40 years." This phenomenal trend has continued during the past 100 years. A century ago males reached final height attainment at 23 years and girls had menarche at 17 years. Since then each generation has matured more rapidly, entering adolescence six months to 1 year sooner, and each generation has been about one inch taller than the preceding one. Thus we are maturing about 25 per cent faster today than 100 years ago. Intelligence quotients at age 11 years are also distinctly higher. It is not possible to state whether this latter phenomenon is a direct corollary of the faster pace of maturation or whether it is related to the fact that head circumference and thereby brain size has also increased.

Since children of today are more mature and taller than those of the previous generation at the same chronologic age, past growth standards are not wholly appropriate for the present generation. Unfortunately, adult society and educational systems have generally failed to keep step with this advancing pace of maturation in terms of curriculum, age of college entrance, age of employment, and, in a more general sense, the age at which an individual is treated as an "adult."

The reason for this dramatic change is unknown. Better nutrition and relative lack of serious childhood disease are major considerations. Increased outbreeding with consequent "hybrid vigor" has been conjectured. Regardless of cause, animal studies imply that the more rapidly a species matures, the shorter is the life span. Thus, some of the evidence of earlier aging (such as atherosclerosis) in recent generations may be partially related to the more rapid pace of biologic aging in the earlier stages of life.

FACTORS IN GROWTH

The basic capacity for growth and for pace of maturation are polygenic determinations, with at least some of the genes being on the X and Y chromosomes. Thus, the most common causes of small stature in well-fed children represent the lower end of the normal polygenic spectrum for statural size and maturational rate, respectively, as summarized in Table 1–1.

TABLE 1–1 FEATURES OF FAMILIAL SMALL STATURE VERSUS FAMILIAL SLOW MATURATION

	Familial Small Stature	Familial Slow Maturation
Frequent family history of	Short stature	Late adolescence
Size at birth	Normal	Normal
Growth during childhood	Slow	Slow
Maturational rate	Normal	Slow
Onset of adolescence	Normal age	Late onset
Final height attainment	Usual age, short	Late age, normal
General evaluation	Otherwise normal	Otherwise normal

Given an adequate genetic endowment, with cells which have a normal capability for growth, there are a host of factors which must be functioning adequately or be available in order to allow for the innate growth capacity. Some of these are listed in Table 1–2, and a few are discussed below. The types of problems listed seldom give rise to significant growth deficiency during fetal life; hence the onset of growth deficiency is usually after birth.

Nutrition. The most common worldwide cause of growth deficiency is malnutrition. Because of deficiency in energy or other nutri-

TABLE 1–2   SECONDARY GROWTH DEFICIENCY RELATED TO HUMORAL FACTORS

Problem	Reason for Growth Deficiency	Diagnostic Studies
Nutritional a. Inadequate intake b. Partial intestinal obstruction c. Malabsorption	Nutritional deficiency	Response to adequate intake Roentgenograms Absorption, enzyme studies
Deprivation syndrome	Neglect, abuse, nutritional	Response to environmental change Home and family investigation
Mental deficiency	Unknown	
Cardiac defect a. Left-to-right shunt b. Cyanotic	?Rapid circulation time ?Hypoxia, sluggish circulation	Cardiac evaluation
Respiratory insufficiency	?Low-grade hypoxia	
Renal dysfunction	Acidosis Polyuria with dehydration Rickets	Urine pH, serum electrolytes, CO_2 Urine concentration Serum calcium, phosphorus
Hypothyroidism	Deficit, energy metabolism	Serum protein-bound iodine
Pituitary growth hormone deficiency	?Diminished lipolysis, amino acid transport to cell	Stimulated serum growth hormone values

Metabolic disorders such as hypercalcemia, hypophosphatemic rickets, galactosemia, glycogen storage disease, salt-losing congenital adrenal hyperplasia, etc.

Chronic infectious disease

Prenatal causes: maternal toxemia, severe malnutrition, heavy cigarette smoking *(usually mild growth deficiency)*

ent resources there is a slowing in the pace of growth and maturation. This is most evident for adipose tissue, muscle, and skeletal growth. However, one of the gravest concerns is malnutrition which occurs during the critical period of increasing brain cellularity. Studies on rats have clearly shown a permanent residual deficit of brain size and cellularity, with compromised brain function, secondary to malnutrition during the period of increasing brain cellularity. The findings in the human are similar; in the wake of prenatal and early infancy malnutrition there may be a permanent deficit in head circumference, brain DNA (cell) content, and subsequent intellectual performance. Hence adequate nutrition is critical to normative growth and development, especially during the periods of increasing cell number for a particular organ tissue.

Hormones. Thyroid hormone is necessary for a normal rate of energy metabolism. Lack of thyroid hormone causes a marked postnatal slowing of linear growth and an even more striking lag in rate of maturation, and the individual is sluggish in activity. Hypothyroidism in fetal life and early infancy can result in residual mental deficiency, but onset of hypothyroidism after infancy does not permanently impair brain development and function. This is another example of serious permanent residua when the problem exists during the critical period of cellular growth in the brain.

Pituitary growth hormone plays a role in glucose, free fatty acid, and amino acid metabolism, and also in skeletal growth. When it is deficient there is a synchronous slowing down in the pace of growth and maturation, and the individual tends to have slight truncal adiposity. Brain development and function are not affected, possibly because the growth deficiency is not clinically manifest in congenital hypopituitarism until late in the first year of postnatal life or thereafter, and hence does not occur during the critical period of increasing brain cellularity.

CATCH UP GROWTH

When there is a secondary cause of growth deficiency, such as in the foregoing examples, a restoration of the missing factor will result in a dramatic acceleration of growth and maturation. This will usually continue until the level of maturation (bone age) has returned to expectancy for chronologic age, after which the individual will resume a more usual rate of growth and maturation. This applies to those tissues which still have the capacity for increasing their cell number. These phenomena imply that the biologic clock of life is still ticking away during the period of secondary growth deficiency, and upon its correction the individual will tend to catch up to the stage of development where he would have been if the problem had not existed. The adequacy of the catch up growth will depend upon the timing, severity, duration, and nature of the secondary growth deficiency. In general, any serious setback will have its impact, small though it may be, on eventual size. For tissues such as the brain it is often not possible to catch up in cell number when the problem existed during the early critical period; hence there can be permanent residua of deficient brain function.

* * *

Hopefully, this section will have provided the reader with a feeling for the dynamic nature of the process of growth and development. At no stage is the individual static; hence the evaluation of a given individual at a particular moment in time must always be viewed in relation to the past and future in terms of both interpretation and prognostication.

Critical events which occur during growth and development may alter the form and function of the mature individual. But once having attained that mature form, the nature of the individual continues to change in time. For growth and aging are a continuum, the one following upon the other. As you shall see in the next chapter, many aspects of aging tend to be a reversal or loss of the processes involved in growth—a degrowth.

REFERENCES

Bayer, L. M.: and Bayley, N.: Growth Diagnosis. Chicago, University of Chicago Press, 1959.

Bell, E. (Ed.): Molecular and Cellular Aspects of Development. New York, Harper & Row, 1967.

Blais, M. M., Green, W. T., and Anderson, M.: Lengths of the growing foot. J. Bone Joint Surg., 38-A:998, 1956.

Cheek, D. B.: Cellular growth hormones, nutrition, and time. Pediat., 41:30, 1967.

Falkner, F. (Ed.): Human Development. Philadelphia, W. B. Saunders Company, 1966.

Garn, S. M., and Rohmann, C. G.: Interaction of nutrition and genetics in the timing of growth and development. Pediat. Clin. N. Amer., 13:353, 1966.

McCance, R. A.: Food, growth, and time. Lancet, 2:621, 1962.

Needham, A. E.: The Growth Process in Animals. Princeton, New Jersey, D. Van Nostrand Company, Inc., 1964.

Stuart, H. C., and Prugh, D. G.: The Healthy Child, His Physical, Psychological, and Social Development. Cambridge, Mass., Harvard University Press, 1964.

Tanner, J. M., Goldstein, H., and Whitehouse, R. H.: Standards for children's height at ages 2–9 years allowing for height of parents. Arch. Dis. Childh., 45:755, 1970.

Thomson, A. M.: The evaluation of human growth patterns. Am. J. Dis. Child., 120:398, 1970.

Watson, E. H., and Lowrey, G. H.: Growth and Development of Children. 5th ed. Chicago, Year Book Medical Publishers, 1967.

Winick, M.: Fetal malnutrition and growth processes. Hospital Practice 34:33, May, 1970.

Zarrow, M. X. (Ed.): Growth in living systems. International Symposium on Growth Held at Purdue University, 1969. New York, Basic Books, Inc., 1969.

CHAPTER TWO

BIOLOGY OF AGING

EDWIN L. BIERMAN
WILLIAM R. HAZZARD

The process of aging begins with conception and ends with death. The study of this process is the science of gerontology. Because the aging process proceeds gradually and inexorably to death, its study has been largely neglected by investigators preoccupied either with the more positive processes such as growth and development or with specific, often dramatic disease entities. As a result we know relatively little about aging. What follows, then, is necessarily highly preliminary and largely in the nature of a catalog of possible mechanisms whereby aging may take place.

Why do people die? Apparently individuals do not die "of old age," but of specific disorders or diseases. Therefore one can define "aging" and "senescence" as the underlying process that leads to an increased probability of disease. In simpler terms, aging represents a progressive decline of vigor and resistance with the passage of time. Even if we escape wars, accidents, and diseases, aging proceeds at a rate which differs little from person to person, so that there are heavy odds in favor of dying between the ages of 65 and 80. Some will die sooner, and a few will live into the ninth or tenth decade. However, at the present time there appears to be a virtual limit on the life span, however lucky, robust, and free of disease one remains. If this process of aging were not a factor in our lives, and if we kept throughout life the same resistance to stress, injury, and disease which we had at age 12, it has been estimated by Comfort that half of us alive today might expect to live another 700 years. In point of fact, however, the maximal human life span has rarely been firmly documented to have exceeded 110 years.

THE PROCESS OF AGING

General

The process of aging is easy to demonstrate by examination of mortality curves. If death were a random event, the mortality rate

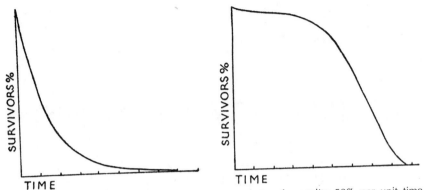

Figure 2-1 *Left:* Survival curve at a constant rate of mortality 50% per unit time. *Right:* Survival curve of a population which exhibits senescence. (From Ageing: The Biology of Senescence, by Alex Comfort. Copyright (c) 1956, 1964 by Alex Comfort. Reprinted by permission of Holt, Rinehart and Winston, Inc.)

would be constant with time, and the survival curve of such a population would be semi-logarithmic (Fig. 2–1), like that of a radioactive isotope or of water glasses in a cafeteria. The survival curve of a population that exhibits senescence, however, is strikingly different (Fig. 2–1). It shows an initial gradual decline followed by a sharp increase in mortality rate with time so that a rectangular-shaped curve results. Translated into numbers, the probability of dying doubles approximately every eight years. The human population curve clearly shows the impact of the aging process, even in groups which have increased mortality rates due to such devastating infectious diseases as infantile diarrhea and tuberculosis, which are prevalent in underdeveloped countries or in the disadvantaged population in the United States (Fig. 2–2). The conquest of such diseases has resulted in a shift of the survival curve to the typical one of aging by a reduction in the mortality of the younger age groups (Fig. 2–3). This increase in life expectancy has been due almost entirely to the reduction in mortality from such specific diseases, but this conquest of disease has not appreciably altered maximum life span, which remains at 90 to 100 years. As a result of the reduction in mortality from disease in younger age groups, allowing more people to reach the upper limit, we are left primarily with aging and age-linked diseases in adult clinical practice. Moreover, the proportion of the population in the United States over age 65, which was 10 per cent (20 million) in 1970, is steadily increasing. Thus the medical, sociological, and economic implications of the aging process loom ever larger in our projections of the future needs of our population.

Aging is clearly not unique to man but occurs among all animals. The oldest known animal, the Galapagos turtle, has been estimated to reach 175 years of age. Of the mammals, man has the longest life span. Unicellular organisms are probably the only form of life which may not age, since they divide into two new cells and thus could the-

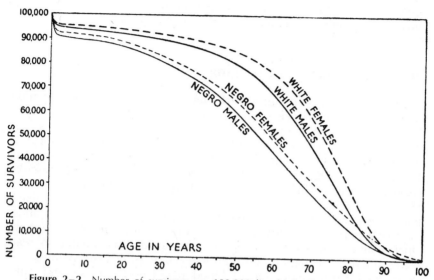

Figure 2-2 Number of survivors per 100,000 live births, by race and sex: United States, 1939–41. (From Ageing: The Biology of Senescence, by Alex Comfort. Copyright (c) 1956, 1964 by Alex Comfort. Reprinted by permission of Holt, Rinehart and Winston, Inc.)

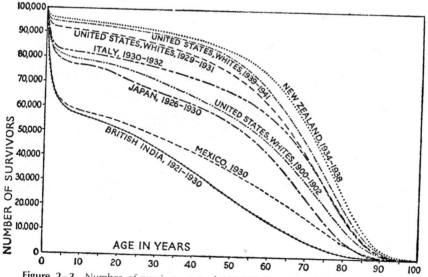

Figure 2-3 Number of survivors out of 100,000 live male births, from recent life tables for selected countries. (From Ageing: The Biology of Senescence, by Alex Comfort. Copyright (c) 1956, 1964 by Alex Comfort. Reprinted by permission of Holt, Rinehart and Winston, Inc.)

oretically go on forever. This in itself suggests that aging is in some way a function of multicellular existence. In multicellular organisms, aging occurs at various levels of organization: organs and organ systems; tissues; cells; subcellular particles; and molecules.

Organ and Organ System Aging

The examination of aging at the level of organs and organ systems suggests that many processes begin to decline long before death. Thus their measurement may provide an estimate of the physiologic age of an individual, which is a far better index of his rate of aging than his chronologic age. Such physiologic aging is apparent in man after the age of 30 (Fig. 2–4) and some functions, notably cardiovascular work performance and sexual function in males, clearly reach their peak at the end of the adolescent growth period. There is a nearly linear decline in most integrated body functions at the rate of about 1 per cent per year in adult life. In addition, many homeostatic systems which continue to function well at rest may become unable to react to stress and perturbation and thereby become progressively impaired. Examples include regulation of blood pH, blood glucose, and pulse rate, to mention only a few. As a result, older persons are characteristically less effective than young people in meeting environmental challenges and require a longer time to readjust their internal environment after displacements occur. None of these functional decrements appears to be a fundamental cause of the aging process in the whole

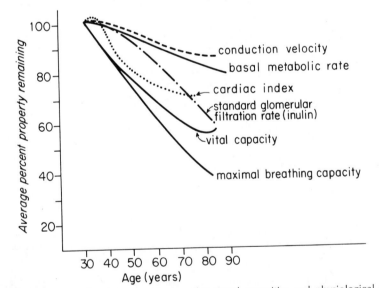

Figure 2–4 Decline in various human functional capacities and physiological measurements with age. (Adapted from Shock, N. W. *In* Strehler, B. L., Ebert, J. D., Glass, H. B., and Shock, N. W.: The Biology of Aging. Washington, D.C., American Institute of Biological Sciences, 1960, p. 22.)

organism, but rather a result. The impact of these age-linked functional changes on diagnostic criteria for certain diseases is an important problem, which will be discussed in detail in Chapter Ten. It is sufficient to say that aging is not limited to any organ or system. This suggests that a fundamental feature of the aging process might be apparent in tissues or cells, or even at some lower level of organization.

Tissue and Cellular Aging

Tissue and cellular aging can be examined in three major categories: noncellular material, multiplying cells, and nonrenewing cells. Much attention has been focused on noncellular interstitial tissue and, in particular, on collagen, the major element of connective tissue in the skin, skeletal, and vascular systems. Clearly, if collagen became altered so that diffusion of metabolites from circulation to cells were impaired, a generalized decrease in organ function with time would be explained.

Properties of connective tissue normally change in the direction of increased cross-linking and stiffness and loss of elasticity. Whether these connective tissue changes, though clearly important in such tissues as skin and arteries, are a fundamental factor in the aging process is still unresolved. In multiplying cells, arrangements of cells become less regular and there is less homogeneity in cell size, so that tissues become less well organized with time. Of particular importance in tissues in which cells tend to be nonrenewable is the loss of cells with time, and a consequent decrease in functioning cell number. For example, all areas of the cerebral cortex lose cells with age, and muscle mass decreases. Although this loss might account for some aspects of functional deterioration, changes must also be taking place in those cells that remain in the body.

An interesting aspect of cellular aging is the accumulation in cells of substances which are not metabolized and may, in fact, be harmful. One such example is a fluorescent pigment called "lipofuscin" or "age pigment," which is deposited in certain tissues of many species, in cells that turn over very slowly, such as in brain and heart muscle. This pigment may occupy as much as 5 per cent of the volume of the heart muscle cell in a 70-year-old individual. Lipofuscin contains a large amount of lipid, presumably representing auto-oxidation products derived from generated cell membranes, possibly lysosomes. The deposition of this pigment may play some role in the decreased functional capacity of certain cells and tissues with age. Also, a high proportion of elderly individuals have been found at autopsy to have a proteinaceous substance called *amyloid* in their tissues, particularly in brain, heart, and pancreatic islets. This, too, may contribute to functional impairment.

The multiplicity of factors controlling cell replacement, regeneration, and wound healing are also of central interest in an appraisal of the biologic nature of the aging process, since these functional processes decline with time. In tissue culture, human cells do not divide indefinitely but have a finite capacity for division which decreases with age. For example, embryonic cells divide about 50 times in culture, those from a 20-year-old divide about 30 times, and cells derived from older donors divide about 20 times.

With regard to subcellular and molecular aging, no characteristic biochemical sign of oldness in cells or molecules has yet been described. However, most of the rather fanciful theories on the nature of the aging process are concerned with molecular interactions within specialized cells. There are theories concerned with the functional deterioration of cells that no longer divide which invoke such processes as exhaustion of irreplaceable enzymes and denaturation of proteins and macromolecules. However, there is no evidence that the gradual decline of overall metabolic rate with age is related to decreased function of existing cells, rather than to a loss of cells from tissues. There are also theories that relate to cell differentiation at the molecular level. For example, errors in the reading out of the genetic code may be related to the aging process. Thus, if there occurs a progressive accumulation of faulty copying in clonally dividing somatic cells (such as mutation or cross linkages in RNA and DNA), some of the progressive functional deterioration seen in the aging organism might be explained. If a somatic cell were to undergo such a genetic change, it would become a different cell, one which might not perform its original function. Chromosomal aberrations, which may be a rough index of mutations, do accumulate in mammalian cells such as liver. Perhaps an aging cell may even represent an alternative to a neoplastic cell.

An interesting theory suggests that aging may represent an autoimmune process. In other words, a mutation of immunological cells could produce immune reactions to one's own native tissues and might lead to cell dysfunction and death. Serum autoantibodies to various cellular antigens as, for example, thyroid, stomach and nuclei, are found with greater frequency in older individuals. Monoclonal gamma globulin "paraproteins" also appear to accumulate with age. Perhaps also involved is the age-related increase in amyloid deposition which has already been noted.

One theory which has few proponents today is the historical hormonal imbalance theory. The early discoverers of hormones, particularly the sex hormones, were fully convinced that they had the key to the prevention of aging. This even led to the therapeutic use of tiger testicle extracts! Unfortunately, such treatment with sex hormones has been ineffective in providing eternal youth. Furthermore, it is well recognized that gonadal senescence, as seen in male castrates or with surgically-induced early menopause in the female, does not result in somatic senescence.

General Factors Affecting Aging

Unknown features of the specific biologic process of aging appear to be inherited. Short life spans seem to be inherited in that a predisposition to a fatal disease like cancer or heart attack may be genetically determined. The reverse also appears to hold true in that longevity also seems to be inherited. Parents of centenarians and nonagenarians appear to have lived much longer than parents of individuals dying at an earlier age. Sex also appears to affect longevity, with the advantage to the female. This is not confined to the human species but extends to most animals as well. One theory advanced to explain this phenomenon has to do with sexual exhaustion. In several species, it is true that the male dies soon after reproductive activity ceases. There is good evidence against this idea in the case of man. The mortality figures for clergymen in England show that Anglican and Protestant clergy had only 70 per cent of the general male mortality; the mortality of the celibate Roman Catholic clergy was 105 per cent. It would seem that the virtues of sexual abstinence as a factor in promoting longevity have been overemphasized. In contrast to many Western writers, who until quite recently continued to proclaim the harmful consequences of sexual excess, Indian and Chinese sages thought that continued sexual activity in man was the way to eternal youth. Although this may be an extreme view, death rate figures for the United States appear to show that married persons have a mortality rate which is one and one-half to two times lower than that of widowed or divorced persons. Undoubtedly, there are other factors involved as well.

Alteration of Aging by Experiment and by Disease

Despite our lack of fundamental knowledge about aging, there have been several approaches to the experimental alteration of the aging process. One approach proceeds from the concept that life is programmed like a computer so that an organism goes through a fixed sequence of operations involving growth, differentiation, and aging. Under such circumstances, aging might occur because a program had run out with no further built-in instructions. As a result, guidance and control mechanisms would progressively fail, not unlike the progressive failure of homeostasis which occurs in the aging organism. This has logically suggested that the faster the rate of growth and differentiation, the faster the aging process. One experimental approach has been to retard the growth rate by underfeeding. This has led to prolongation of life in many species. In the classical experiments of McKay, rats were fed diets deficient in calories but adequate in all other respects for up to three years. Their growth retardation was associated with a decreased incidence of many chronic rat diseases, and survival well beyond their usual life span. In a sense they were put into "dietary cold storage" and thereby kept artificially young. The mechanism of this prolongation of life with growth retardation is unknown.

However, the reverse experiment, an attempt to accelerate growth and development by treatment with an agent such as growth hormone, does not shorten life. Attempts to accelerate aging by other means have also been relatively unsuccessful. Radiation may be an exception. Exposure to significant amounts of x-radiation shortens life span, but it is not clear whether such radiation results in accelerated aging or chronic toxicity. If one excludes the induction of tumors, cataracts and hair loss, radiation does not alter causes of death but lowers the age at which animals die from them, which is the typical property of the aging process. This continues to be an interesting area of investigation.

One "experiment of nature" may exist in man in the form of an extremely rare disease called adult progeria, or Werner's syndrome, which superficially resembles accelerated aging. People with this disorder present between the ages of twenty and forty with grey hair, thin and atrophic skin, hair loss, a high-pitched squeaky voice, cataracts, skin ulcers, and short stature. In this disorder the most frequent causes of death are related to connective tissue tumors and vascular atherosclerosis. However, many of the features of the aging process, such as collagen changes and age pigment deposition, are not found in this syndrome. Although the mortality curve is shifted earlier in time, there is not a proportional increase in all the causes of death or all the features of the aging process. Therefore, this syndrome is thought to be a caricature of aging, exaggerating the ectodermal features of the aging process but not simply representing premature or accelerated aging. It may be, however, that accelerated aging, if not generalized in man, may occur in individual organs and organ systems asynchronously with that of the rest of the body, as, for example, seems to occur in the pre-senile brain syndromes. It is always difficult to separate changes due to disorders of specific tissues and organs from effects of the aging process *per se*.

* * *

There is a lack of understanding of the nature of some of the biologic fundamentals of the aging process, its relation to other time-related processes, such as cessation of sexual function, and its relation to growth, tissue organization, and development. If the biological scientist is asked whether human aging is ever likely to be controlled or even influenced, at present he can only answer that until the nature of the processes involved are known, he can make no predictions. But we as health professionals must face, rather than ignore or approach with professional disdain, the clinical consequences of the aging process. Despite some progress from the efforts of social medicine, behavioral medicine, medical science, and rehabilitation professionals, our society at present is finding it difficult to cope with the increased number of people reaching later life without any dramatic change in biologic age. From the social point of view, it must be realized that an increase in longevity which would result from even a limited control of aging might produce a major revolution in social patterns.

Future possibilities for the treatment of aging such as the replacement of young organs for old, the use of drugs that counteract radiation effects, and the use of drugs or procedures that counteract antibody-antigen reactions will compound these difficulties, and their use must be weighed in the total social context. Perhaps it might be possible to modify the rate of aging, thus lengthening the period of adult vigor without increasing the ultimate life span or producing an ageless man. Such a modification would present a nearly square survival curve, with its limit short of the century mark. If this situation came to pass, we would have realized one facet of life peculiar to Huxley's *Brave New World*, where people remained apparently young and vigorous until an advanced age and then died quickly at "approximately the usual time."

REFERENCES

Comfort, Alex: Ageing: The Biology of Senescence. New York, Holt, Rinehart & Winston, Inc., 1964.

Comfort, Alex: The Process of Aging. New York, Signet Science Library, 1964.

Goldstein, S.: The biology of aging. N. Engl. J. Med., *285*: 1120–1129, 1971.

Kohn, R. R.: Principles of Mammalian Aging. Englewood Cliffs, New Jersey, Prentice-Hall, 1971.

Strehler, B. L.: Time, Cells, and Aging. New York, Academic Paperbacks, Academic Press, 1962.

CHAPTER THREE

PREPARATION FOR NEW LIFE

DAVID W. SMITH

The decision to start a new life, to have a child, is the most important one made by the individual relative to the future of mankind. Society is increasingly shifting its perspective toward quality of life rather than quantity of life. Disease and malnutrition, tragic and unwanted, were the major partially limiting factors on population size in the past. The predominant mortality prior to old age was in the first year after birth. Figure 3–1 shows the dramatic reduction in infant mortality from 1915 to 1965. This relative control of disease has increasingly shifted the responsibility for population stabilization to man himself. Today, population stabilization means the average couple having one to two children, and this obviously requires control of reproduction. The means of achieving control are presently available as summarized in Table 3–1. Unfortunately, 44 per cent of births from 1966 to 1970 were unplanned and, of these, one-third were unwanted.

Population stabilization will allow for ever-increasing concern and attention to the quality of life for our children-to-be. The first consideration is to have children who will not be handicapped early in life by problems related to physical and mental development. This concern should begin prior to conception in order to affect some of the major causes of mortality and handicapping morbidity during the early critical period of development. Figure 3–2 shows the major causes of infant death in 1965. Many of these same disorders are the major causes of handicapping morbidity. Most of these deaths and morbidity are due to problems which had their advent prior to birth. For example, the number one cause of infant death and morbidity is being born too soon, prematurity; and the number two cause is problems in morphogenesis, malformation. A significant portion of this mortality and handicapping morbidity is preventable by the concerned preparation for new life prior to conception and throughout the early period of development.

26

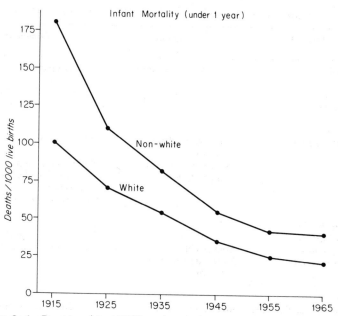

Figure 3–1   Drop in white (400%) and non-white (450%) infant mortality during 50 years in the United States. (Data from United States Public Health Service, National Center for Health Statistics.)

FACTORS TO CONSIDER IN THE PREPARATION FOR NEW LIFE

Following are some factors which can affect a new life and which should be considered in the preparation for having a child. Many of these are presented in more detail in Chapter 4.

Maternal Age.   The ideal maternal biologic age for reproduction would appear to be from 18 to 30 years of age. The neonatal mortality is almost twice as high for babies born of 40- to 45-year-old women and 4 times as high for women beyond the age of 45 years. The likelihood of chromosomal abnormality in the offspring increases progressively beyond the maternal age of 35, as illustrated in Figure 3–3 for the occurrence of 21-trisomy Down's syndrome (mongolism).

Paternal Age.   The likelihood of a fresh gene alteration (mutation) increases with older paternal age, there being about a tenfold increase in the possibility of the offspring having a fresh mutant gene disorder from the paternal age of 30 to 60 years. Specific disorders due to a single mutant gene include achondroplasia, Marfan's syndrome, Apert's syndrome, acrodysostosis, and certain other rare disorders. Though such conditions are rare in comparison to chromosomal abnormalities (related to older maternal age), their frequency of fresh occurrence is related to older paternal age.

Maternal Nutrition.   Ideally, it is advantageous for the woman to

TABLE 3-1 MEANS OF REPRODUCTIVE CONTROL

Method	Action	Comment
Hormonal	Inhibition of ovulation	Most preparations 100% effective
Estrogen		Some major side effects
Progesterone		Reversible means of control
Mechanical		
Intrauterine device	? altered tubal egg transport	97% effective
	? inhibition of ovum implantation	Side effects: Expulsion of device, bleeding, cramps, infection
		Reversible means of control
Other Mechanical		
Coitus interruptus		Low patient acceptance
Jellies; foams	Spermacidal	Reversible means of control
Diaphragm; condom	Mechanical barriers to sperm	
Surgical		
Ligation of vas deferens —male	Mechanical barrier to sperm	No effect on sex hormone production or sexual performance in either sex.
Ligation of Fallopian tubes—female		Permanent means of control
Termination of Pregnancy		
Menstrual extraction immediately following missed period		Little or no anesthesia required; Outpatient procedure
Suction curettage prior to 10–12 weeks' gestation		Some form of anesthesia needed; Outpatient procedure
Saline induction, late abortion		Increased risk; hospitalization; psychological sequellae; combine with contraceptive advice

be well nourished *prior* to conception and to maintain good nutrition throughout the pregnancy, anticipating a weight gain of approximately 20 to 30 pounds, based on her pre-pregnant size. A diet rich in high quality protein is essential and a pattern of weight gain that reaches 10 pounds at 20 weeks' gestation is desirable.

Maternal Medications, Drugs, Alcoholism, Heavy Cigarette Smoking. The potentially deleterious effects of a variety of chemical agents on early development are summarized in Chapter Four, Prenatal Life and the Pregnant Woman. It is safest if the woman avoids taking any medication about the time of conception and throughout pregnancy unless there is a very strong indication for its usage and the medication is not recognized as being definitely harmful to the developing fetus (see Chapter Four). Ingestion of alcohol in moderation has not

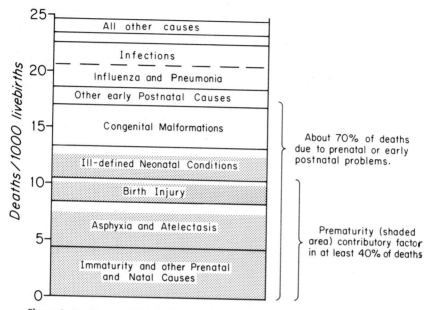

Figure 3-2 Causes of infant (first year) mortality in the United States in 1965. (Data from United States Public Health Service, National Center for Health Statistics.)

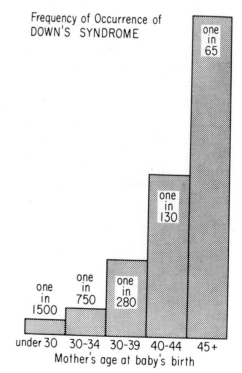

Figure 3-3 Progressive increase in incidence of 21-trisomy Down's syndrome during the latter stages of a woman's reproductive life. (Adapted from Mikkelsen, M., and Stone, J.: Human Heredity, 20:457, 1970, reproduced with permission.)

been shown to be harmful. However, excessive drinking, with associated malnutrition, is deleterious to fetal growth and development. Maternal cigarette smoking habits influence fetal size, and the incidence of prematurity increases with the number of cigarettes smoked.

Rh Incompatibility. The prospective parents should know their Rh blood type. Rh sensitization of the Rh-negative mother by an Rh-positive fetus and potential damage to subsequent Rh-positive fetuses can now be prevented, as set forth in Chapter Four.

Maternal Infectious Disease. A serological test for syphilis should be considered prior to conception, and any active disease at that time or during the pregnancy should be promptly treated. This is one infectious disease of the fetus which can be cured by medical therapy. Gonorrhea should be treated, especially prior to delivery, at which time the baby may become infected.

All children should be vaccinated against rubella in an effort to prevent the pregnant woman from having contact with, and being infected by, this agent during the first 4 months of gestation, since rubella infection of the fetus is a very serious disease (see Chapter Four).

If the woman has active urinary tract infection, this should be treated prior to conception.

Maternal Noninfectious Diseases or Disorders. Certain maternal disorders create an increased risk of a problem in fetal development. When the disorder can be effectively managed *prior* to conception, this is ideal. When it cannot be managed in such a manner as to reduce the risk to the fetus, then the potential parents should be informed about the risks, to enable them to make an intelligent decision to have or not to have a child. The former category, which can be managed, includes hypothyroidism and hyperthyroidism, and the latter category includes heart disease, hypertension, chronic renal disease, and diabetes mellitus. For the woman who has had diabetes mellitus for several years there is an increased risk of miscarriage, stillbirths, and neonatal problems in adaptation, plus a threefold greater than usual risk (6 per cent) of the baby's having a malformation problem.

Inheritable Disorders, Genetic Counselling. For families in which there is an individual with a serious genetically determined disorder, the risk for any family member's having an offspring with the same type of disorder should be determined. This determination will enable a couple to take this risk into consideration in the decision to have or not to have children. For a few disorders it is now possible to detect an affected fetus by early amniocentesis (see Chapter Four), allowing for early termination of that pregnancy if the fetus is affected. This method is also applicable to the older mother, who has an increased risk of having a child with a chromosomal abnormality. Amniocentesis and chromosomal studies of the early fetal cells in which there is a serious chromosomal abnormality can indicate the need to have a pregnancy terminated.

PRACTICAL MEASURES IN PREPARATION FOR NEW LIFE

Ideally, it would be advantageous for most of the foregoing information to become general public knowledge, and for each new life to start as a *wanted* individual whose prospective parents had prepared for the event prior to conception and throughout the period of pregnancy. This preparation should include a preconceptual evaluation of the couple for Rh typing and determination of any risk of offspring having a serious genetically determined disorder when such a disorder is present in one or more family members. The prospective mother should be evaluated for the presence of any nutritional deficiency, active infectious disease, or metabolic disorder which might compromise the early development of a fetus. Remediable disorders should be treated *prior* to conception. For nonremediable disorders, the couple should understand the potential risk to the woman in becoming pregnant, as well as the risk to the fetus. All women should be informed of the optimal maternal life situation for the fetus during pregnancy and for preparation for childbirth. Such measures will do more to reduce infant mortality and handicapping morbidity than any therapeutic measures instituted after birth.

By these means the preparation for new life could achieve the goal of enhancing the quality of life for each new individual.

REFERENCES

Nelson, W. E., Vaughan, V. C., and McKay, R. J.: Textbook of Pediatrics. 9th ed. Philadelphia, W. B. Saunders Co., 1969, pp. 1–12.

Niswander, K. R., and Gordon, M.: The Collaborative Study of the National Institute of Neurological Diseases and Stroke; The Women and Their Pregnancies. Philadelphia, W. B. Saunders Co., 1972.

Report of the Presidential Commission on Population Growth and the American Future. Washington, D. C., U. S. Government Printing Office, 1972.

CHAPTER FOUR

PRENATAL LIFE AND THE PREGNANT WOMAN

DAVID W. SMITH
DOUGLAS DER YUEN

The average duration of human pregnancy, counting from the first day of the last menstrual period, is about 280 days, or 40 weeks. Since the interval between the onset of menstruation and ovulation averages approximately 13 days, the mean duration of actual pregnancy, counting from the day of conception, is closer to 267 days. Prolongation of pregnancy by as much as 2 to 3 weeks beyond the expected date of confinement is common (8 to 12 per cent) and generally not abnormal. A small number of infants in prolonged pregnancy develop dysmaturity, so called "postmaturity syndrome."

Prenatal Life
DAVID W. SMITH

The genetic endowment that guides the morphogenesis and function of an individual is contained within the fertilized ova, the zygote. After the first few cell divisions, differentiation begins to take place, presumably through activation or inactivation of particular genes, allowing cells to assume diverse roles. The entire process is programmed in a timely and sequential order, with little allowance for error, especially in early morphogenesis. The following are a few of the phenomena which are critical in morphogenesis: migration of cells; aggregation of like cells; controlled mitotic rate; controlled cell death; inductive interaction between variant tissues; and high energy requirement during the most active period of differentiation for a particular tissue.

LIFE SITUATION

Physical

Figures 4–1 through 4–15 show the progression from fertilization to the 7-month fetal stage of development. The relative rates of linear and weight growth are shown in Figure 4–16, and charts showing the normal ranges of growth during late fetal life are in the appendix. The Negro fetus, which normally matures faster and has a shorter gestational period, is slightly heavier than the Caucasian fetus until about 35 weeks of gestation; thereafter the Caucasian fetus grows more rapidly. Hence, at full-term birth the Caucasian baby is usually larger than the Negro baby, though not more mature.

Physiologic*

General. The early fetus is approximately 94 per cent water, and by full term is 69 per cent water. Weight gain is accelerated during the last eight weeks of fetal life by the accumulation of adipose tissue.

Fetal blood has a low oxygen tension (30 mm Hg), partly because

---

*See also the Perinatal section of Chapter 5, especially for cardiovascular and pulmonary development and function.

(Text continues on page 38.)

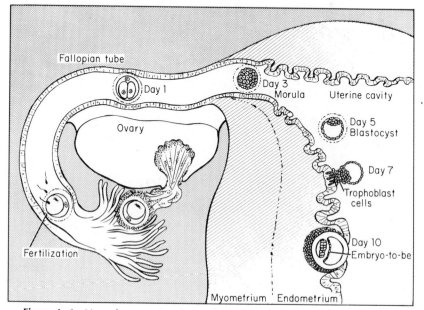

Figure 4–1 Normal progression during *the first 10 days,* from fertilization in the Fallopian tube to implantation in the uterus.

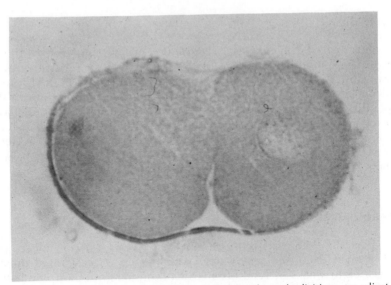

Figure 4–2 *Two cell stage,* within zona pellucida. The early divisions are reliant on the maternal cytoplasm of the ova for nutrition, and occur without enlargement of the ovum.

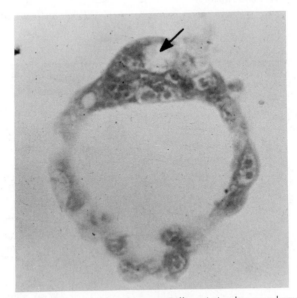

Figure 4–3 *Four to five day blastula stage.* Differentiation has now begun. The embryonic cell mass shows the first indication toward an amniotic space (arrow). The cells above it will become trophoblasts, capable of invading the lining of the uterus. At this stage there are about 108 cells, of which 8 will become endoderm and ectoderm, the initiation of the embryo-to-be.

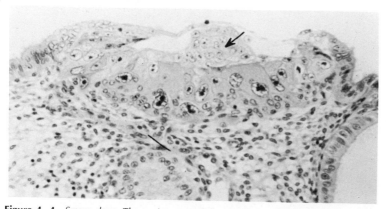

Figure 4–4 *Seven days.* The major part of the conceptus, the cytotrophoblast, has invaded the endometrium, and the embryo-to-be (arrow) is differentiating into two diverse cell layers, the ectoderm and the endoderm. The invading syncytiotrophoblast cells must now produce chorionic gonadotropin, thus maintaining the corpus luteum of the ovary and maintaining the pregnancy. The presence of this hormone in the mother's urine is one early test of pregnancy.

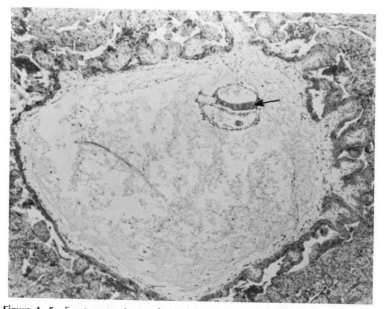

Figure 4–5 *Fourteen to sixteen days.* The thicker ectoderm (arrow) has its continuous amniotic sac, whereas the underlying endoderm has its yolk sac. Major changes will now begin to take place. Nutrition is by diffusion at this stage of development. The chorionic villi of the placenta are now forming. As the embryo bulges forth into the uterine cavity the chorion will become denuded in that area.

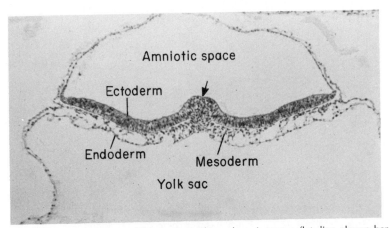

Figure 4–6 *Seventeen to eighteen days.* The embryo is now a flat disc, shown here in transverse section. Mesoblast cells migrate from the ectoderm through Hensen's node (the hillock marked by the arrow) and the primitive streak to specific locations between the ectoderm and endoderm, there constituting the highly versatile mesoderm. The formation of most organ tissues results from an interaction between mesoderm and adjacent ectoderm or endoderm. Anterior to Hensen's node the notochord develops, providing axial support and influencing subsequent development such as that of the overlying neural plate.

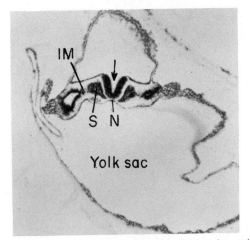

Figure 4–7 *Twenty-one to twenty-three days.* The midaxial ectoderm has thickened and formed the neural groove (arrow), partially influenced by the underlying notochord (N). This groove will fuse dorsally to form the neural tube. Lateral to it the mesoblast has now segmented into somites (S), intermediary mesoderm (IM), and somatopleura and splanchnopleura as intervening stages toward further differentiation. Vascular channels are developing *in situ* from mesoderm; blood cells are being produced in the yolk sac wall; and the early heart is beating. Henceforth development is extremely rapid with major changes each day. The next 3 to 4 weeks are the era of major organogenesis during which incomplete or faulty development may leave the individual with residual malformation.

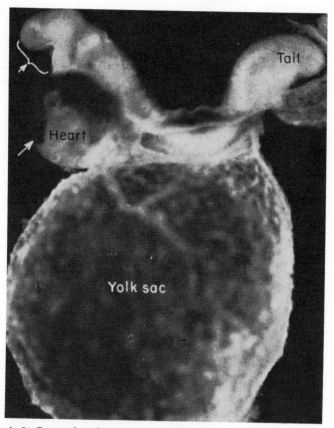

Figure 4–8 *Twenty-four days.* The forepart of the embryo is growing rapidly, especially the anterior neural plate. The lateral portions are growing downward while the head and tail are curling downward also in their growth. Soon the body wall will be fused and the embryo will be in a C-shaped position. The cardiac tube (lower arrow) under the developing face (upper arrow) is now functional. The yolk sac will now rapidly regress.

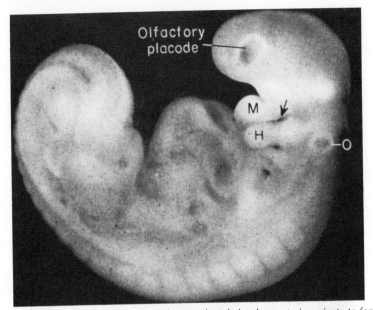

Figure 4–9 *Twenty-six days.* The olfactory placode has begun to invaginate to form the nasal pit. Between it and the mandibular process is the area of the future mouth, where the buccopharyngeal membrane, with no intervening mesoderm, is breaking down. Within the recess of the mandibular (M) and hyoid (H) processes the future external auditory canal will develop (arrow), and dorsal to it the otic placode (O) is invaginating to form the inner ear. The relatively huge heart must pump blood to the developing placenta as well as to the embryo proper. Foregut outpouchings and evaginations will now begin to form various glands and the lung and liver primordia. Foregut and hindgut are now clearly delineated from the yolk sac. The somites, which will differentiate into myotomes (musculature), dermatomes (subcutaneous tissue), and sclerotomes (vertebrae), are evident on into the tail, which will gradually regress.

of the admixture of arterial and venous blood in the intervillous space of the placenta. The fetus does well by virtue of having a high level of fetal type hemoglobin relative to oxygen-carrying capacity and because he can better utilize anaerobic metabolism for his energy needs. Thus, the fetus and the newborn may be able to withstand periods of hypoxemia more successfully than can mature persons. The early energy needs are predominantly met by glucose through entrance of pyruvate into the energy-generating cycle. The young embryo also uses the pentose shunt pathway, which allows production of pentose necessary for RNA and DNA synthesis, to a greater extent than the mature person. Later in fetal life, protein and fat become part of the energy resource, with increasing generation of high-energy ATP.

Placenta. This organ, fetal in origin, serves as liver, lung and kidney for the fetus. It is responsible for fetal nutrition and homeostasis. In addition, it provides a large number of protein and steroid hormones and enzymes such as chorionic gonadotropin, estrogen, progesterone, alkaline phosphatase, diamine oxidase and others. Progesterone appears to be one of the poorly understood factors involved in preventing uterine contractions and may affect the duration of gestation. Prostaglandins also may be important in the maintenance of the uterine homeostasis. If the fetus is dying, the first measurable hormonal change may be a decrease in maternal urinary estriol excretion. Precursors of this steroid are produced by the fetal adrenal, modified by the fetal liver, metabolized in the placenta and then excreted into the maternal urine.

The developing placenta is relatively large in early fetal life; by 15 weeks the fetus proper has equalled the placenta in weight, and thereafter surpasses it in size. New cells are added in the placenta until about 32 weeks; thereafter the growth rate is less rapid, and degenerative aging changes are sometimes evident by birth. At birth the placenta weighs about 460 gm (14 per cent of fetal weight). If the pregnancy goes beyond about 40 gestational weeks, the placenta may no longer be an adequate resource; postmature babies may show indications of undernutrition.

The vascular villous bed of the placenta has a surface area of about 160 square feet. Substances with a molecular weight of less than a few hundred, such as most anesthetic gases and drugs, pass through by direct or "facilitated" diffusion. Caution must therefore be exercised

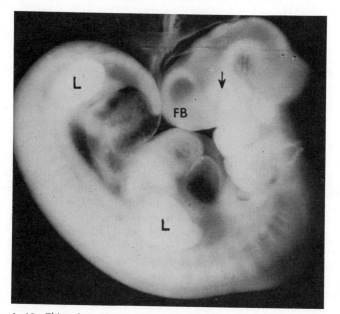

Figure 4–10 *Thirty days.* The brain is rapidly growing, and its early cleavage into future bilateral cerebral hemispheres is evident in the telencephalic outpouching of the forebrain (FB). To the right of this is the developing eye, with the cleft optic cup (arrow) and the early invagination of the future lens from surface ectoderm. From the somatopleura the limb swellings (L) have developed. The loose mesenchyme of the limb bud, interacting with the thickened ectodermal cells at its tip, carries all the potential for the full development of the limb. The liver is now functional and will be a source of blood cells. The mesonephric ducts, formed in the mesonephric ridges, communicate to the cloaca, which is beginning to become septated, and the yolk sac is regressing.

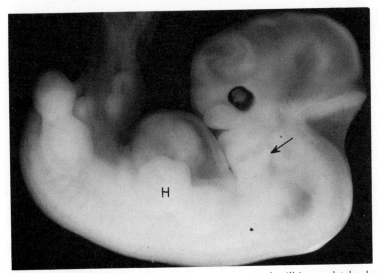

Figure 4–11 *Thirty-six days.* The retina is now pigmented, still incompletely closed at its inferior medial margin. Closure of the lip is nearly complete. The hillocks of His are forming the early external ear (arrow) from the adjacent borders of the mandibular and hyoid swellings. The hand plate (H) has formed with condensation of mesenchyme into the five finger rays. The lower limb lags behind the upper limb in its development. The ventricular septum is partitioning the heart. The ureteral bud from the mesonephric duct has induced a kidney from the mesonephric ridge, which is also forming gonad and adrenal. Cloacal septation is nearly complete; the infraumbilical mesenchyme has filled in all the cloacal membrane except the urogenital area; and the genital tubercles are fused, whereas the labioscrotal swellings are unfused. The gut is elongating, and a loop of it may be seen projecting out into the body stalk.

in both the nature and dosage of agents administered to the pregnant woman. Lipid solubility, protein binding and other factors affect placental transfer. The diffusing gradient favors a slightly higher fetal level of many amino acids, water-soluble vitamins, calcium, phosphorus, magnesium, potassium and inorganic iodide ions. The transfer of iron seems to be unidirectional to the fetus. There is selective transfer of a few large proteins, such as maternal immunoglobulin G (IgG), which increasingly crosses to the fetus after four to five months, providing passive immune protection against certain infectious agents during the first few postnatal months. No maternal anterior pituitary hormones and relatively little maternal thyroxin cross the placental barrier; hence the fetus is generally self-reliant in terms of its endocrine function. As an "auxiliary liver" the placenta synthesizes albumin and alpha and beta globulins, degrades certain molecules, stores glycogen, and makes fructose.

Minor placental leaks may occur during pregnancy, allowing a few blood cells to exchange, but the most common time for this to occur is during placental separation following delivery, when a significant fetal-maternal transfusion may occur. This is the critical time for the Rh-negative mother; the time when she may become sensitized

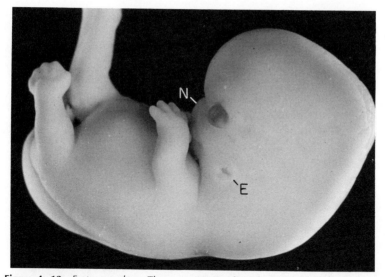

Figure 4-12 *Forty-one days.* The nose (N) is relatively flat, and the external ear (E) is gradually shifting in relative position as it continues to grow and develop. A neck area is now evident, the anterior body wall has formed, and the thorax and abdomen are separated by the transverse septum (diaphragm). The fingers are now partially separated, and the elbow is evident. The major period of cardiac morphogenesis and septation is complete. The urogenital membrane has now broken down, yielding a urethral opening. The phallus and lateral labioscrotal folds are the same for both sexes at this age.

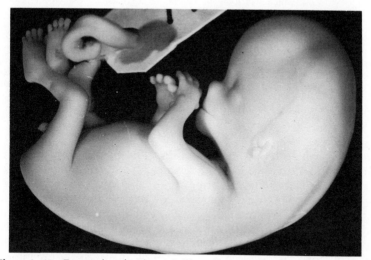

Figure 4-13 *Ten-week male.* The eyelids have developed and fused, not to reopen until four or five months. Muscles are developed and functional; normal morphogenesis of joints is dependent on movement; and primary ossification is occurring in the centers of developing bones. Ossification begins at 7 weeks in the clavicle and by birth all the primary centers are ossified with only the secondary centers at the knee being ossified by that time.

In the male the testicle has produced testosterone and masculinized the external genitalia with enlargement of the genital tubercle, fusion of the labioscrotal folds into a scrotum, and closure of the labia minora folds to form a penile urethra; these structures are unchanged in the female.

Figure 4–14 *Three and one-half month male.* The fetus is settling down for the latter two-thirds of prenatal life. The morphogenesis of the lung, largely solid at this point in development, will not have progressed to the capacity for aerobic exchange for another three to four months. The skin is increasing in thickness, and its accessory structures are differentiating. The deciduous teeth are now developing from the interaction between invaginating ectoderm, which will form the enamel, and adjacent mesenchyme, which will form the dentin and pulp. The permanent dentition begins mineralizing at birth and is complete by about 15 years.

The fetus is active in its aquatic environment, but it is not until 4 to 5 months that the mother usually discerns the movement. Thereafter, it is seldom that a day passes without activity being noted. The amniotic fluid is being swallowed and continually replaced, predominantly by urination. It is now possible to insert a needle into the amniotic space and withdraw 5 to 10 ml of fluid (amniocentesis) for studies of the fluid or fetal cells contained therein.

During the next few months there is a major addition of neuronal cells within the brain.

by the Rh-positive fetal red blood cells. The period during labor and delivery is also a time when serious maternal and sometimes fetal blood loss can occur secondary to rupture of aberrant fetal vessels in the membranes or premature separation of part of the placenta. A large reservoir of blood exists in the placenta at the time of birth and the blood volume of the newborn can be greatly influenced by "early" versus "late" clamping of the umbilical cord.

Circulation. By several weeks of age, diffusion is no longer an adequate means of supplying nutrition to the conceptus, and a circulatory system develops. The pulsatile tubelike heart folds upon itself with rotation, septation and valvular development contributing to its final form. Vascular channels generally form *in situ,* and these coalesce and change in accordance with the tissue within which they develop. The work and size of the early heart are relatively great since it must also supply the placenta, yolk sac, and membranes.

The red blood cells which are initially nucleated are first produced in the yolk sac, then in the liver and spleen, and from 7 to 8 weeks are increasingly developed in the bone marrow. Under a stress such as the hemolysis of erythroblastosis fetalis, red blood cells may continue to be produced in the liver and spleen in addition to the marrow. Leukocytes are produced from about 40 days of age onward.

Hemostasis. Maturation of the clotting components into an effective hemostatic mechanism continues throughout gestation and in part during early infancy. Extensive hemorrhage occurs in most early abortuses, in which all hemostatic components are poorly developed. Premature infants have imperfect platelets, fragile vessels, and low levels of several clotting factors, and hemorrhage is relatively common. In full-term babies, only platelet function and certain clotting factors (principally the vitamin K factors) are incompletely developed, and bleeding is rare.

Immune System. Early lymphocyte stem cells derive apparently from the thymus. Early in fetal life the stem cells appear to differentiate into two populations. One group, termed T-cells, are thymus-dependent and reside primarily in the bone marrow; they are associated with delayed or cellular immunity. The other, termed B-cells, populate the lymph

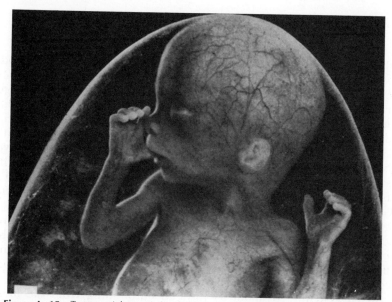

Figure 4-15 *Twenty-eight-week fetus.* At about this stage the lung has matured to the extent of usually allowing for some aerobic exchange, but it is a very hazardous time to be born. The major cause of death from this period of development till adulthood is prematurity, being born too soon. The major reason for death in the premature is respiratory insufficiency.

Adipose tissue now develops and the fetus will normally double in weight during the next 2 months and be mildly obese at full term birth. Testicular descent into the scrotum occurs at about this time in development. The lung becomes increasingly capable of aerobic oxygen exchange in late fetal life.

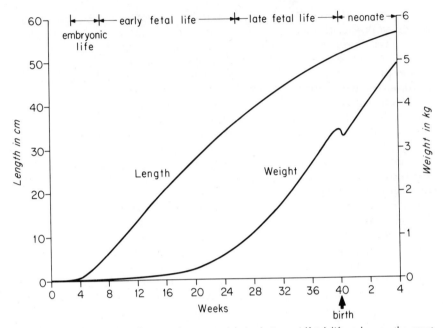

Figure 4-16 The most rapid linear growth is during midfetal life, whereas the most rapid advancement in weight is in late fetal life.

nodes and spleen, and differentiate further into the normal antibody-producing (immunoglobulin) cell line, including plasma cells. The responsiveness of the immune system to antigenic stimulus is rarely challenged during fetal life. Indeed, one of the unique phenomena surrounding pregnancy is the unresponsiveness of the mother or infant to the foreign antigens unique to the other. The absence of the rejection of what is to all intents and purposes a prolonged homograft remains an unsolved mystery. Nevertheless, there is good evidence that the fetus, though it has perhaps a limited immune capacity, is capable of response. The humoral response may be partially modified by the transfer of maternal IgG to the fetus, beginning at about 16 weeks.

The embryo and the early fetus have an active macrophage defense system and lack the usual tissue injury response involving polymorphonuclear cells and fibrosis. This difference helps to explain the absence of fibrous scars at sites damaged in early development; instead, the damaged part may be reduced in size or missing.

Renal System. At about 31 days an outbudding from the mesonephric duct induces the metanephros to begin the formation of the kidney. This outbudding progressively arborizes to become the calyceal system, with collecting ducts which anastamose with the tubules and their glomeruli of metanephric origin, which continue to form until about 35 weeks. Renal tubular function is present from 8 weeks, and some water reabsorption from 11 to 12 weeks. However, the distal tubules are short and, hence, concentrating ability is limited. There is also limited ability to acidify the urine.

Amniotic Cavity. The amount of amniotic fluid increases from about 50 ml at 12 weeks to 400 ml at 20 weeks. Early in pregnancy it is a transudate of maternal serum reaching the amniotic cavity through the fetal skin, salivary glands, tracheobronchial tree and through the placenta, membranes, and cord. After 20 weeks' gestation, fetal urine assumes an increasing role and late in pregnancy is the predominant source of amniotic fluid. There is a dynamic fluid exchange such that in a matter of three hours the fluid is totally replaced. Removal of amniotic fluid is accomplished mainly through fetal swallowing plus absorption through the fetal lung, skin, cord and amnion.

From 13 to 14 menstrual weeks onward it is possible to insert a needle through the lower abdominal wall and uterus of a pregnant woman and obtain 5 to 10 ml of amniotic fluid. This is presently done at the parents' request when there is a known high risk of having a child with a serious disorder detectable in early development. For example, chromosome studies of cultured amnion cells from amniotic fluid can be done to exclude a fetal chromosomal abnormality. Similarly, enzyme studies can be performed to exclude, for example, a homozygous fetus with Tay-Sachs disease, when parents are carriers of the mutant gene for this autosomal recessive disorder. Sex can be determined in the fetus of a woman who is a known carrier for an X-linked recessive disorder such as hemophilia, in which case the male fetus would have a 50 per cent risk of being affected. Having obtained the definitive information, the parents can then elect to terminate an undesirable pregnancy prior to fetal extrauterine viability.

Intestine. Swallowing and peristalsis occur early, but there is usually no passage of the thick, dark intestinal accumulation called meconium until after birth. Earlier passage resulting in meconium staining of amniotic fluid may indicate that the fetus has, at some time, experienced distress. Trypsin is present from 16 weeks, and amylase by birth.

Behavioral Components. The neural groove closes, mitoses result in increasing numbers of neurones which migrate out from the basilar layer, the anterior neural tube develops into the brain, and axone processes move out while those within the brain and spinal cord form networks. Myelinization of certain axones begins at 4 to 5 months and generally coincides with functional capacity. Fetal motor activity has been noted from 8 weeks, though the mother does not generally feel fetal movement until about 17 weeks. Any period of prolonged inactivity after 4 to 5 months should give rise to concern about a fetal problem. Functional activity proceeds from cephalad to caudad, and stereotyped reflexes are combined and superseded by increasingly complex patterns as brain centers begin to coordinate the activity. Thus, initially jerky activity becomes more smooth and sustained.

Cerebellar development is relatively late. This is the presumed reason why the 7- to 8-month-old premature baby is relatively hypotonic, with irregular jerky movements, whereas the full-term baby is mildly hypertonic, and only slightly jerky in its movements.

FETAL PROBLEMS

Mortality and Morbidity. The highest mortality is in the earliest stages of development when serious errors in morphogenesis often do not allow continued development. The studies of Hertig *et al.* indicated that only about 50 per cent of fertilized ova survive to become a recognized pregnancy. Following recognition of the pregnancy, the spontaneous abortion rate is reported as being from 10 to 25 per cent. Most of these occur in the first 5 to 8 weeks of pregnancy. The reasons for this high early mortality are not clearly delineated, but at least one major cause is chromosomal abnormalities, discussed later in this section. The lower limit of birth weight for viability of a premature is 500 to 700 gm. Some of the problems which lead to fetal morbidity and death in the latter stages of fetal life are presented below.

Prematurity and Prenatal Growth Deficiency. A clear distinction should be made between the premature baby and the one with prenatal growth deficiency. About one-third of babies weighing less than 2500 grams at birth represent the latter situation and are *not* premature.

Prenatal growth deficiency is a rather gross sign which may be the consequence of one of a number of genetic or environmentally determined causes, some of which are presented below or in the tables. It is important to appreciate that the baby with prenatal growth deficiency, though usually more mature than the premature of comparable weight, is more liable to develop problems of neonatal adaptation such as hypoglycemia or hypocalcemia within the first few days after birth than is a normally grown infant of comparable gestational age.

Prematurity, with its attendant problems of early adaptation to the extrauterine environment, is the number one cause of death in early infancy. The main reason for death is respiratory insufficiency secondary to immaturity of the lung, which will be discussed in the next chapter. The premature baby is also more likely to have intraventricular hemorrhage, sepsis, hypoglycemia, hypothermia, acidosis, hyperbilirubinemia, and/or periods of malnutrition. These can be lethal or leave permanent residua, especially in terms of brain development and function. An attempt should be made to determine the cause of prematurity, which can be maternal or fetal in origin. Some of the causes are set forth in Tables 4–1 and 4–2.

Placental Problems. Placental insufficiency can result in secondary fetal malnutrition. A low uterine placement of the placenta (placenta praevia) can result in premature separation or even laceration of the placenta as the cervix begins to dilate in late pregnancy. This can result in serious maternal blood loss and, on occasion, fetal bleeding; it is also one cause of premature delivery.

Infectious Problems. The early fetus is generally an excellent culture medium for many viral agents. Once a viral agent is acquired through maternal viremia, or via the vaginal route (rarely), it tends to cause chronic, widespread fetal disease. In early fetal life there may be no inflammatory response and no fibrosis. Hence, the residua may simply be missing cells and incomplete development. Serious disease

TABLE 4–1 SOCIOLOGIC SITUATIONS WHICH MAY RELATE TO A FETAL PROBLEM

Sociologic	Potential Fetal Problem
Lower socioeconomic status	Prematurity
Older woman, first pregnancy	Prematurity
Incestuous union	Mental deficiency (presumed autosomal recessive)
Older maternal age	Autosomal trisomy syndromes

may occur in tissues which are not altered by the same viral agent in the mature person. A notable example is the rubella agent (German measles), which, for unknown reasons, must usually be acquired during the first 12 to 16 weeks to cause fetal disease. Such viral agents may give rise to a fetal immunoglobulin M (IgM) antibody response, but this is usually insufficient to rid the fetus of the viral agent. The IgM response can be utilized at birth as a nonspecific indicator of prenatal infectious disease, since IgM does not cross in significant amounts from the mother and is provoked only by an antigenic stimulus to the fetus.

Table 4–3 lists some of the fetal pathogenic infectious agents and their potentially damaging effects, *if* the fetus survives the insult.

Rupture of the membranes before the onset of labor places the fetus at risk for both premature labor and infection. If it occurs at or near term, about 90 per cent of women will go into labor during the next 24 hours. If labor does not ensue, then serious thought should

TABLE 4–2 MATERNAL METABOLIC OR DISEASE PROBLEMS

Maternal	Potential Fetal Problem
Diabetes mellitus	Obesity, respiratory insufficiency, neonatal hypoglycemia, malformation (6%)
Hypertension	Prematurity
Toxemia of pregnancy	Prematurity, growth deficiency, respiratory insufficiency
Hyperthyroidism	Transient thyrotoxicosis
Untreated phenylpyruvic oligophrenia	Microcephaly, mental deficiency
Cardiac disorder, especially cyanotic	Growth deficiency, prematurity
Incompetent cervix	Prematurity

TABLE 4-3   FETAL INFECTIOUS DISEASE

Maternal Infection	Potential Fetal Disease
Rubella during first trimester	Deafness, heart defect, cataract, mental deficiency, chorioretinitis, growth deficiency
Syphilis*	Deafness, mental deficiency, osteitis, chondylomata
Toxoplasmosis*	Hydrocephalus, microcephaly, chorioretinitis, mental deficiency
Cytomegalic inclusion disease	Microcephaly, hydrocephalus, chorioretinitis, mental deficiency, hepatitis
Herpes simplex (usually via vaginal route)	Meningoencephalitis
Coxsackie B	Myocarditis
Serum hepatitis	Hepatitis
Vaccinia	Severe generalized vaccinia
Bacterial sepsis	Sepsis

*From *primary* maternal infection. Secondary infections seldom lead to parasitemia.

be given to induction of labor. Spontaneous labor occurs less frequently if the fetus is premature, but induction of labor is not indicated. As the interval between rupture of membranes and delivery increases, so does the risk of amnionitis. Should infection occur, treatment consists of antibiotics and prompt delivery (vaginally or by cesarean section). There is no place for prophylactic antibiotics to prevent amnionitis.

Chemical and Drug Problems. During the period of rapid growth and differentiation, the embryo and fetus may be more susceptible to the toxic effect of a chemical agent than is the mature mother, as was dramatically indicated by the thalidomide disaster. Table 4-4 lists some of the *known* presently available agents which can cause a problem for the fetus.

Nutritional Problems. Though the parasitic embryo and fetus will generally thrive at the expense of a mildly malnourished mother, his development may be compromised in a seriously malnourished mother. Of special concern in this regard is the mid- to late-fetal period, during which time there is a major addition of neurones within the fetal brain. It is now recommended that the woman gain about 20 to 30 pounds during a pregnancy, depending upon her weight prior to the pregnancy. Little or no salt restriction is necessary; a diet high in good quality protein is essential.

TWINNING. About one in 80 pregnancies consists of twins, with about 30 per cent being monozygotic (identical twins). Twins grow at the usual rate until 30 weeks, to a combined weight of about 4000 gm, and thereafter tend to grow at a slower rate. The rate of growth is often unequal, especially for identical twins, who at times have a placental vascular communication and therefore suffer from unequal exchange. Twins are likely to be relatively undernourished at birth and are more prone to prematurity and problems of neonatal adaptation.

Immunologic Problems. If the fetus is Rh-positive and the mother Rh-negative, the fetal red cells can sensitize the mother to produce anti-Rh-positive antibodies. The maternal antibodies can cross the placenta and result in hemolytic destruction of fetal Rh-positive red blood cells during that pregnancy or subsequent pregnancies, giving rise to the disorder known as erythroblastosis fetalis. The most likely time for a mother to receive a significant dose of fetal red blood cells is at delivery. As the placenta separates, the mother often receives a small transfusion of fetal blood into her circulation. If she is Rh-negative and the baby Rh-positive, these fetal red cells can stimulate a permanent maternal antibody response. These fetal red blood cells can be rapidly destroyed before they cause sensitization by giving the mother high titre anti-Rh antibody (Rhogam), which thereby prevents her from being sensitized. Thus, every Rh-negative woman who delivers an Rh-positive offspring should be given the hyperimmune gamma globulin within 72 hours of the delivery.

TABLE 4–4   MEDICATIONS AND DRUGS

Maternal	Potential Damaging Effect on Fetus
Aminopterin	Skeletal dysplasia, multiple defects
Methyl mercury	Brain dysfunction
Androgenic steroids	Masculinization of external genitalia in female
Tetracyclines	Discoloration with or without hypoplasia of enamel in developing teeth
Iodides or propylthiouracil	Goiter, due to block in thyroxine synthesis
Narcotic addiction	Postnatal irritability, lethargy, seizures
Heavy cigarette smoking	Mild growth deficiency, average of 400 gm less in birth weight
Alcoholism	Growth deficiency, developmental lag

This prevention of Rh sensitization has now made ABO blood group incompatibility a more common incompatibility problem. The situation of maternal-O, fetal-A or B is the most frequent circumstance encountered but, since the type O mother already has anti-A or anti-B agglutinins from early life, this cannot be prevented in the manner of the above-mentioned Rh sensitization. Furthermore, the *first* pregnancy is a potential for ABO incompatibility problems, whereas this rarely occurs for Rh incompatibility unless the Rh-negative mother has been previously sensitized by an Rh-positive transfusion. The major risk of ABO incompatibility is unconjugated hyperbilirubinemia in the perinatal period, secondary to the hemolysis.

Sociologic Situations and Fetal Problems. Table 4–1 lists a few of the fetal problems which can be related to a maternal sociologic situation. Of these, the most important is the increased frequency of prematurity in women of lower socioeconomic status. The reasons for this are not clearly understood, though relatively poor nutrition, crowding, and poor general maternal health and care are considered to be factors.

Maternal Metabolic or Disease Problems. Table 4–2 lists a few of the maternal disorders which can have an adverse effect on the fetus. It should be appreciated that the cause of maternal toxemia of pregnancy may derive from the fetal placenta.

Multifactorial-Common Malformation Problems. Multifactorial is herein meant to imply the combined effect of many genes—polygenic—plus environmental effects. Present evidence in the human implies that polygenic inheritance, interacting with as-yet-unrecognized environmental factors, is the major mode in the causation of most of the more common single localized defects in morphogenesis. Examples include isolated cleft lip, cleft palate, most cardiac defects, pyloric stenosis, meningomyelocele, anencephaly, dislocation of the hip, and club foot. Taken together, these defects make up over half of the 2 per cent of babies born with a recognized malformation problem. For normal parents who have one child with such a defect, the recurrence risk for the same type of anomaly is 3 to 5 per cent for their next offspring. The risk for the offspring of an affected parent who marries a normal individual is of the same magnitude, 3 to 5 per cent. As yet we do not know of any environmental alteration which would reduce the liability for any one of these more common single localized defects in morphogenesis.

Chromosomal Abnormality Problems. Faulty chromosomal distribution leading to genetic imbalance occurs in at least 4 per cent of pregnancies. For most of these this is a lethal situation, as indicated by the fact that 25 per cent of spontaneous abortions are due to a chromosomal abnormality. About one in 200 babies born has a chromosomal abnormality and some of these, such as 18 trisomy and 13 trisomy tend to be sublethal, with most infants dying in the early postnatal period. Figure 4–17 summarizes the occurrence and types of chromosomal abnormalities found in early life.

Other Malformation Problems. There are many individually rare malformation problems which account for about a third of the babies born with a problem in morphogenesis, polygenic (multifactorial) and

CHROMOSOMAL ABNORMALITIES

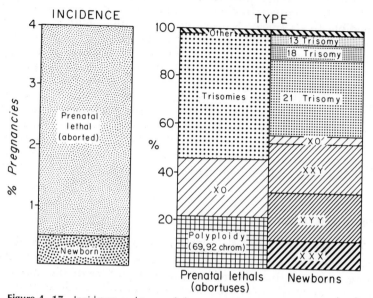

Figure 4–17 Incidence and types of chromosomal abnormalities in early life.

chromosomal abnormalities accounting for the majority. This remaining one third includes patterns of anomaly due to a single mutant gene (autosomal dominant), of which most represent a fresh gene mutation from unaffected parents. Others are due to a pair of mutant genes (autosomal recessive) or an X-linked mutant gene. Rarely, one encounters a malformation problem for which an environmental causation is clearly implied, but for many no cause is apparent.

The Pregnant Woman
DOUGLAS DER YUEN

LIFE SITUATION AND COMMON DISORDERS

Emotional Changes

In addition to the many physiologic changes of pregnancy, certain emotional changes also commonly characterize pregnancy; in fact, some multiparous patients recognize the onset of pregnancy by the appearance of personality changes. Mood changes, such as temporary mental depression, emotional instability with unprovoked crying spells and mental irritability, occur not infrequently. Mental and physical exhaustion, with somnolence and fatigue, are common during pregnancy. Occasionally, pregnant patients develop bizarre cravings for strange or inedible foods (pica). Nausea alone or with vomiting is frequently encountered during early pregnancy. The exact cause is not known, but the symptoms are usually self-limited and respond to appropriate therapy, invariably disappearing after the first trimester of pregnancy. Only between 1 and 5 per 1000 vomit so severely that they require hospitalization (hyperemesis gravidarum). Most women experience a progressive decrease in sexual desire during pregnancy that returns to normal after pregnancy. The many physical and emotional changes of pregnancy may be worrisome and bothersome to the patient, and she needs reassurance from her obstetrician and the nursing staff that the changes are a physiologic part of normal pregnancy.

Physiologic Changes

Systemic and Metabolic. The pregnant patient has a different "look" than the nonpregnant female. This is not only due to the enlarging abdomen, but also to the gait and posture of the patient. The changing center of gravity produces a progressive lordosis of the spine and results in backache, a common complaint during pregnancy (Fig. 4–18). The average weight gain during pregnancy should approximate 25 pounds. At term most of this weight gain is accounted for by the weight of the fetus, placenta, amniotic fluid, physiologic edema, and enlarging uterus, breasts, and blood volume (Table 4–5). Proper dietary habits are important, and a diet consisting of at least one gram of protein per kilogram of body weight of the mother is the minimum daily requirement for proper fetal growth and development. The fetus demands a large amount of iron from the maternal system (300 mg), and does this at the expense, not only of the mother's iron stores, but also of the mother's hemoglobin. An additional 500 mg of iron is required for the expanded red cell volume of pregnancy. If the maternal iron stores are seriously depressed, iron deficiency anemia may manifest itself. During pregnancy the plasma volume increase is greater than the increase in red cell mass, so one normally sees a slight drop in the hematocrit, but this is never more than 2 or 3 per cent. The blood leukocyte count is usually normal or slightly elevated during pregnancy but may rise markedly, to levels of 25,000 or more during labor and early puerperium (period after delivery). Several blood coagulation factors are increased during pregnancy, including fibrin, fibrinogen, and factors VII, VIII, IX and X. Clotting times, however, do not differ significantly from those of nonpregnant women.

The hormonal changes of pregnancy affect many organ systems. Dilation of the ureter and renal pelvis occurs, along with an increased tortuosity and decreased motility of the ureter (Fig. 4–19). These changes, primarily induced by placental hormones, may be responsible for the increased incidence of pyelonephritis (renal infection) during pregnancy. In the digestive tract the gastric emptying time is

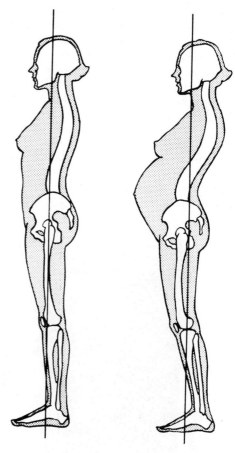

Figure 4-18 The progressive lordosis of the spine during pregnancy produces characteristic changes in gait and posture and may result in backache.

increased and constipation is a common complaint, both due to hormonally decreased bowel motility and pressure from the enlarging uterus. The uterus may also displace the appendix upward, which may

TABLE 4-5 PHYSIOLOGIC WEIGHT GAIN IN PREGNANCY

Fetus	7.5 lbs
Placenta	1.5
Amniotic Fluid	2.0
Hypertrophy uterus	2.0
Hypertrophy breasts	2.0
Blood volume increase	2.0
Extravascular fluid (edema)	5.0
Total	22.0 lbs

confuse the unsuspecting clinician when appendicitis develops during pregnancy (Fig. 4–20). Heartburn, common during pregnancy, is most likely caused by reflux of acid secretions into the lower esophagus. Gallbladder emptying may also be delayed, and it is recognized that pregnancy may predispose to the formation of gallstones. Other endocrine induced anatomic changes include breast enlargement and increased pigmentation of the nipple and areola (Fig. 4–21). Striae occur along the sides of the breasts, and a venous pattern can frequently be seen. Early in pregnancy colostrum can be expressed from the nipples. Striae and a prominent venous pattern may also be present over the abdominal wall (Fig. 4–22). Vascular spiders and palmar erythema are frequent and are possibly related to the hyperestrogenemia. A prominent pigmentation, called the linea nigra, may appear over the midline of the abdomen and umbilicus (Fig. 4–23). A butterfly pigmentation,

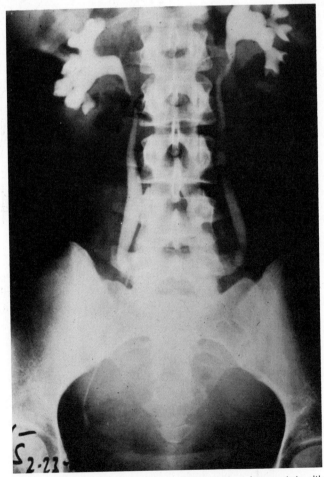

Figure 4–19 An intravenous pyelogram depicting the characteristic dilation of the ureter and renal pelvis, along with an increased tortuosity of the ureter that normally occurs during pregnancy.

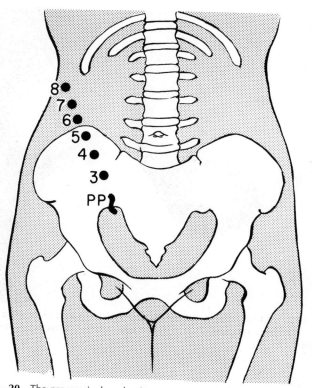

Figure 4–20 The progressively enlarging uterus may displace the appendix upward so that the site of pain and tenderness may vary if appendicitis occurs during pregnancy.

chloasma—"mask of pregnancy"—frequently appears over the face. This same feature may appear in some women when taking oral contraceptives.

Endocrine changes that occur during pregnancy include enlargement of the thyroid gland, with increased serum protein bound iodine (PBI). Since thyroid binding globulin is also markedly increased, the amount of unbound, or effective, hormone is not appreciably higher. The basal metabolic rate (BMR) progressively increases to as high as plus 25 per cent, but most of this increase in oxygen consumption is the result of metabolic activity of the fetus.

Though there is little morphologic change in the adrenal gland, there is a considerable increase in the circulating glucocorticoid, cortisol. Although much of it is bound in the serum by the protein transcortin, the amount of free, active hormone is increased. There is also a considerable rise in aldosterone (the adrenal salt retaining hormone) excretion during pregnancy. This appears to be the result of elevation in the levels of renin, renin substrate and angiotensin, especially during the latter half of pregnancy. The relationship of the augmented renin-angiotensin system and toxemia of pregnancy is still not clarified.

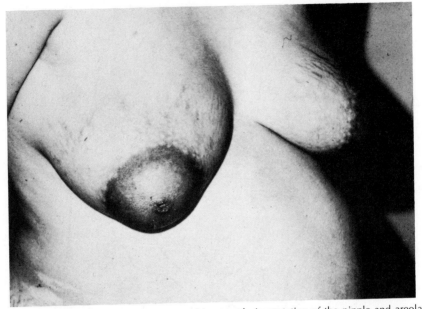

Figure 4–21 Breast enlargement and increased pigmentation of the nipple and areola are common changes of pregnancy. Striae and an accentuated venous pattern over the breasts may often be seen.

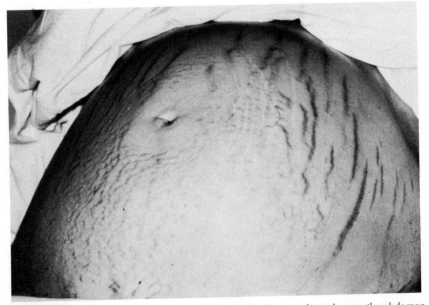

Figure 4–22 Striae gravidarum are reddish, slightly depressed streaks over the abdomen that occur in about one-half of all pregnancies.

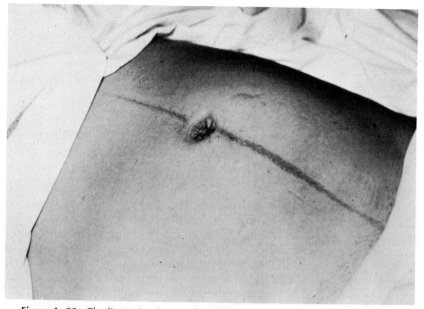

Figure 4–23 The linea nigra is a predominent brownish pigmentation over the midline of the abdomen and umbilicus.

Adrenal androgen, as judged by urinary 17-ketosteroids, appears to be unchanged during pregnancy.

Pregnancy has a "diabetogenic" effect on the patient. Preexisting diabetes may be aggravated, and certain patients may develop a typical glucose tolerance curve of diabetes only during pregnancy. The normal patient, after the 26th week of pregnancy, has a reduced sensitivity to insulin, resulting in higher compensatory circulating insulin levels. It appears that reduced sensitivity to insulin is primarily the result of chorionic somatomammotropin (HCS), a protein hormone secreted by the placenta. Reduced glucose tolerance occurs when compensatory insulin secretion fails to increase adequately. Other contributory factors to the "diabetogenic effect of pregnancy" are the degradation of insulin by the placenta and increased levels of estrogen and free cortisol in the plasma which may antagonize the action of insulin.

Renal. In addition to the anatomic changes of the urinary system previously mentioned, striking functional renal changes may also accompany pregnancy. Glomerular filtration rate (GFR) increases early in pregnancy, as much as 50 per cent by the beginning of the second trimester. Renal plasma flow (RPF) increases to a lesser degree. The apparent GFR and RPF may be lower if measured in the supine or standing position, rather than the lateral recumbent position. This is the result of vena caval venous obstruction, reduced cardiac output, and lowered RPF and GFR. Tests of renal function will be altered by normal pregnancy. Increased GFR may lower blood urea nitrogen (BUN) and creatinine values by as much as one-third (Table 4–6). Urine concentration tests are misleading because pregnant women

TABLE 4-6 PRACTICAL TESTS OF RENAL FUNCTION

	Nonpregnant	Pregnant
Serum creatinine	1–1.5 mg %	0.5 mg %
Serum urea nitrogen	10–20 mg %	9 mg %
Serum uric acid	3–6 mg %	3 mg %
Endogenous creatinine clearance	65–145 cc/min	105–220 cc/min

tend to accumulate fluid (edema) by day, and mobilize and excrete this fluid at night while recumbent, resulting in a dilute morning urine specimen. A physiologic glucosuria is fairly common in pregnancy, due to the increase in GFR which may exceed the tubular reabsorptive capacity for filtered glucose. Although glucosuria may be physiologic, the possibility of diabetes mellitus cannot be ignored, and such patients should be evaluated for abnormal glucose metabolism.

Cardiovascular. Many cardiovascular changes are associated with pregnancy. There is an increase in red cell mass and plasma volume, and, therefore, an increase in blood volume. The cardiac output and heart rate increase early in pregnancy and remain elevated throughout most of pregnancy (Table 4–7). "Physiologic" systolic heart murmurs are commonly encountered during pregnancy, and increased blood volume results in some diffuse heart enlargement and an increase in pulmonary vascular markings. Late in pregnancy the enlarged uterus plays an important role in maternal cardiodynamics. In the supine and semirecumbent positions the uterus produces complete venous occlusion of the inferior vena cava, and many women complain of dizziness or faintness when they assume these positions (Fig. 4–24). Approximately 12 to 15 per cent of women become hypotensive and even faint when they assume the supine position late in pregnancy. This is known as the "supine hypotensive syndrome." Partial obstruction of the abdominal aorta and common iliac arteries also occurs.

TABLE 4-7 CARDIOVASCULAR CHANGES ACCOMPANYING PREGNANCY

% Change	Pregnancy*
Cardiac output	30–50 %
Heart rate	10–15 %
Stroke volume	20–40 %
Blood volume	20–100 %

*Maximum changes, not necessarily at term.

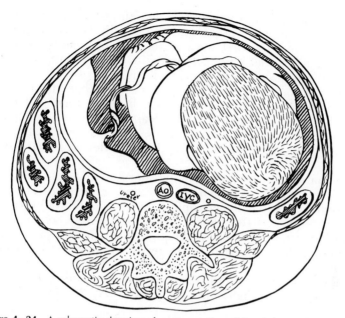

Figure 4-24 A schematic drawing of a cross section of the abdomen during late pregnancy. From the anatomic relationships it can be seen how the pregnant uterus can compress the inferior vena cava and aorta when a woman assumes the supine or semi-recumbent position. This may result in the "supine hypotensive syndrome."

The venous obstruction produces a marked increase in the venous pressure of the legs, and edema of the lower extremities is very common and normal during pregnancy. This also contributes to the common development of varicose veins of the legs and vulva, and of hemorrhoids.

Pulmonary. Few respiratory changes occur during pregnancy. Ventilation per minute increases early and progressively as pregnancy advances. The hyperventilation that accompanies pregnancy is, at times, confused with serious dyspnea. This is not related to altered mechanics of respiration, but appears to be hormonally stimulated. Progesterone has been shown to lower blood pCO_2, possibly by increasing the sensitivity of the respiratory center to stimulation by CO_2. In spite of the enlarging uterus, diaphragmatic excursion and vital capacity remain unaltered.

The Pregnant Uterus

As early as the sixth to eighth week of gestation, pregnancy can be diagnosed by pelvic examination, as one can palpate an enlarged and softened uterus.

The vagina and cervix become congested and cyanotic (Chadwick's sign). On bimanual examination there is softening at the cervical-fundal junction (Hegar's sign) and the fundus of the uterus assumes a globular shape. At approximately 4 months of gestation the uterus becomes an extra-pelvic organ and can readily be palpated abdominally. At this time the first signs of fetal skeletal calcification can be detected on abdominal x-ray. At approximately 5 months of gestation the uterine fundus reaches the umbilicus (Fig. 4–25). Around the middle of the fourth month of gestation the mother may first appreciate fetal movement (quickening), and between then and the fifth month of gestation fetal heart tones can be detected with the fetal stethoscope. Fetal heart beat can be detected as early as the twelfth week of gestation with the aid of the doppler device, which augments the sound.

The marked enlargement of the uterus is made possible mostly by individual muscle cell hypertrophy and stretching. The uterine muscle cell at term has hypertrophied more than tenfold (Fig. 4–26). The uterus contracts throughout pregnancy. These contractions are frequent and occasionally hard enough that the mother or an observer can recognize them in the latter stages of pregnancy (Braxton-Hicks contractions).

In the primigravida and occasionally in the multigravida the patient will experience "lightening," approximately 2 weeks prior to the

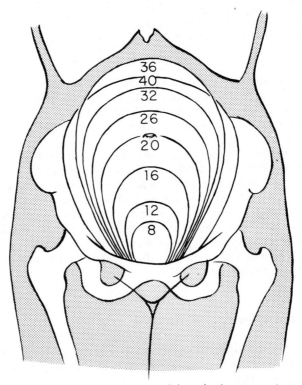

Figure 4–25 A schematic representation of the enlarging uterus at monthly intervals throughout pregnancy. By the fifth month of pregnancy the top of the uterine fundus normally reaches the umbilicus.

Figure 4–26 A cross-sectional sketch of individual uterine muscle cells illustrating the relative sizes and shapes in the nonpregnant state as compared with the pregnant and post-partum states.

onset of labor. This signals the descent of the fetal presenting part into the pelvis. The patient becomes aware that breathing is easier as the pressure against the diaphragm is partially relieved. Pelvic pressure sensations, bladder pressure and discomfort low in the pelvis are not infrequent at this time.

REFERENCES

Prenatal Life

Assali, N. S. (Ed.): Biology of Gestation. Vol. II. The Fetus and Neonate. New York, Academic Press, 1968.

Cohlan, S. O.: Teratogenic agents and cogenital malformations. J. Pediat. *63*:650, 1963.

Dawes, G. S.: Foetal and Neonatal Physiology. Chicago, Year Book Publishers, Inc., 1968.

Hertig, A. T., Rock, J., and Adams, E. C.: A description of 34 human ova within the first 17 days of development. Amer. J. Anat. *98*:435, 1956.

Langman, J.: Medical Embryology. 2nd ed. Baltimore, Williams and Wilkins Company, 1969.

Moore, K.: The Developing Human: Clinically Oriented Embryology. Philadelphia, W. B. Saunders Co., 1973.

Niswander, K. R., and Gordon, M.: The Collaborative Study of the National Institute of Neurological Diseases and Stroke: The Women and Their Pregnancies. Philadelphia, W. B. Saunders Company, 1972.

Potter, E. L.: Pathology of the Fetus and the Infant. Chicago, Year Book Publishers, Inc., 1961.

Schaffer, A. J.: Diseases of the Newborn. 3rd ed. Philadelphia, W. B. Saunders Company, 1971.

Silverstein, A. M., and Lukes, R. J.: Fetal response to antigenic stimulus. Lab. Invest. *11*:918–932, 1962.

Singer, J. E., Westphal, M., and Niswander, K.: Relationship of weight gain during pregnancy to birth weight and infant growth and development in the first year. Obst. Gynec. *31*:417, 1968.

Smith, D. W.: Recognizable Patterns of Human Malformation. Philadelphia, W. B. Saunders Company, 1970.

Villee, D. B.: Development of endocrine function in the human placenta and fetus. New Engl. J. Med. *281*:473–484, 533–541, 1969.

The Pregnant Woman

Hellman, L., and Pritchard, J.: William's Obstetrics. 14th ed. New York, Appleton-Century-Crofts, Inc., 1971.

Ruch, T., and Patton, H. (Eds.): Physiology and Biophysics of Digestion, Metabolism, Endocrine Function and Reproduction. Philadelphia, W. B. Saunders Company, 1973.

Taylor, E. S.: Beck's Obstetrical Practice. 8th ed. Baltimore, Williams & Wilkins Company, 1966.

CHAPTER FIVE

PERINATAL LIFE FOR THE MOTHER AND BABY

Labor and Delivery

KENT UELAND

In order to understand labor, one must have some knowledge of uterine muscle physiology. During labor, contractions of the uterine muscle result in progressive shortening of that muscle, that is, the muscle never returns to its original precontractile length. It is through this mechanism that normal contractions produce a progressive thickening of the upper uterine segment (fundus), while effecting cervical dilatation and effacement (thinning) of the cervix and lower uterine segment. Although the uterus does not have an identifiable pacemaker as such, like the A-V node in the heart, it does have spontaneous rhythmic contractile activity of varying frequency and intensity in both the nonpregnant and the pregnant state. Normal contractions of the pregnant uterus exhibit fundal dominance. The contractions originate in the fundus (at either cornua) and propagate down the uterus to the lower uterine segment and cervix (Fig. 5-1). The contractions are longest and most intense in the fundus and, as a result, the muscle retracts toward it, causing a thinning of the lower uterine segment. Physiologically, the lower uterine segment is a passive structure; anatomically, it consists mainly of elastic tissue fibers interspersed with a few muscle fibers.

Labor can be defined as painful uterine contractions that lead to the expulsion of the fetus. The uterine contractions of labor have the major characteristics of frequency, intensity and duration. Normal contractions should occur between two and five times every 10 minutes. As labor progresses they tend to become more frequent. During the early first stage of labor, the intrauterine pressure generated by a contraction reaches an average of 40 to 60 mm Hg. Normally this intensity increases as labor advances, and it is not unusual to see contractions

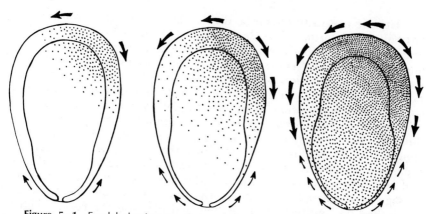

Figure 5-1 Fundal dominance of a normal uterine contraction, with propagation toward the passive lower uterine segment.

as strong as 70 to 80 mm Hg or more late in the first stage and in the second stage of labor. The duration of contractions does not seem to change appreciably during labor, and ordinarily varies from 45 to 90 seconds. Generally, the more intense the contraction, the longer it lasts. Uterine tonus is defined as the pressure that remains in the uterus between contractions. The average tonus in early labor approximates 5 mm Hg, whereas late in labor it can be as high as 12 mm Hg. Rupture of membranes almost invariably lowers uterine tonus at any stage of labor.

Although contractions are rhythmical, they do not occur at regular intervals. Similarly, the intensity and duration may vary, but a contraction following the longest pause is usually the strongest (Fig. 5-2).

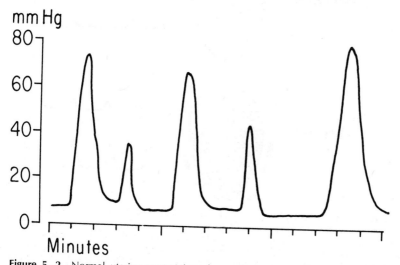

Figure 5-2 Normal uterine contractions frequently vary in intensity, frequency and duration throughout labor.

Uterine contractions can be divided into three types: normal, subnormal and abnormal. The characteristics of normal contractions have already been described. Subnormal contractions tend to occur less frequently than normal contractions, have an amplitude of less than 40 mm Hg and a duration of less than 30 seconds. However, both subnormal and normal contractions have fundal dominance. Abnormal contractions, on the other hand, lack fundal dominance, and the focus initiating the contraction may be located anywhere in the uterus. Ordinarily, they are less intense and occur less frequently than normal contractions. Rarely do they constitute the only type of contraction occurring for any length of time. Typically, they are mixed with normal and subnormal contractions. Understandably, the higher the percentage of abnormal contractions, the more protracted the labor, because they are ineffective in dilating and effacing the cervix. Figure 5–3 schematically presents the characteristics of the three major types

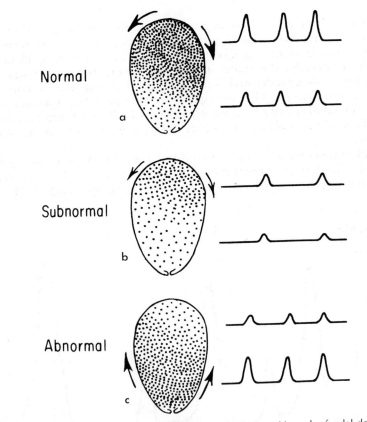

Figure 5–3 Three major types of uterine contractions. a. Normal—fundal dominance with downward propagation, of normal frequency and with the highest pressure in the fundus. b. Subnormal—fundal dominance with downward propagation, of less than normal frequency and intensity. c. Abnormal—lack of fundal dominance or reversed propagation, commonly of less than normal frequency and duration and with the highest pressure at the site where the contraction is initiated.

of uterine contractions. Note the frequency of contractions and the amplitude, both in the fundus and lower uterine segment.

The three basic types of uterine contractions can be identified clinically. During the peak of a normal contraction the uterus cannot be readily indented on abdominal palpation. Vaginal examination at the height of a normal contraction shows the cervix to be tightly applied to the presenting part. This indicates fundal dominance, as the cervix and lower uterine segment are being retracted cephalad. Subnormal contractions are readily indentable abdominally, and on vaginal examination the cervix is not as firmly applied to the presenting part as in a normal contraction. Abnormal contractions may or may not be indentable abdominally; frequently they are. However, on vaginal examination during the peak of the contraction the cervix hangs loose and the examining fingers can readily be passed between the cervix and the presenting part.

Labor is divided into three stages. The first stage begins with the onset of painful uterine contractions and ends when the cervix is completely dilated and retracted. According to Friedman's labor curve, the first stage of labor can be subdivided into two major phases, latent and active (Fig. 5–4). The latent phase begins with the onset of labor and ends when the cervix begins to dilate progressively. During this phase cervical effacement and softening occurs. In primigravid women the latent phase should not exceed 10 hours, and in multigravid women it should not exceed 6 hours. The active phase begins when the cervix starts dilating at a steady rate, normally at about 4 cm of dilatation, and ends with complete dilatation and retraction of the cervix. In the active phase of labor, cervical dilatation should normally proceed at a rate exceeding 1.2 cm per hour in the primigravida and 1.5 cm per hour in the multigravida. Not infrequently, the rate of dilatation is similar in both groups of patients. The average duration of the active phase is 4 to 5 hours in the primigravida and 3 to 4 hours in the multigravida. If one can accurately time the onset of labor, the total duration of the first stage of labor is approximately 12 hours for primigravidas and 7 hours for multigravidas. However, it is important to understand that it is frequently difficult to pinpoint exactly when labor begins, making it impossible to accurately establish the duration. In addition, the cervix is commonly partially dilated and effaced at the onset of labor (primigravida more effaced and less dilated than multigravida), which frequently results in a very short, or even absent, latent phase of labor. Under these circumstances, the length of labor would be greatly reduced, as most of the time spent in labor is attributable to the obscure latent phase.

The second stage of labor may also be subdivided into two major phases. The descent phase begins with complete cervical dilatation and retraction, and ends when the presenting part reaches the pelvic floor or #4 station (approximately 4 cm below the plane of the ischial spines). Normally, 10 uterine contractions should be sufficient to achieve this in both primigravidas and multigravidas. Not infrequently, in primigravidas, the vertex is on the pelvic floor at the time of complete cervical dilatation and retraction, and these patients do not have a

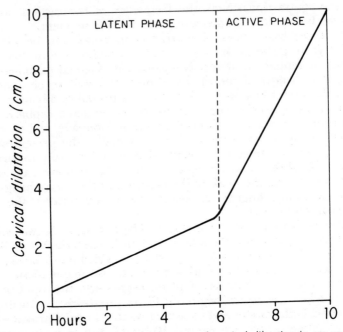

Figure 5–4 Modified Friedman labor curve of cervical dilatation in cm and time in hours, showing the two major phases of the first stage of labor—latent and active.

descent phase in the second stage of labor. A low presenting part at the onset of labor, or rapid descent early in labor, are favorable signs and frequently signify a short labor. A persistently high station suggests a relative cephalopelvic disproportion.

The pelvic floor phase starts when the presenting part reaches the pelvic floor (between contractions) and ends with delivery of the fetus. For primigravidas an average of no more than 20 contractions should be required, while in the multigravidas 10 contractions should be sufficient.

In the first stage of labor two major forces are normally involved: (1) the force of uterine contractions and (2) the resistance of the cervix. Under certain abnormal conditions the resistance of the bony pelvis may also play a role. In the second stage of labor three major forces are involved: (1) uterine contractions, (2) maternal bearing-down, and (3) the resistance of the bony pelvis. Maternal bearing-down efforts are vital and constitute about 50 per cent of the expulsive forces during the second stage of labor.

The third stage of labor begins with the delivery of the fetus and ends with the delivery of the placenta. Placental separation almost invariably occurs with the first one or two contractions following delivery of the fetus. This stage of labor should usually be completed within 4 to 6 minutes, and rarely longer than 10 minutes.

Normally, in the primigravida at the onset of labor the presenting

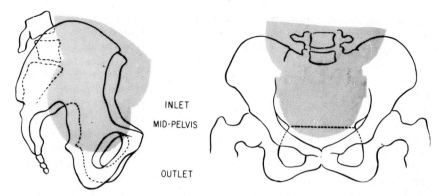

INLET

MID-PELVIS

OUTLET

Figure 5-5 Schematic representation of the relationship between the presenting part and the level of the ischial spines. When the vertex becomes engaged (at 0 station) the largest diameter of the fetal head (biparietal) has negotiated the inlet of the pelvis.

part is engaged, at 0 station. This means that the presenting part is at the level of the plane of the ischial spines (Fig. 5-5). In the multigravida this occurs less commonly and the vertex may remain unengaged or at a minus station during early labor. As labor progresses, the presenting part descends into the pelvis. The type of pelvis frequently determines the position of the vertex during descent. Position of the vertex of the fetus refers to the relationship of the occiput to the maternal pelvis. For example, if the occiput is to the mother's right side and the sagittal suture directly transverse, the position is occiput right transverse (ORT). If, on the other hand, the occiput is to the right and anterior, and the sagittal suture oblique, then the position of the vertex is occiput right anterior (ORA) (Fig. 5-6). With a normal gynecoid pelvis, descent occurs in the transverse or largest diameter of the pelvis. However, in those women who have an anthropoid pelvis

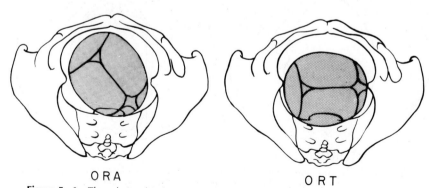

ORA

ORT

Figure 5-6 The relationship between the fetal occiput and the maternal pelvis. ORT—occiput right transverse—fetal occiput is on the mother's right side and the sagittal suture in a horizontal position. ORA—occiput right anterior—the fetal occiput is on the mother's right side and the sagittal suture is directed obliquely.

(with a long anterior-posterior diameter) descent occurs in the occiput anterior or occiput posterior position, again oriented to the largest pelvic diameter (Fig. 5–7). As the head descends, it normally flexes and rotates when it encounters the resistance of the soft tissues of the pelvis, and normally the vertex appears on the pelvic floor in the occiput anterior position. In patients receiving conduction anesthesia the soft tissues of the pelvic diaphragm are relaxed and frequently the contractions are subnormal, so that the normal rotation is either delayed or does not take place at all, resulting in a higher incidence of abnormal positions, such as occiput posterior and occiput transverse. This can readily be corrected by augmenting the contractions with an intravenous infusion of a dilute solution of synthetic oxytocin.

The mean duration of labor for the primigravida is 14 hours and for the multigravida, 8 hours. Labor may be prolonged at any stage and major deviations from the expected normal may be produced by alterations or abnormalities in any of the following: (1) the power,

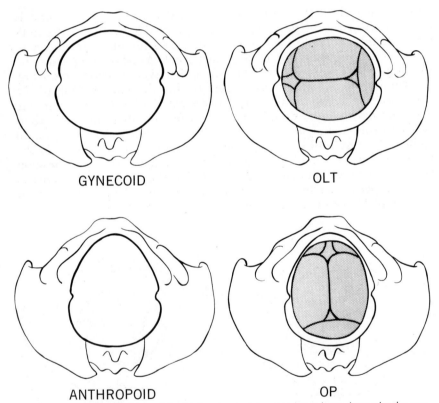

GYNECOID OLT

ANTHROPOID OP

Figure 5–7 The position of the fetal vertex is determined to a large degree by the configuration of the maternal pelvis. The anterior-posterior diameter of the fetal vertex orients itself to the largest pelvic diameter. In the normal gynecoid pelvis the vertex descends in the occiput transverse position as shown. If the pelvis is anthropoid, with a large anterior-posterior diameter, the fetal vertex engages and descends most commonly in the occiput anterior or occiput posterior position.

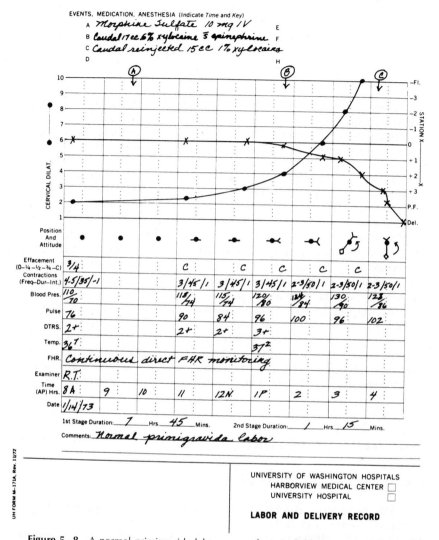

EVENTS, MEDICATION, ANESTHESIA (Indicate *Time* and Key)

A *Morphine Sulfate 10 mg / V* E
B *Caudal 17 cc 6% xylocaine 5 epinephrine* F
C *Caudal reinjected 15 cc 1% xylocaine*
D H

1st Stage Duration: __7__ Hrs. __45__ Mins. 2nd Stage Duration: __1__ Hrs. __15__ Mins.

Comments: *Normal primigravida labor*

UH FORM M-171A, Rev. 1 U72

UNIVERSITY OF WASHINGTON HOSPITALS
HARBORVIEW MEDICAL CENTER ☐
UNIVERSITY HOSPITAL ☐

LABOR AND DELIVERY RECORD

Figure 5–8 A normal primigravida labor curve of cervical dilatation and descent. The two curves usually cross at 5 to 7 cm dilatation. Note the rotation and flexion of the vertex as it descends. The heavy dot signifies the lowest portion of the presenting part. The open triangle represents the posterior fontanel, the diamond the anterior fontanel and the connecting line the sagittal suture.

i.e., uterine contractions, maternal bearing-down efforts; (2) the passage, *i.e.*, cervix, bony pelvis; or (3) the passenger, *i.e.*, fetus. An understanding of the normal physiology of labor enables one to identify the underlying cause, or causes, of significant abnormalities and to direct appropriate therapy to correct the problem. Figure 5–8 shows the labor chart of cervical dilatation and descent in a normal primigravid labor.

The Perinate

RICHARD P. WENNBERG

DAVID E. WOODRUM

W. ALAN HODSON

There is no age in life when adaptive requirements are so compressed in time and so critical to continued survival as the period surrounding birth. This precarious transition from fetus to infant extends beyond the moment of delivery and is often referred to as "perinatal adaptation."

During the first nine months of life the human lives in an aquatic environment and in a parasitic relationship with his mother. The placenta plays a vital role in growth, metabolic homeostasis, gas exchange and excretory function; it shares or totally usurps the vital regulatory functions of nearly every major organ in the body, including the gut, kidney, liver, neuroendocrinologic systems, and lung. At birth, these placental functions are abruptly interdicted, and many body organs must suddenly assume for the first time the peculiar postnatal functions for which they are genetically programmed.

During the 28-day neonatal period, approximately one in 50 liveborn humans will die, and perhaps one in 25 will suffer difficulties such as perinatal asphyxia or have a congenital defect which will adversely affect the future lives of both infant and family. The risks of birth are high and are in large part related to a failure to meet the physiologic and biochemical adaptive requirements of the perinate.

THE PERINATAL SITUATION

Cardiopulmonary Adaptation

The most critical adaptive requirement at birth is the delivery of oxygen to tissue and the elimination of carbon dioxide. Several major changes in the cardiopulmonary system must occur in the first minutes of life in order to ensure intact survival.

Late Fetal Circulation. During fetal life blood flows through four channels which normally close after birth: the umbilical arteries and vein, the ductus venosus in the liver, the foramen ovale lying in the atrial cardiac septum, and the ductus arteriosis connecting the pulmonary artery with the descending aorta as shown in Figure 5–9. Following oxygenation in the placenta, blood flows into the fetus via the umbilical vein. Approximately 50 per cent of the umbilical venous blood enters the liver, perfuses the hepatic parenchyma, and is collected in the hepatic venous system before entering the inferior vena cava (IVC). The remaining 50 per cent of umbilical venous flow is shunted, via the ductus venosus, through the liver into the IVC, where

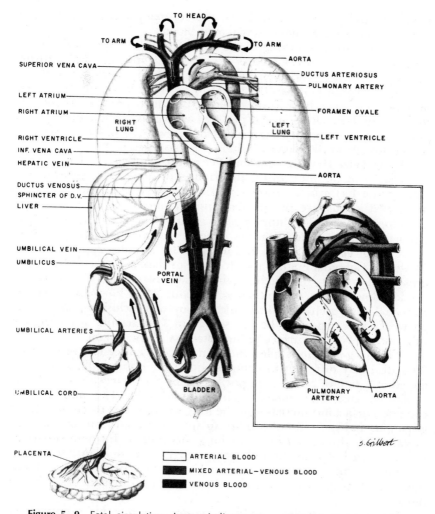

Figure 5-9 Fetal circulation. Arrows indicate course of blood. Oxygen saturation is highest in the umbilical vein and progressively lower in the vessels to the head and neck, the aorta, and, finally, the inferior vena cava below the liver, which has the most desaturated blood. The insert illustrates the course and distribution of blood in the fetal heart and large vessels more clearly. Note that the oxygenated placental blood entering the heart via the inferior vena cava flows preferentially to the left ventricle and head. (From Bonica, J. H.: *Principles and Practice of Obstetric Analgesia and Anesthesiology.* Philadelphia, F. A. Davis Co., 1967; adapted from Ross Clinical Aid No. 1, Fetal Circulation, Ross Laboratories, Columbus, Ohio 43216. Reproduced with permission.)

it mixes with blood returning from the lower body. Because of the anatomical juxtaposition of the IVC and the foramen ovale, most of the well-oxygenated blood from the IVC passes directly into the left atrium. This blood enters the left ventricle and subsequently perfuses the coronary arteries, the upper body and the head, via vessels originating from the arch of the aorta. Thus, the coronary and cephalic vessels are perfused with the most oxygenated blood.

Venous blood returning to the heart from the upper body via the superior vena cava (SVC) flows preferentially into the right atrium, the right ventricle, and then into the pulmonary artery. Only 10 per cent of this blood perfuses the fetal lungs, while the other 90 per cent bypasses the lungs by flowing through the ductus arteriosus into the descending aorta. Roughly 50 per cent of the blood flow through the descending aorta perfuses the lower body, and the other 50 per cent passes directly to the placenta where it is reoxygenated.

Lung: Fetal Development and Perinatal Adaptation. The state of maturation of the lung which determines its ability for gas exchange is the major factor in the successful transition to extrauterine life. Well-developed alveoli are not present until about the time of birth (38 gestational weeks). The lung appears glandular initially and has a high glycogen content. The bronchial generations are completed by about 16 weeks of gestational age, and terminal air saccules appear at about 24 weeks. Cuboidal epithelial cells begin to flatten, and capillary plexuses develop near the potential air surface. Structural differentiation would allow limited gas exchange at about 24 to 25 weeks. Type II epithelial cells, rich in cytoplasmic osmiophilic inclusions, form after 25 weeks and appear to be the source of "surfactant," a lipoprotein substance providing surface tension stability in the alveoli.

The lung *in utero* is filled to about 40 per cent of its capacity with fluid distinctly different in composition from amniotic fluid. It is secreted at a rate of about 3 ml per kilogram per hour with some being swallowed and some mixed with amniotic fluid. The phospholipid content (surfactant) increases in the lung over the last three months of gestation, and the ratio of lecithin to sphingomyelin concentrations in the amniotic fluid is an index of lung maturation. In those situations where an early termination of pregnancy may be indicated, sampling of amniotic fluid permits an antenatal assessment of the risk of development of respiratory distress syndrome with hyaline membrane disease.

Intermittent shallow, rapid respiratory movements occurring *in utero* are probably related to fetal electrocortical activity which varies with fetal sleep states. The onset of regular rhythmic respiration at birth is most likely due to asphyxial changes in the blood gases which stimulate peripheral and central chemoreceptors. Other nonspecific changes such as a decrease in environmental temperature and an increase in tactile, proprioceptor, visual and auditory stimuli may help to stimulate the first breath. With the first breaths, air replaces the fluid in the lungs, and the partial pressure arterial of oxygen (PaO_2) rises, followed by closure of the fetal cardiovascular shunts. The increase in PaO_2 stimulates closure of the ductus arteriosus and constriction of the umbilical arteries. Increased blood flow through the lungs increases the right atrial pressure in the heart, effecting closure of the foramen ovale. The ductus arteriosus is functionally closed within 3 to 4 hours of birth.

Nutritional Adaptation

Fetal growth accelerates dramatically early in the third trimester. With a normal placenta and a healthy mother, the fetus will double its weight in the last six weeks of gestation. A part of this late growth is manifested as an increase in glycogen and lipid stores which will assure nutrition for the newly born infant prior to the establishment of adequate oral intake. In the full-term infant, these glycogen stores may be depleted by 24 hours of age. The prematurely born infant has little or no nutritional reserve and is vulnerable to nutritional deficiency since adequate oral intake may take some time to establish.

Homeostatic mechanisms modulating the blood level of nutrients prior to birth are shared by mother, placenta and fetus. The fetus receives a relatively constant influx of nutrients and maintains a blood glucose level at 70 to 80 per cent of maternal values. Following birth, the infant's blood glucose concentration falls, stabilizing between four and six hours of age at 45 to 60 mg per 100 ml. Homeostatic mechanisms for regulating blood glucose normally adapt rapidly to the postnatal environment, although several days or weeks are required before gluconeogenic and other regulatory mechanisms reach maximum potential. If an infant is very premature, or if he has had placental insufficiency with resulting decrease in glycogen stores, he may develop hypoglycemia within the first days of life, if not supplied with an exogenous source of glucose.

It is therefore important to establish and maintain an adequate nutritional intake soon after birth. Sucking and swallowing reflexes, important in accomplishing oral intake, are well integrated by 32 to 33 weeks of gestation. Most digestive enzymes are present in both premature and mature infants, and lactase, required for digesting the principal sugar in milk, is found in greater abundance in newborns than in adults.

The perinate will normally lose about 5 per cent of its birth weight during the first two to three postnatal days, largely due to an adjustment in total body water. With adequate nutrition (about 120 cal/kg/day), the infant will then gain 20 to 25 grams a day during the first four postnatal months.

Temperature Regulation

The deep body temperature of the newborn commonly falls 1 to 2 degrees centigrade during the first few minutes after birth. A number of factors are responsible for this rapid heat loss at birth: evaporation of amniotic fluid from the skin, a relatively high skin to room temperature gradient at birth, and a relatively high ratio of surface area to mass in the newborn. The premature is even more susceptible to cooling in the first moments after birth.

It is uncertain whether the thermal stress at birth is advantageous or deleterious. While cooling may serve as a stimulant for the initiation of breathing, marked heat loss is associated with an increased infant mortality. There is also evidence that postnatal cooling inhibits recovery from metabolic acidosis and potentiates hypoglycemia.

Both full-term and premature infants respond to a cold environment by peripheral vasoconstriction and by increasing heat production. Heat is produced by increasing the metabolic rate rather than by shivering. Not only cooling, but also overheating of the newborn influences resting metabolic rate. A naked full-term newborn infant has a minimum oxygen consumption at rest when placed in an environment of about 32° C, the "neutral thermal environment." If an infant is premature, has respiratory distress, or is otherwise ill it is important to minimize oxygen requirements for thermogenesis by preventing heat loss in the delivery room and by placing the infant in a neutral thermal environment. In the delivery room, heat loss may be minimized by rapidly drying the infant following birth and by placing him under a radiant heat source.

Host Defense to Infectious Disease

Infections occur more often in the neonatal period than at any other age. Although cellular immunity is apparently normal, the newborn's serum is deficient in opsonic factors which potentiate phagocytosis of foreign antigens such as bacteria. The newborn appears to have a deficient inflammatory response and localizes infections poorly. Since the newborn normally has had little previous antigen exposure, passive immunity is limited to a large supply of maternal immunoglobulin G (IgG), which selectively crosses the placenta. Maternal IgM and IgA do not readily cross the placenta, and exist in low concentration in the newborn infant.

As a result of these numerous handicaps, the newborn, and especially the prematurely born infant, is susceptible to infections by organisms for which circulating IgM, opsonization, and efficient tissue localizations are essential defense mechanisms. These organisms include most gram negative bacilli, group B beta-hemolytic streptococci and staphylococcus aureus.

Renal Adaptation

The fetal kidney produces urine, which contributes significantly to the amniotic fluid volume. However, the usual renal functions of removing waste products and maintaining acid-base, electrolyte, and blood volume homeostasis are accomplished for the most part by the placenta. Thus, a fetus with bilateral renal agenesis (absent kidneys) may survive until shortly after birth.

The principles of renal function are identical in the perinate and adult, although the newborn kidney does not achieve maximum function until one to three months of age (Table 5–1). The glomerular

TABLE 5-1 COMPARATIVE RENAL FUNCTION IN NEWBORN, INFANT, AND ADULT

	Kidney Weight (gms)	Glomerular Filtration Rate (ml/min/1.73M²)	Maximum Tubular Excretory Capacity TMPAH (mg/min/1.73M²)	Concentrating Capacity (m osm/l)	Acidifying Capacity	
					pH	H+ excretion (mEq/min/1.73M²)
Newborn	22	45	16	600–1100	6.0±.3	16–40
6 month old	40	115	60	800–1200	4.8±.2	65–200
Adult	300	125	80	800–1500	4.8±.2	65–200

filtration rate in both premature and full-term infants is about 45 ml/min/1.73 m², compared with 125 ml/min/1.73 m² in adults. Renal tubular transport is diminished at birth; the newly born has a lower transport maximum for bicarbonate and para-amino hippuric acid (PAH), cannot excrete a sodium load as efficiently as an adult, and has a limited capacity to excrete ammonia in response to an acid load.

The newborn is also limited in his ability to concentrate or dilute urine. The adult kidney will excrete urine varying in concentration from 50 to 1500 mOsm per liter, depending upon the amount of water intake, in order to preserve a serum solute concentration of 300 mOsm per liter. Many newborns can concentrate their urine only to 600 to 700 mOsm per liter under conditions of water deprivation. This may be related in part to the low urea load to the kidney of newborns, which results in a diminished urea concentration in the medulla of the kidney and, therefore, a low total solute concentration in the urine.

The limitations in renal function have great clinical relevance in regard to fluid and electrolyte therapy and feeding, acid-base balance in a sick infant, and the administration of drugs such as kanamycin and penicillin, which depend upon renal tubular excretion for elimination.

Hepatic Detoxification

Most drugs and toxic endogenous substances are either excreted unchanged through the kidneys (*e.g.*, penicillin) or modified by the liver to facilitate excretion by the kidney (*e.g.*, chloramphenicol) or hepato-biliary system. Most hepatic detoxifying enzymes have very low activity *in utero*. Substances normally catabolized by the liver cross the placenta and are detoxified and excreted by the maternal liver.

One such detoxifying enzyme, glucuronyl transferase, conjugates bilirubin, a breakdown product of heme, with glucuronic acid. Conjugation transforms the lipid-soluble bilirubin into a water-soluble bilirubin diglucuronide, which can then be excreted via the biliary tract into the gut.

The nine-month fetus produces 20 to 30 mg of bilirubin each day, but most of this crosses the placenta and is excreted by the maternal liver. Following birth, the perinate is confronted with an accumulation of unconjugated bilirubin until the hepatic conjugating and excreting mechanisms become adequate. The serum bilirubin concentration in most term infants continues to rise until about the third day, then gradually decreases to a normal adult value of less than 1 mg per 100 ml. In normal infants, bilirubin concentration will usually not exceed 11 to 12 mg per 100 ml, and in most cases will remain much lower. This degree of bilirubinemia, acquired through the normal adaptive processes, is referred to as "physiologic jaundice of the newborn." If the infant produces more bilirubin than usual, as in the case of hemolytic disease caused by maternal antibodies destroying fetal red cells (Rh or ABO incompatibility), considerable amounts of bilirubin may accumulate in the serum.

Unconjugated bilirubin is toxic to cellular systems and if allowed to reach high concentrations may cause irreversible brain damage (kernicterus), resulting in mental retardation, athetoid cerebral palsy, deafness, or death. Kernicterus usually occurs only when the bilirubin concentration exceeds 20 to 24 mg per 100 ml. At this concentration of bilirubin, loci on serum albumin which bind bilirubin tightly become saturated, potentiating transfer of bilirubin into tissues. When the bilirubin concentrations reach dangerous levels, they may be lowered by an exchange transfusion which replaces the jaundiced blood with fresh donor blood.

Hematologic Adaptation

The production of red cells is controlled largely through a humoral factor, erythropoietin. Levels of erythropoietin increase in the normal fetus with increasing gestational age, leading to a high level in cord blood at term. The red cell mass in the newborn is relatively high (about 17 gm of hemoglobin per 100 ml) and the reticulocyte count is also high (2 to 6 per cent at birth). From the second day through the first six to eight weeks of life, erythropoietin is normally not measurable in either blood or urine. During this time, red cell production does not keep pace with body growth and red cell destruction, and by two to three months of age hemoglobin concentration will drop to about 11 gm per 100 ml, the so-called physiologic anemia of infancy.

At birth, about 80 per cent of hemoglobin is in the form of fetal hemoglobin (Hgb-F), with only about 20 per cent adult type hemoglobin (Hgb-A). By four to five months of postnatal age, normal adult values of Hgb-A are found. The mechanism regulating the change from Hgb-F to Hgb-A is unknown. Hgb-F has a higher oxygen affinity than Hgb-A, resulting in a left shift of the oxygen-Hgb association curve. This shift might facilitate oxygen transfer across the placenta from mother to fetus, but at the same time might inhibit oxygen unloading to tissue. Thus, it is uncertain whether Hgb-F conveys any physiologic advantage to the fetus with regard to oxygen delivery.

Neurologic Adaptation

During the latter half of pregnancy there is a rapid proliferation of brain cells. Proliferation (increased DNA content) decreases after birth and reaches adult levels by about five months of age. In contrast, brain RNA, protein, and weight (reflecting cell size) increase linearly from mid-gestation through the first year of life. Myelin lipids (cerebroside and sulfatide) exist in low concentrations at birth, and by the first year of life reach only about 20 per cent of adult content.

Other than its role in sustaining and regulating vital functions such as temperature and breathing, the nervous system has few recognized adaptive requirements in the perinatal period. Functionally, the human brain is very immature at birth, and the newborn's movements are guided largely by primitive reflexes with relatively little cortical control. In fact, an infant can be born without a cerebral cortex (hydranencephaly) and behave almost like a normal newborn. In contrast to most species, the human infant requires several weeks before he effectively finds his way to the breast, months before he will be able to ambulate, and years before he can protect himself from adverse climates (by clothing himself) and other life-threatening situations. Consequently, the human is born into a situation of prolonged maternal dependency that is unique among animal species. His successful adaptation to the first years and his preparation to face future adaptive crises are therefore inextricably linked to skillful mothering and an appropriate adaptive response to his birth by his parents.

COMMON PROBLEMS OF THE PERINATE

Asphyxia and Fetal Monitoring

Fetal asphyxia is an important contributor to infant mortality and a major cause of mental retardation and cerebral palsy. Fetal asphyxia may result from any of the following: insufficient uterine blood flow (maternal hypotension, tonically contracted uterus); interference with placental gas exchange (premature separation of the placenta, placental scarring); and umbilical cord compression (cord wrapped around neck of fetus, knot in the umbilical cord, prolapse of cord through cervix).

Recent electronic advances in continuous monitoring of fetal heart rate and uterine activity have improved our ability to detect fetal asphyxia during labor. The fetal heart rate may be monitored continuously, indirectly by means of transabdominal ultrasound, or directly by attaching an electrode to the presenting part of the fetus through the cervix. Uterine contractions can be monitored externally by use of an abdominal transducer (tocodynamometer), or internally by means of an intrauterine pressure catheter inserted through the cervix and attached to a pressure transducer. Mild asphyxia may cause an increase in the baseline fetal heart rate or loss of its normal beat to beat irregularity, and moderate to severe asphyxia may result in pronounced deceleration of the heart rate in association with uterine contractions. The pattern of deceleration of the heart rate in relation to the uterine contraction provides some clues as to the cause of fetal asphyxia. Uterine contractions serve as a recurring stress to the fetus by reducing the placental intervillous blood flow or, if placental exchange is already compromised, there is compression of the umbilical cord. Periodic uterine contractions can cause transient fetal asphyxia which can become severe. Fetal heart rate patterns are broadly classified into the following three types based on the time relationships between the heart rate deceleration and the uterine contractions: early decelerations, late decelerations and variable decelerations (Fig. 5–10).

Early decelerations appear to be a normal vagal reflex slowing of the heart rate, occurring simultaneously with uterine contractions. They are attributed to fetal head compression and are ordinarily not related to fetal distress. Late decelerations are a slowing of the heart rate, occurring after the onset of the uterine contraction, that persist beyond the contraction. They are abnormal and are frequently caused by insufficient placental oxygen—so-called "uteroplacental insufficiency." Variable decelerations are variable in onset, shape, and duration and are usually caused by umbilical cord compression. Variable decelerations are the most common fetal heart rate pattern associated with the clinical diagnosis of fetal distress. By recognizing the causes of acute fetal distress, initial obstetrical management can be directed at correcting the underlying pathophysiology, e.g., changing maternal position to reduce cord compression, treating maternal hypotension, or reducing uterine hypertonus to correct uteroplacental insufficiency. If these measures are unsuccessful within a reasonable period of time, delivery is indicated to prevent permanent and severe damage to the infant.

Occasionally, fetal heart rate monitoring may give ambiguous or incomplete information about the status of the fetus during labor. Therefore, fetal capillary blood sampling can be utilized to evaluate the acid-base status of the fetus. This can be an invaluable technique providing vital adjunctive information. This, combined with continuous fetal heart rate monitoring, provides complete information about fetal condition. Normally, fetal capillary blood pH tends to decline slightly near the end of the first stage and during the second stage of labor. Normal fetal pH should be above 7.25. A pH between 7.20 and 7.25 is equivocal and bears repeating. A pH less than 7.20 indicates fetal acidosis and must be repeated, while a pH of 7.15 or less shows severe acidosis, requiring prompt delivery of the compromised baby. The technique has several disadvantages in that it requires meticulous technique, is time consuming and cumbersome, and does not give instantaneous information. One must also obtain simultaneous maternal acid-base data, and sampling must be done serially to establish a trend. A single random sample may be meaningless.

Meconium staining of the amniotic fluid is another sign of fetal

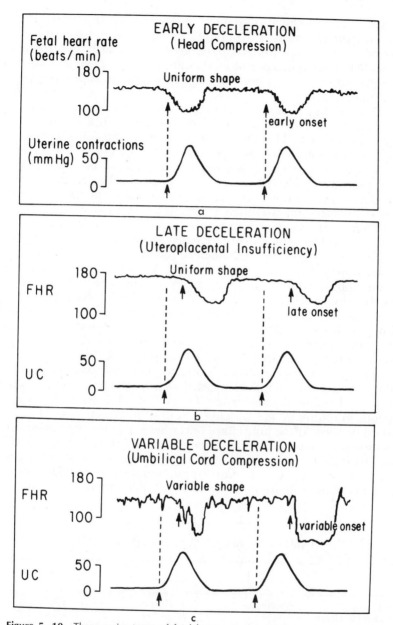

Figure 5–10 Three major types of fetal heart rate deceleration patterns. *a.* Early deceleration—thought to be due to fetal head compression and not normally related to fetal asphyxia. This pattern is uniform in shape and has its onset at approximately the same time as the uterine contraction. *b.* Late deceleration—thought to be due to decreased placental blood flow during contractions—acute uteroplacental insufficiency and is an indication of acute fetal distress. This pattern is usually uniform in shape but has its onset late in the contraction of the uterus and persists beyond the completion of the contraction. *c.* Variable deceleration—thought to be due to umbilical cord compression; is the most common pattern associated with clinically diagnosed fetal distress. The pattern is variable in shape, time of onset and duration.

asphyxia. The intestinal contents of the fetus contain a dark greenish mucoid material called "meconium." Meconium is not passed into the amniotic fluid except under conditions of stress such as cerebral hypoxia. Recognition of signs of fetal asphyxia may sometimes make possible prevention of fetal brain damage or death, by appropriate obstetrical intervention.

Fetal asphyxia most often occurs during the terminal stages of labor and is the most common cause of severe central nervous system depression at birth. The severely asphyxiated infant will appear flaccid and cyanotic. There may be a period of no respiratory effort followed by a period of gasping. Lesser degrees of asphyxia may be associated with irregular respirations, mild slowing of the heart rate (to about 100 per min), cyanosis and occasional movements of the extremities. It is customary and useful to record the condition of the newborn at 1 minute and again at 5 minutes of age, using an Apgar score (see Table 5–2). The Apgar score is based on a maximum of 2 points assigned to each of five parameters: heart rate, respiratory effort, muscle tone, reflex irritability and color. A score of 2 or less indicates severe asphyxia; 3 to 5, moderate asphyxia; and 6 to 7, mild asphyxia. The healthy newborn rarely has a 1 minute Apgar score of 10 as the extremities are not completely pink. Low Apgar scores are correlated with a high infant mortality, especially at lower gestational ages. Infants with Apgar scores of 2 or less, and weighing less than 2000 grams, have a mortality rate approaching 80 per cent.

The treatment of asphyxia is directed at rapid oxygenation of the baby. The airway should be cleared of secretions, amniotic fluid or blood, and followed immediately by oxygen administration. If spontaneous respirations are absent, a resuscitation bag and face mask should be used. If the lungs have never been aerated, high inflationary forces may be needed to initiate ventilation; a spontaneously breathing newborn may generate 50 to 80 cm H_2O negative transthoracic pressure with the first breath. Care must be taken to ventilate with an appropriate air volume in order to avoid tissue injury. The full-term

TABLE 5–2 APGAR EVALUATION METHOD

Sign	0	1	2
Heart rate	Absent	< 100/min.	> 100/min.
Respiratory effort	Absent	Weak cry Hypoventilation	Good strong cry
Muscle tone	Limp	Some flexion of extremities	Well flexed
Reflex irritability (response to stimulation of feet)	No response	Some motion	Cry
Color	Blue; pale	Body pink, extremities blue	Completely pink

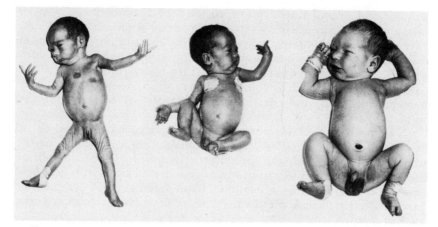

Figure 5–11 Infants (left to right) were born at 28 weeks, 33 weeks, and 40 weeks of gestation. Note the increase in subcutaneous tissue mass and flexion tone with increasing gestational age.

infant has a total lung capacity of 300 ml and a tidal volume of only 25 ml. In a severely depressed infant, alkali (sodium bicarbonate) should be administered via the umbilical vein to buffer noncarbonic acids which have accumulated subsequent to anaerobic metabolism. Cardiac massage is necessary if the heart rate falls below 50 per minute. The importance of immediate recognition and treatment of neonatal asphyxia cannot be overemphasized. The appropriate management requires a person in attendance who has knowledge and skills pertaining to the specific problems in the newborn and who can provide undivided attention to the baby.

Prematurity

Figure 5–11 shows a comparison of two prematurely born babies to a full-term baby. An infant is considered premature when born prior to the thirty-seventh week of gestation. Formerly infants with a birth weight of less than 2500 grams (5½ pounds) were considered to be premature. Recognition of intrauterine growth deficiency resulting in low birth weight infants born later than the thirty-seventh week of gestation has led to the abandonment of birth weight as a satisfactory index of maturation. The term "low birth weight," therefore, includes normal and undergrown premature infants as well as undergrown full-term infants (see Appendix for normal standards).

The incidence of prematurity in the United States is about 7.5 per cent, but varies from a high of 16 per cent in low socioeconomic areas to about 3 per cent in middle and upper income communities. There is no apparent racial predilection. Populations with very low neonatal and prenatal death rates, such as the Scandinavian countries, have a very low prematurity rate. Since neonatal morbidity and mortality are related to prematurity, one of the most important solutions to lowering infant mortality is the prevention of prematurity. Unfortunately, the causes of premature labor are poorly understood. Many maternal situations, such as young unwed mothers, multiple pregnancy, maternal infection, and cervical incompetence, are associated with a higher incidence of prematurity.

The problems of the premature are in large part related to unreadiness for both immediate and late adaptation to extrauterine life. Frequent problems of the premature include: hyaline membrane disease; asphyxia; periodic apnea; inadequate nutrition; jaundice; poor temperature regulation; infections; hypoglycemia; and anemia. Of these problems, hyaline membrane disease is by far the most common cause of death.

Hyaline Membrane Disease

Hyaline membrane disease (idiopathic respiratory distress syndrome) affects approximately 75,000 infants each year in the United States, of whom 25,000 die. The disease occurs in 15 per cent of all premature infants in inverse proportion to gestational age (see Table 5–3). Although there is insufficient supportive evidence, factors such as antepartum bleeding or delivery by caesarian section, in addition to prematurity, may increase the susceptibility to the disease.

Characteristically, the infant will show signs of respiratory distress in the delivery room, accompanied by tachypnea, expiratory grunting and retractions of the chest wall. The disease progresses in severity for 48 to 72 hours, during which time the respiratory rate may increase to 120 per minute, accompanied by severe xyphoid, subcostal and intracostal retractions, nasal flaring, and cyanosis. Recovery, if it occurs,

TABLE 5–3 INCIDENCE AND MORTALITY OF HYALINE MEMBRANE DISEASE (HMD) RELATED TO GESTATIONAL AGE

Gestation	Incidence of HMD	Mortality in Affected
40 weeks	0.05%	5%
36 weeks	0.7%	5%
34 weeks	20%	10%
32 weeks	40%	15%
28 weeks	66%	95%

requires several days, the duration varying with the severity of the disease.

The chest radiograph reveals a characteristic reticulogranular pattern with an air bronchogram, due to the focal collapsed areas of the lung contrasted with overexpanded airspaces.

Pathophysiology. At autopsy the lungs are airless, appear liverlike and do not float in water. On histologic section there is a "Swiss cheese" pattern with overexpanded bronchioles and alveolar ducts and patchy areas of atelectasis. The dilated terminal air spaces are lined with membranes which contain plasma proteins. These membranes are not present early in the disease and are thought to be a result of either altered surface forces in the lung or capillary endothelial damage or both. The membranes are not a necessary component of the disease, hence many have preferred to rename the disease "idiopathic respiratory distress syndrome."

The extensive alveolar collapse severely restricts oxygen transfer to the blood. Pulmonary arterial blood courses through atelectatic lung without oxygenation, causing a right to left shunting of the blood. Therefore, hypoxia is the major pathophysiologic event. Metabolic acidosis due to the anaerobic metabolism of hypoxia tissue may ensue.

The focal atelectasis causes a decrease in lung compliance, hence the chest wall retractions, tachypnea and nasal flaring. The expiratory grunt is probably an attempt to prevent alveoli from collapsing.

Etiology. The precise etiology is not understood. Pulmonary immaturity seems to be the most important factor. Studies on maturation of the lung indicate that surfactant, the proteolipid substance responsible for lowering surface tension, and thus preventing collapse at end expiration, is not present until about the twenty-eighth week of gestation. The type II alveolar epithelial cells, responsible for surfactant production, are either absent or lacking in the cytoplasmic osmiophilic inclusions which manufacture or store surface active phospholipids. By 34 to 38 weeks there is usually a sufficient alveolar lining layer to prevent hyaline membrane disease. Other developmental features of the fetal lung, such as structural maturation of terminal air spaces including alveoli, may be important.

Treatment. The treatment of hyaline membrane disease is primarily supportive, in attempts to maintain physiologic homeostasis. Sometimes ventilatory support is necessary to provide an adequate arterial oxygen and carbon dioxide tension. The ambient temperature and the temperature of inspired gases is carefully controlled and monitored to keep the infant within his zone of thermal neutrality, thus maintaining minimal oxygen consumption. Acid-base and fluid balance are maintained with intravascular infusions of 10 per cent glucose in water, and $NaHCO_3$, sodium and potassium are added when indicated. The application of a positive end-expiratory pressure appears to be beneficial in preventing alveolar collapse and improving pulmonary oxygen exchange.

The long-term outlook for survival from hyaline membrane disease is favorable and lends strong support to continued efforts at vigorous management in the neonatal period.

REFERENCES

Perinate

Avery, M. E.: The Lung and its Disorders in the Newborn Infant. 2nd ed. Philadelphia, W. B. Saunders Company, 1968.

Cornblath, M., and Schwartz, R.: Disorders of Carbohydrate Metabolism in Infancy. Philadelphia, W. B. Saunders Company, 1966.

Dawes, G. S.: Foetal and Neonatal Physiology. Chicago, Year Book Medical Publishers, 1968.

Maisels, M. J.: Bilirubin. Pediat. Clin. N. Amer., *19*:447–501, 1972.

Nelson, N. M.: On the etiology of hyaline membrane disease. Pediat. Clin. N. Amer., *17*:943–965, 1970.

Oski, F., and Naiman, J. L.: Hematologic Problems in the Newborn. 2nd ed. Philadelphia, W. B. Saunders Company, 1972.

Stave, U. (Ed.): Physiology of the Perinatal Period. 2 vols. New York, Appleton-Century-Crofts Division, Meredith Corp., 1970.

CHAPTER SIX

INFANCY: THE FIRST TWO YEARS

WALDEMAR H. WENNER
BEVERLY VANDER VEER

The few-days-old infant who is discharged from the hospital nursery is an organism with remarkable potential. He will become a very different creature in the two years of life that this discussion will cover. Dramatic changes will take place in his various components. Such aspects as physical growth, physiologic maturation, behavioral development, and social and emotional responsiveness are considered separately below, and each is quite complex. It is important to stress that this is an artificial separation, for convenience in presentation, and that in the infant each system develops in functional interaction with all others and has an immediate impact upon them. Similarly the effect of problems originating in one aspect of the maturing human will frequently also be manifested elsewhere.

LIFE SITUATION

During the first two years, physical changes relate most dramatically to the organism's becoming larger. Except for changes in the nervous system, physiologic changes are less far reaching than those necessary at birth to adjust to extrauterine existence. Behavior changes are such that the infant shows progressively greater control over his activities as he is more and more able to modify what he does to attain a desired goal. In the area of social interaction, the baby shows progressively greater independence of others while, at the same time, showing increasing ability to initiate and sustain, not just passively receive, interaction with others. This interaction allows differentiation of a variety of emotions and is the basis of his learning to cope with

85

his own and others' feelings. During the first years of life, the "others," in our culture, are usually the immediate family.

Physical

Among the many possible measures of physical growth, the following are commonly used in the clinical evaluation of young children (see Chapter 1, Growth, for further discussion and the Appendix for more detailed standards and graphs).

Weight. At birth, approximately two-thirds of term infants will weigh between 6 and 8½ pounds. According to a useful rule of thumb, this can be expected to at least double by four to six months (12 to 17 pounds) and triple by one year (18 to 25½ pounds). An average weight at two years, roughly quadruple the birth weight, will be 27 pounds (23½ to 31½ pounds). From this range of normal weights, one can see that there are large individual variations in growth. A child is expected to maintain his position relative to his peers if he is making adequate progress. Thus, a child who was average at one year (22 pounds) and at the third percentile at two years (23¼ pounds) would have lost ground relative to his peers instead of achieving his expected incremental gain. This should elicit concern and require careful consideration of causes for this lag even though he had actually gained weight.

Length. At birth, two-thirds of infants will range from 19 to 21 inches. In the first six months, there is an average increase of 5½ inches. During the second six months, the increase averages 3 inches. The whole of the second year of life has an average increase of only 4½ inches. Growth is more rapid in the extremities than in the trunk, and hence body proportions change.

The rate of increase in height appears to be under the control of different mechanisms during various periods of childhood and adolescence. During the first year of life, size at birth (see Chapter 1, for relationship to size of parent) and nutrition are major determining factors for increase in length. Thereafter, the genetic background appears to play a greater role in growth rate, and eventual adult height can be estimated with some predictive efficiency from about two years onward.

Head Growth. The occipital-frontal circumference measurement is commonly used to clinically evaluate head growth, though the growth is really volumetric. Growth of the head is used as a gauge of the growth of the brain, and alterations from normal raise concern about too rapid or too slow a change in the nervous tissue or fluid contents of the cranium. At birth, the average head circumference is about 13½ inches, with a normal variation of about one inch larger or smaller in full-term infants. In the evaluation of subsequent measurements, the use of a graph, a detailed list of age norms, or growth rate norms are mandatory for proper interpretation of head circumference growth. The growth roughly follows a negatively accelerated logarithmic curve; therefore, deviations from normal are most quickly apparent during the first months of most rapid growth (see section on brain in Chapter 1).

The posterior fontanel is usually closed by two months of age, while the larger anterior fontanel is usually open until 9 to 18 months of age; however, in exceptional cases, this may have wider variation. For example, we have personally observed an anterior fontanel closed to palpation at four months and one that was palpably open until 27 months, in children who were otherwise "normal."

Teeth. During the first two years, the infant changes from a creature having no teeth to one having between 16 to all 20 of his deciduous teeth. In addition, during these two years, the calcification of all the permanent dentition begins, with the exception of the second and third molars. See the Appendix for the normal schedule of tooth eruption.

It is necessary to note that the above discussion of physical growth relates to studies done on Caucasian children. It has been found that African-American infants tend to be somewhat smaller. Relatively less normative data exist on physical growth in groups such as Oriental-Americans and others. Socioeconomic status, which seems closely allied to nutrition, is also an influence. Such environmental influences can affect the manifestation of genotypic characteristics.

There are, additionally, differences between the sexes: during the first two years of life, boys weigh slightly more on the average, are slightly taller, and have slightly greater head circumferences than girls.

Measures of physical growth are useful parameters to follow relative to the quality of care and health of an infant. During the first two years of life, when growth is especially rapid, deviations in growth rate can be extremely useful indices of a problem.

Physical changes during the first years of life bring about corresponding change in the child's situation. At the start he was easily carried about by his mother; at the end he has become more than an armful to most mothers. Fortunately, during this time, he also learns to walk so that he isn't carried except in unusual circumstances.

Physiologic

With extrauterine existence, there are a host of basic cellular physiologic changes in adaptation toward the new environment. After this adjustment, no similarly remarkable changes occur during the first two years of life.

The kidney becomes better able to handle a solute load as it becomes increasingly able to concentrate its urinary output during the first months of life. The early immaturity necessitates modification of cow's milk, if it is used in feeding (see Planning appropriate nutrition in section on Wellness Care in this chapter).

The immune response system of the infant at birth has been shown capable of reacting to antigenic stimuli. Until such stimuli are present, usually from infection or immunization, the infant has little or no immune globulin of his own. He is born with placentally transmitted maternal immune globulins which, during the first months of life, provide gradually decreasing protection from certain of the infectious diseases against which the mother had had antibodies. As he grows older, the infant's own immune globulin production becomes increasingly efficient (see section on Infections, under Common Problems, in this chapter).

Nervous System. One of the remarkable changes in the physiology of the nervous system is related to the immense increase in interneuronal connections, chiefly because of the arborization of dendrites. This increases the opportunity for nerve cells to influence each other's electrophysiologic state, which is the basis of nervous tissue activity. Another change relates to the conduction times within the nervous system, which become more rapid as the fibers become larger, as the cellular membranes mature, and as the fiber investments, including the myelin sheath, develop.

A third change relates to the electroencephalographic (EEG) tracings obtained at different ages. It appears that part of the change in the EEG relates to maturation of dendritic arborization. The changes are generally toward the persistence of ever more rapid rhythms and greater rhythmic patterning as the organism matures through the first two years. At term birth, there is differentiation on the EEG between waking and sleeping, which is difficult to discern in the preterm infant before eight months of gestation. Wave patterns which foreshadow the adult alpha rhythm (10-to-13-cycle-per-second patterns that appear over the occiput when awake with eyes closed) are seen in the three-month-old infant. At first, they are slower, but with increasing maturity they progress to the adult rhythm by 10 to 12 years of age.

There are practical consequences of these and other changes:

a) When convulsions occur in early postnatal life, they usually have different manifestations than in later life. Convulsions appear to depend upon cortical dendritic interconnections for their more typical general body tonic-clonic behavior in the mature individual.

b) The threshold for convulsions seems to alter, there being a greater susceptibility of the child under four to six years of age to brief convulsions as an accompaniment of fever, even in the absence of any brain abnormality.

c) The infant's pattern of sleep and wakefulness changes drastically during the early months of life. At birth, he awakens recurrently, usually after sleeping less than four hours, eats, and returns to sleep, often less than an hour after awakening. Sleep occurs indiscriminately in the day and night, taking up about two-thirds of the 24-hour day. Parents are usually awakened from sleep several times during the night by their new infant's crying. As the infant becomes older the ability to sustain sleep increases, so that by four months of age one episode of sleep lasting more than eight hours is usual each day. Additionally, this eight-hour sleep regularly occurs at night, which partially explains why two-thirds of sleep is at night by 16 weeks. Change in the amount of sleep is relatively small during this time, decreasing little more than one hour. Duration of wakefulness changes less dramatically than duration of sleep, with the longest period of wakefulness increasing from not quite two and one-half hours at one week to a bit more than three and one-half hours at 16 weeks. The quality of behavior while awake changes dramatically, as discussed below.

Physiologic maturation of the central nervous system (CNS) is influenced by the adequacy and timing of contributions, such as stimulation and nutrition, from the environment. This fact has been associated with a concept of "critical periods" in development. The concept is also applied outside the realm of physiology. Examples of the interplay of CNS maturation and environment are the sensory deficits resulting from lack of appropriate sensory stimulation during early life. Such lack can lead to permanent defects in the underlying neuronal substrate. In man, unilateral amblyopia (functional blindness) can result from suppression of the diplopic image in a non-alternating strabismus (cross-eyed) situation. In animal experiments, blindfolding one eye during early life leads to failure of myelinization of the optic nerve to that eye, with consequent permanent abnormal function, accompanied by normal myelinization and function in the unpatched eye. Other experiments with young animals have shown permanent failure of maturation of certain retinal elements in eyes exposed in early development to blue light only, with subsequent failure to respond to other colors.

The embryologist's concept of a "critical period" during which an organ must develop if it is to mature normally was used by ethologists to label the apparently brief fixed time during which imprinting occurs in certain species. Imprinting is the name applied to the type of learning that occurs in some birds shortly after hatching in which they automatically follow a moving object and for the rest of their lives follow similar objects when they appear. It has been suggested that a similar paradigm is operative in young primates deprived during their early life of social contacts with mothers and peers. Such animals have subsequent deficits in adaptive and social behaviors.

In addition to the human amblyopia mentioned above, a persuasive application of this theory to the human infant is the permanent impairment of intellectual ability that results from nutrition which is inadequate to support the continued multiplication of cells in the central nervous system during the first few postnatal months.

The theory is often extended into the social and educational arenas, perhaps because the CNS underlies human activities in both. Since there is relatively little knowledge of the correspondence between physiologic maturation of the CNS and the emergence of specific behaviors, such an extension can be questioned. The appropriateness of its application, for example, in the social area as an explanation of responses to "inadequate mothering" is controversial. A major question relative to these wider applications concerns the irreversibility of the effects of deficits in early social experience and cognitive stimulation. It can be noted that commercial promotion of the early use of "educational toys" relies somewhat on this theory.

Behavior

What children do—the way they act, behave, or perform—changes as they become older. As with physical growth or physiologic maturing, these changes in children's capabilities have been assessed as a means of determining the health of an individual. The descriptions separate various aspects; motor acts are separated from language and communication skills; adaptive behaviors are often distinguished from personal-social skills. This specific separation was used by Arnold Gesell and his colleagues in their seminal presentation of an age-graduated series of characteristic and age normative behaviors arranged into a measuring instrument. This instrument related increasing age to behavioral attainments somewhat as a ruler relates ascending ordinal numbers to accumulating units of length. Age normative behaviors are those that appear in the repertoire of many children as they pass through a relatively brief age span as, for example, walking independently is normative for infants 12 to 15 months of age. Many others have followed their lead in constructing developmental scales which allow an observer to specify the maturational attainment of a child regardless of his age. An example of this would be the statement that a person who is taking his first independent steps is like the usual child of about 12 months in this type of behavior even if the person is showing the skill precociously at eight months or with significant delay at 24 months.

A mnemonic (Table 6–1) for the progression of motor abilities in the maturing infant is presented because of the central organizing quality this group of skills has relative to the way the infant interacts with his environment. This motor skills mnemonic can in turn form an association framework for remembering key achievements in other areas of development. Motor abilities include both gross bodily control and finer motor coordination (postural reactions, head balance, sitting, standing, creeping, walking, prehensory approach to an object, grasp, skill in manipulation of the object, and release). The mnemonic consists of aligning three-month chronologic intervals with key skills that illustrate the cephalocaudal progression of motor control. The motor skills do not suddenly appear in the infant's repertoire, but rather are preceded by a series of increasingly better approximations. For the purposes of the mnemonic, skillful, purposeful, easily repeatable or common motor acts are associated with the age at which they are expected in the course of normal development, though more than a few children will already have had these skills for some time before the age at which they are listed.

The numerous skills of the older infant are based upon earlier skills. The two-year-old child running and walking up and down stairs using a banister shows better balance than that needed for simple walking. Looking beyond that time, at 30 months he will be able to walk on tip-toe and jump in place, and at three years will be able to jump off a low (12 inch) platform.

In the mnemonic, the use of the hands is mentioned only at the nine-month age. The adeptness with which a person uses his hands is often described as fine motor skill. This skill, which is little more than

TABLE 6-1 MNEMONIC FOR MOTOR DEVELOPMENT

Age	Anatomic Progression	Motor Skill
Birth (full term)		Suck, breathe, and swallow in a coordinated fashion*
3 Months		Directed vision—reaching for objects with eyes
6 Months		Sit with head erect when hips are supported; reach for objects, though grasp of them is immature
9 Months		Sit unaided indefinitely; grasp, using opposition of thumb and fingers (pincer grasp)**
15 Months***		Walk unaided

*This motor skill can be better appreciated if compared to the necessity of passing a feeding tube into the stomach of an infant born at 28 rather than 38 weeks of gestation.

**Sitting unaided indefinitely is but one of the skills children acquire with control over movement at the hips. Creeping (moving on hands and knees), getting from a prone into a sitting position and back to prone—all of these become a part of the child's activities about this age.

***The jump from 9 months to 15 months (an exception in the 3-month interval part of the mnemonic) can be thought of as an analogue of the growth curves discussed above and presented in the Appendix. They have a negatively accelerated logarithmic form that required longer times to elapse for succeeding "equivalent" gains in weight and, in this case, skills.

nascent at 5 or 6 months, reaches an almost adult level during the course of the second half of the first year of life. Initially, during that brief span, the child secures small objects such as 1-inch cubes using the ulnar aspect of his hand. At the end, he characteristically takes such an object using the distal portions of the digits on the radial side of his hand (see Fig. 6–1); or, more simply, the location of the object on being grasped moves across the palm toward the thumb and distally during this time. The opposition of the thumb to the other fingers in prehension is a part of this increase in deftness with small objects. When the volar portions of the distal phalanges of the thumb and index or third finger are used, the grasp is called a pincer grasp. The opposite of grasping, the ability to release an object, also shows an orderly progression in skill, but is acquired after the ability to grasp.

Changes in the area of adaptive behavior during the first two years are also great. Adaptive is the adjective applied to behaviors in which the child solves simple problems and shows increasing resourcefulness in exploiting various objects. This is exemplified by the following enumeration of some changes in expected play with 1-inch cubes at different ages. The infant of one month will give little evidence he even sees such a cube on a table unless conditions are "just right." At four months of age, it will not only be quite obvious he sees the cube, but his hands become active. He can be seen to look from his hands to the cube. Touching of the cube may be infrequent even though he tries hard to effect a contact. A month later his infrequent touching will advance to ease in touching and occasional grasping. He will have

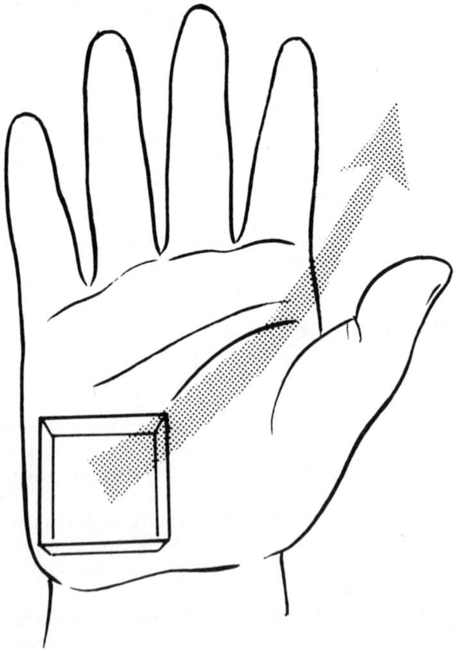

Figure 6–1 Schematization of changes in the portion of the hand used to grasp a one-inch cube during the second six months of life.

a solution to the "problem" of how to get hold of an object in front of himself—no mean feat. By about six months, the infant will be able to examine a cube more thoroughly by transferring it from one hand to the other rather than by simply grasping it. The transfer also shows the beginnings of "voluntary" release, a fine motor skill exercised when opening one hand and closing the other. By nine months of age, he will routinely exploit the cubes in another way by combining them, banging them together, and matching them. By about one year, the infant's combining will be more specific and will include attempts to build a tower by releasing a cube on top of another. By 15 months, he will usually be successful in solving the problem of tower building, but only with two cubes. The problem of taller towers is only gradually solved. By 18 months, he can stack three cubes; at 21 months, five. By 24 months, he may add a block or two to his vertical stack, but also is able to align the cubes horizontally, having as it were, acquired a new dimension in which to arrange them.

The increase in the complexity of activities and the refinement of skill that is shown in the above activities has parallels in the "play" that can be elicited with other sorts of materials. Such is the stuff of which developmental tests are made. It is additionally possible to examine such activities for clues as to how a child thinks about his world. Jean Piaget has done just this. His considerations, though not particularly useful in providing age-related measures of developmental progress for the clinician, do provide a fascinating vantage point from which to view the maturation of play. For example, Piaget noted that at one age (about 6 to 8 months in most children) an infant, though interested in a pocket watch when he can see it, acts as if it had ceased to exist when it disappears behind a pillow. Later, a quite different thing happens: the infant immediately pulls the pillow aside to secure the just hidden watch. Piaget concluded that at one stage in development objects have an evanescent existence for the infant. Later, objects acquire subjective permanency. He further suggests that during the first 18 months of life a child builds basic concepts of reality on the basis of information available from his senses and his motor activities.

Communication with others by crying is the core of the infant's early "language." By two years of age, sounds with specific symbolic function (words) will be used in combinations to communicate. While the complexities of this stunning change in capabilities are outside this survey, it can be briefly noted that some words are both understood and used by one year of age. As imitation is important in these changes, parents should be encouraged to talk to and with their infants.

Personal-social behaviors are those that reflect the infant's acquisition of culturally approved activities as, for example, toilet training and self-help skills such as self-feeding. After maturation of the infant to biologic readiness, these behaviors show variation in their timing and specifics dependent to a great extent upon parental expectation and customary practice.

Individual variation exists in the time at which skills are achieved. Also, the latitude for attainment of these skills within normal limits changes as the child grows older. The full-term newborn who does not show the ability to coordinate breathing, sucking, and swallowing within 24 to 48 hours of birth falls outside normal latitude. At the other end of the mnemonic, walking can be normally, though rarely, delayed to 18 months.

Because of this individual variation, no one behavior is sufficient to characterize the developmental age of an infant. Rather, several behaviors from each of the different areas (motor, language, adaptive, personal-social) need to be observed and their usual ages of attainment compared. Standardized infant tests do this and are either useful as screening devices (the DDST, see Appendix) or as more definitive evaluations (Bailey, Gesell), depending upon the number of items and resultant extent of behaviors sampled.

Social

Growth toward social and emotional independence proceeds under the stimulus of interaction between the child and others. Initially, the "others" are usually quite limited—often only the mother. In our culture, the child's caretakers continue to be the chief others; it is often well beyond two years before important and usual stimuli for growth include interaction with age peers. Both the child and his caretakers contribute to this interaction and are affected by it.

The contribution of adults to growth-promoting interaction has various adjectives applied to it—acceptance, support, guidance, stability, encouragement, stimulation, and protection. Parents and others provide these in varying quality and quantity.

Infants also vary in their contribution to interactions. Some of the variability originates in the infant's unique characteristics, such as temperament, tolerance of new situations, reactivity, activity, cuddliness, and other qualities. Stability or unchangeableness in such characteristics also may produce changes in social interactions. Some changes may relate to age. For example, an active three-month-old infant kicking vigorously in his crib will have a different input to his interactions than an equally vigorous two-year old racing about his household. Furthermore, what the infant seeks from interaction fluctuates. When he is tired, he needs more support than when he is fully rested. In the latter state, the 18-month-old child may leave his mother and get into "trouble" if she doesn't follow; in the former, he may actively seek a parent and protest her leaving, as parents of many under-two-year-olds know from the experience of putting their child to bed.

One aid to conceptualizing the variability in such interactions is a circumplex such as Figure 6–2, which relates to the dimension of dependence-independence. The adult's axis is a continuum from "only fulfilling dependency needs" to "supporting only movement toward independence." At one end, for example, might be the theoretical mother who "does all" for her child, actively smothering his efforts at autonomy. At the other end might be the essentially *laissez faire*

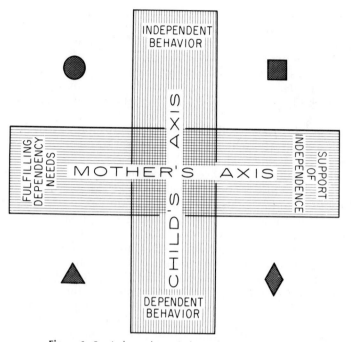

Figure 6–2 A dependence-independence circumplex.

parents, whose caretaking activities cease once the essentials of barest physical needs are met. Generally mothers manage to occupy the middle range of this continuum, supporting their child's strivings for independence and supplying his dependency needs. The child's axis is a continuum from seeking to have things done for him to strident demands for independence.

In Figure 6–2, the ■ would be the position in the circumplex of a mother-child dyad in which the child is quite independent and whose mother is easily able to support this. The ▲ would locate a dyad consisting of a dependent child whose mother finds satisfaction fulfilling his needs. The ◆ would be the position of a dyad that would contain internal conflicts. The mother would want the child to be independent, a common situation of mothers who are pregnant when their child is still quite young, as if they were preparing the way for the new baby whose demands may limit the amount of time available for the older child. The child in this dyad would be one who wanted his mother to do many things for him. The remaining position, ●, represents a dyad in which the child robustly seeks independence from a mother who infantilizes him. Such a pattern is not rare among mothers with their "last" baby.

There are other areas of interaction, and potential circumplexes to display them, in which variations in infants' predispositions may match or fail to match family characteristics: calm, quiet, orderly families may be disrupted by a particularly energetic, active baby; families who take pleasure in being constantly on the go may have to restructure their lives somewhat if their infant is one who cannot tolerate irregular hours and frequent changes in people and places.

The process of social maturation has markers that can be used to assess its adequacy. Failure to demonstrate these may raise questions about the child, his parent or their interaction. Some of these include the following:

Early social response really consists of two responses that are present together in relatively clear form by about six to eight weeks: following the parents (and other objects) visually and responding to social stimulation with a smile. Both have antecedents which can be detected in some infants as early as the neonatal period. These very early social-like responses undoubtedly play an important role in shaping parental social reactions toward the infant. They, as it were, allow the infant to seduce his parents.

Spontaneously responding with a smile to the stimulus of a human face soon follows at two to four months. By this time, the infant is not a passive recipient of social overtures but is clearly seeking interaction.

Sober regard of new faces, or, not infrequently, the manifestation of greater anxiety by crying and in other ways showing that strangers are recognized as strangers, comes into the infant's repertoire at about eight months of age. Occasional children show this earlier.

Looking to the mother, as if for reassurance, either when on her lap, or when separated but within visual range, is often seen when development of independent locomotion gives the child the ability to separate himself from his mother. Infants are often less disturbed by the intrusion of unknown adults if they can sustain contact, even if only visual, with their mother. This pattern has many manifestations as the child matures. The toddler will go to his mother for reassurance when confronted with a situation he cannot master. Looking to parents for support wanes as the child becomes capable of coping with a wider variety of situations on his own.

Unpredictability in regard to compliance with requests, as though experimenting with willfulness and autonomy as a person, becomes prominent somewhat before two years.

PREVENTIVE MEASURES: WELLNESS CARE

The physician's role in the infant's growth and development has several aspects which can be subsumed under the term "wellness care," the maintenance of health and the prevention of disease. A physician may offer this care individually or in cooperation with other health care professionals.

Assessment of progress of a child is obviously central to this task. The preceding discussion has sketched some dimensions of such an assessment. If the progress is less than satisfactory, the health care specialist is alerted to look for causes and, if possible, assist the processes of growth and development by remediation.

Anticipatory guidance allows the parents to foresee the changes that will occur in the normal course of growth and development. Ideally, this allows naturally occurring changes in children to be facilitated; at the very least, it prevents such changes from being considered problems.

Counsel regarding parental concerns is another aspect of wellness care. Because of the individuality of children and parents, routine advice will not cover all situations. Sometimes the problems will relate to inadequate or more-rapid-than-usual progress. At other times, after the problem's genesis, duration, degree of disruption, and relationship to other aspects of the child's situation have been elucidated, the problem may be interpreted as being of relatively little concern for the long term progress of the child.

There are about as many ways to provide parental care for children as there are parents and children, the task being quite individual. Support for parents' efforts, unless ill effects are seen or anticipated, allows flowering of their self-confidence about child-rearing abilities. Parents can be further aided if they are educated to routinely ask, "What does my infant want? What does he need?" when they are considering how to provide parenting. In terms of the discussion of social growth sketched above, the child's contribution to a situation and the reasons for those activities need to be considered along with the parents' desires and needs.

There are some other specific tasks which are usually undertaken in providing wellness care:

Immunization of the child against certain diseases such as diphtheria, tetanus, pertussis, polio and rubeola (common measles) is a usual practice. Immunization against rubella (German measles) and mumps is a variable practice. Smallpox vaccine is no longer routinely administered.

Tests for diseases such as tuberculosis (skin test), urinary tract infection (urine test) and anemia (determination of the level of blood hemoglobin) are usually administered.

Planning appropriate nutrition for the infant takes into account the fact that infant diets are different from adult diets. In part, this is because the early diet is totally liquid. Wellness Care must ensure that the diet meets the infant's nutritional requirements. If a nursing mother's diet is appropriate, human milk will be nutritionally close to complete, lacking only three elements. Vitamin D is virtually absent. In most parts of the United States there is insufficient sunlight to ensure adequate conversion of 7-dehydrocholesterol in the skin to vitamin D. Therefore, the nursing infant needs a supplement such as cod liver oil or one of the newer water miscible preparations in a dose which will provide 400 International Units of vitamin D per day. Iron and fluoride are also inadequate in human milk.

Human milk shares these deficiencies with cow's milk, which is commonly modified for use by infants whose mothers choose not to breast feed them. The modification chiefly reduces the osmotic and phosphorous load presented to the infant's immature kidneys by dilution of cow's milk with water. The 20 calories per ounce ratio common to human and undiluted cow's milk is restored by the addition of a carbohydrate such as corn syrup. Modification of cow's milk additionally does involve heating, such as that used to produce evaporated milk. This alters proteins so that a softer curd is produced in the infant's stomach, aiding his digestion.

The commercial addition of iron to infant formulas is frequent. Many advocate the use of iron-fortified milk routinely. If the infant is breast fed, however, or receives an artificial formula without iron supplementation, he can receive iron from other dietary sources.

Almost all commercially available cow's milk has appropriate amounts of vitamin D added (400 IU per quart). The use of skim milk powder or liquid in the preparation of infant formula can result in a dietary deficiency of essential fatty acids in addition to vitamin D deficiency, as this vitamin is fat soluble. Vitamin C may need to be supplemented in infant diets, as its presence in milk depends upon the diet of the lactating mother or cow, the amount destroyed by heating in preparation of formula, and the amount added in commercial processing, as is commonly done in proprietary formulas. Supplementation of vitamin C can be with ascorbic acid (tablets or liquid), which is least expensive, or by the addition of vitamin C containing foods, such as some fruit juices. Either way, the infant should have between 25 to 50 mg of the vitamin each day. With the many vitamin supplemented foods commercially available, hyper-vitamin toxicity with fat soluble vitamins is more than theoretically possible if supplemental vitamins are also used. The major concern is hypervitaminosis D. Also, these supplements are relatively expensive and often unnecessary.

Fluoride is needed in infants' and children's diets for its effect in the prevention of dental caries. If local water supplies contain inadequate amounts (less than 0.8 to 1 mg per day) a supplement should be provided.

Counsel regarding the pace of progression to an essentially adult diet is also a part of wellness care. After the infant is taking about a quart of milk (usually he weighs about 12 pounds and is 2 to 3 months old), other foods are added. With emergence of grasping and chewing at about six months, finger foods are appropriately added. This eventually frees the mother from the burden of hand feeding the child to ensure adequate intake of food. The child's budding independence can also be encouraged. As growth slows in later infancy, maternal concern about decreased intake of food can be lessened. By two years of age, a spoon is relatively skillfully used by a child to convey essentially adult type of foods to his mouth.

If the child assumes independence in his feeding by taking what he wants of offered foods, it is necessary that food to which he has access be balanced and nutritious, with limited offerings of cookies, candy, soda pop, or other snacks.

Education regarding the prevention of illness should include guidelines for the prevention of accidents.

Education should be provided regarding symptoms of illness requiring professional evaluation and care, as well as in ways to provide home care for the child who has common, mild illnesses, such as respiratory tract and gastrointestinal infections, or who is involved in an accident.

The medical and functional status of the child should be determined by periodic physical examinations. Attention to vision and hearing are important parts of these examinations. A "cover-test," looking for "lazy-eye" or amblyopia is possible after three or four months of age, when visual fixation is well developed, and preventive measures can be initiated. Hearing assessment is appropriate, especially if upper respiratory infections, particularly otitis media, have occurred since the last evaluation. Delayed language development also requires determination of auditory acuity.

COMMON DISORDERS

Mortality is higher shortly after birth than at any later age. A large portion of mortality, however, is associated with the problems of establishing extrauterine existence. Thus congenital malformations, immaturity, and infections which are usually limited to the newborn period, are the predominant causes. Beyond the early neonatal period, infections of the respiratory tract and the digestive system are leading causes of death in the United States during the first year of life. From the time of the first birthday until middle adulthood, accidents become the leading cause of death. Respiratory infections, congenital malformations and cancer follow accidents, but even the most common of these has been the cause of only about one-third of deaths attributed to accidents.

Behavioral Disorders

"Infantile colic" is the name often applied to excessive crying in the first three months of life. Colic is a term used for the pain associated with distention of a hollow viscus; for example, renal colic is used to describe the intense pain associated with a stone in a ureter. By analogy, the apparent intense discomfort of infants who cry excessively is often thought to be associated with intestinal disorder. Well-established etiologies are lacking, but theories abound. One theory considers food allergy as a cause and substitution of formulas as appropriate therapy. Another theory leads to therapy involving the parasympathetic blocking agents because they decrease intestinal motility. A number of studies have suggested that parents of an infant who crys excessively are usually tense, supporting an environmental etiology for the disorder. The question of which comes first, the crying infant or the tense parents, needs to be closely examined for this etiology to be accepted.

Curiously, by three months of age, irrespective of what therapy is used, the excessive crying wanes. A study of the amount of infant crying showed the usual pattern to be an increase until six weeks of age, and then a decline to newborn levels or below by three months of age. This suggests that the pattern of crying in infants labeled as having "the three-month colic" may be an exacerbation of a normal pattern.

The excessive crying shown by some infants may in part be related to the immature nervous system's limited ability to modulate stimuli before three months of age. This leads to "overload" and crying. Regularly repeated stimuli such as rocking, swaddling, and lullabyes provide external modulation through the mechanism of habituation.

If this theory is used to plan or recommend therapy, reassurance and offering a prognosis of resolution by three months of age are important aspects. Attention must also be paid to the strain on such an infant's mother, who often feels that her mothering abilities are called into question by her inability to ease the crying of her infant. Limiting the use of medication and formula changing decreases the potential danger of iatrogenic (physician caused) difficulties in relation to a disorder that will cure itself with the further development of the infant.

Infectious, Immunologic Disorders

Diarrhea is of especial concern when it occurs in infants and young children because of their smaller volume of body fluids and the possibility of their losing relatively large amounts of water and electrolytes with their stools. Additionally, the higher metabolic rate associated with their high surface area in comparison to body mass causes acidosis to supervene rapidly when nutritional intake is interrupted by illness. Vomiting, frequently associated with diarrhea, leads to further loss of fluids and electrolytes. Food, especially cow's milk, is a frequent source of the etiologic agent in diarrheal disorders, whether this agent be an infectious one or a bacterial toxin. The fact that milk is an excellent bacterial growth medium requires that this particular food be handled with safeguards against contamination and bacterial growth. Since 1900, improvement in general hygienic conditions has been associated with marked decrease in morbidity and mortality due to severe infantile diarrhea.

Haemophilus influenzae infections are more common in the six-month to two-year age range than at any other time of life. This bacterial agent has a highly age-related incidence. This is of particular significance with regard to planning treatment for meningitis or otitis media in young children, prior to culture identification of the agent. Studies have shown that this susceptibility pattern is associated with an age-related change in the bactericidal activity of human blood against this organism. The bactericidal activity probably is related first to experience with the agent and secondarily to increasing immunologic competence.

Infections due to many agents which involve the lower pharynx, larynx, trachea and bronchi are of most concern in very young children. The inflammatory responses of edema and exudate encroach upon their smaller respiratory passages.

Otitis media is a frequent and potentially handicapping complication of respiratory infections (see next chapter).

Tuberculosis presents a special threat for the child under two years of age. In adults, the body defense mechanisms against this disease tend to localize the infection. In young children, this is less effectively done, with the result that involvement of the CNS with tuberculosis is relatively common if a child acquires this infection. This meningitis has an especially high incidence of mortality and handicapping sequelae. Many consider treatment with antituberculosis drugs mandatory if a child has a familial exposure to tuberculosis or shows a newly positive skin test reaction to tuberculin.

It can be seen from the above examples that there are unique considerations in planning appropriate therapy when one's attention is brought to the young child who has an infection.

Nutritional Disorders

The most common nutritionally caused disorder in the United States is iron deficiency anemia in the 9- to 24-month-old infant. The etiology of this disorder is directly related to the growth processes discussed above. The full-term infant whose mother is in good health is born with iron stores that are adequate until his weight has doubled or more. As growth proceeds, an increasing blood volume is necessary to perfuse the increasing body mass. There is a consequent need for an increase in total body hemoglobin, the oxygen-carrying, iron-containing, red pigment in the blood. Additional iron, after gestational stores are depleted, is supplied through the diet. Milk, the major dietary constituent in young children, has little iron. Dry, prepared baby cereals are one source of dietary iron, and introduction of them into an infant's diet in reasonable amounts (6 to 10 tablespoonfuls of dry cereal per day) at or about three months of age will prevent the anemia.

Neoplasia

There are two important tumors whose occurrence is unique to the early years of life. They are Wilms' tumor of the kidney, and neuroblastoma, which arises in the adrenal medulla or from the perispinal sympathetic chain. Both are most commonly found as an upper lateral abdominal mass on palpation. Treatment involves surgery, usually radiation, and often chemotherapy. Both have a significant survival rate for affected children.

Accidents

Any discussion of disorders common to children, regardless of age, should place accidents at the head of the list, for they are this country's leading causes of morbidity and mortality after one year of age. Moreover, they are appropriately discussed in the context of early development, for not only do the types of catastrophe change as development progresses, but also the means of prevention change concomitantly.

For each accidental childhood death, there are some 840 accidents that do not lead to death. This means, if approximately true, that about one-fifth of all children experience at least one significant accident per year.

What is the epidemiology of accidents in early childhood? These are chiefly *home* accidents—occurring where young children are. The common types of accidents are related to the state of the child's development. Frequently occurring examples in the birth-to-two-year-age range would include the following: an infant rolls over for the first time when his mother has put him down near the edge of a table, and he falls; a ten-month-old, practicing his ability to pick up small objects, secures a screw that has fallen out of a toy, puts this screw into his mouth and inadvertently aspirates it into his lung; an infant sitting in his high chair next to the stove reaches for and secures the handle of a pot, pulls it toward himself and spills its contents, scalding his legs and abdomen; a mother leaves her young baby in the bathtub in order to answer a ringing phone, the baby slips, his head goes under water and he drowns. An example of the single most frequent accident— poisoning—might be the tragedy of the curious exploring toddler who sees his mother take some aspirin for her headache. She leaves the bottle open on a counter top. The toddler moves a chair over, climbs up, and eats some of the pills as he has seen his mother do.

These examples illustrate some of the danger situations which are likely to be present when childhood accidents occur:

1. The child is hungry.
2. The child and mother are tired (late in day).
3. The mother is ill or pregnant, or has pre- or early menstrual tension.
4. The parents are quarreling.
5. The child is in new surroundings (moving, trip).
6. A new and unfamiliar person supervises the child.
7. The child makes a developmental advance for which the parents are unprepared.
8. The child is very active and his parents cannot manage him.

Combinations of these situations increase the accident risk considerably. One can see that stress, disorganization and decreased ability to cope are common to all of these. Indeed, when the level of organization in families is assessed, those households with greater disorganization have more accidents.

Generally, the development of the child affects the methods which can be relied upon to prevent accidents. The young child must be protected. He can assume little responsibility in avoiding burns, poisons, falls, drowning, or being struck by an automobile. By two to three years of age, if taught and helped, he can learn to avoid certain hazards. For example, putting on seat belts can be done by the child as he gets older. Some accidents will happen, but proper care can lessen their consequences. An estimated 500,000 poisonings of children occur each year in the United States; therefore, it is vital that mothers be aware that aspirin can kill, and know that they must secure help for the child who accidentally ingests aspirin.

In summary, two principles can be enumerated: the type of mishap likely to occur changes as the child's development progresses; as development progresses, it becomes possible and appropriate for the child to begin to actively protect himself rather than to rely passively on protection.

Using these principles, the health care professional can provide excellent "therapy" by offering anticipatory guidance about accidents to families.

Child Abuse

Infants and children do not always receive the nurturance they need from their parents. More than a decade ago, awareness that some children had roentgenographic evidence of unexplainable patterns of fractures led to the recognition of the "battered child" as a medical syndrome.

The feelings of horror that accompany thoughts of a defenseless child being injured can interfere with the health care professional's working effectively with this situation. The following comments may put the situation into a workable perspective:

Angry feelings toward children are not limited to those who strike out at infants. They are probably present in most adults who deal with children for more than brief periods of time. What is done with these feelings does differ. Most adults do not strike out or severely deprive children who anger them. The minority of those who are abusive to children, approximately 10 per cent, are psychotic or aggressive psychopaths. The rest have often had beatings or other inappropriate care during their own childhood. They are usually isolated individuals who have limited ways of expressing their feelings, especially anger. Children are often unrealistically expected to make up for some of the things which the parents feel are lacking in their own lives.

The abuse of a child is a desperate cry for help on the part of the battering parent. Health care professionals can and should respond to this request for help. Lessening the isolation, giving some of the mothering that the abusive parent did not get as a child, and providing relief from the strain of caring for the child are means of providing hope for the parent and child.

The first obligation is to be sure the child is protected from further abuse. Hearing the parent's cry for help is an important long-term part of that protection. There are now governmentally designated agencies to assist in providing such care for both child and parent. In all states, non-accidental injury must be reported to these agencies. Hospitalization of the child is usually the initial step in treatment when there has been actual injury.

Prevention of child abuse needs to be a goal of persons who help parents care for their children. To accomplish this, ways are needed to assess the abilities and resources of mothers and fathers. For example, crying is a universal and uniquely irritating activity of infants. It is useful to ask those who care for a child what they do when the baby makes them angry by crying. Understanding how a parent deals with crying can alert the health care professional to potential abuse. Inquiring of a mother what she does when she is unhappy, to whom does she turn for aid, can help her to tell of her isolation. In a similar way, other difficulties in parenting need to be brought into focus. Inquiring about these difficulties makes it possible for parents to ask for help.

All parents need help at least occasionally—for relief from the care of their children or a place to turn when they find themselves overwhelmed. The support which once was provided by extended family kinships needs to be provided in other ways for parents. There is much that must be learned about the most effective ways to prevent inappropriate treatment of children. One way is to be alert to the messages given by the potentially abusive parent before he or she is the agent of injury.

REFERENCES

Brazelton, T. B.: Crying in infancy. Pediatrics, 29:579, 1962.

Bagles, J. A.: Economy in nutrition and feeding of infants. Am. J. Pub. Health, 56: 1756, 1966.

Ginsberg, H., and Opper, S.: Piaget's Theory of Intellectual Development; An Introduction. Englewood Cliffs, New Jersey, Prentice-Hall, 1969.

Kempe, C. H.: Paediatric implications of the battered baby syndrome. Arch. Dis. Child., 46:28, 1971.

Kessen, W., Haith, M. M., and Salapatek, P. H.: Human infancy: A bibliography and guide. In Mussen, P. H. (Ed.): Carmichael's Manual of Child Psychology. 3rd ed. New York, John Wiley and Sons, Inc., 1970.

Meyer, R. J., Roelofs, H. A., Bluestone, J., and Redmond, S.: Accidental injury to the pre-school child. J. Pediat., 63:95, 1963.

Parmelee, A. H., Wenner, W. H., and Schulz, H. R.: Infant sleep patterns: from birth to 16 weeks of age. J. Pediat., 65:576, 1964.

Standards of Child Health Care. Evanston, Illinois, American Academy of Pediatrics, 1967.

Thomas, A., Chess, S., and Birch, H.: Temperament and Behavior Disorders in Children. New York, New York University Press, 1968.

CHAPTER SEVEN

CHILDHOOD

VANJA A. HOLM
NICHOLAS A. WILTZ

The years from the end of infancy to the beginning of adolescence span approximately a decade. It is a time of rapid physical, mental and emotional growth and development. Daily changes are subtle during childhood, but appear dramatic when one compares the gestalt of the infection prone, family dependent, imaginative preschooler to the robust, peer oriented, enterprising child of secondary school age. (Fig. 7–1). Physical, physiologic, and behavioral phenomena change with growth, and thus "normality" changes in the individual who is still developing. Concerned about problems in the child, parents like to say "He'll grow out of it." Before accepting this verdict, the professional should consider the child's state of maturation. Some childhood problems are common and temporary phenomena, some are signs of serious disorder.

(Text continues on page 113.)

Figure 7–1, *A* to *N.* **A photo album showing a brother and sister through childhood.**

A, Ingrid on her second birthday. (note pseudostrabismus).

B, Four months later, with mother (the author) and baby brother, Erik—they call it sibling rivalry (note tibial torsion).

C, Ingrid plays being the mother—makes it easier to get used to brother.

D, We learn to get along by taking turns helping with fun household tasks.

Erik 3, Ingrid 5 years of age.

E, We like to dress up for Easter. (Note stance and body proportions.)

F, Erik at 4 years of age likes to try out big sister's roller skates. (Note: baby fat has disappeared.)

G, Ingrid's first day in school—6 years old. (Note: legs now straight.)

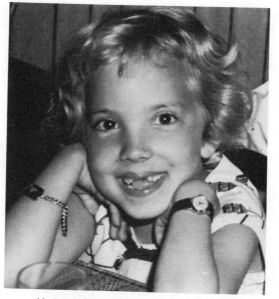

H, A year later, she has lost her front teeth. (Note changes in facial appearance.)

Age 7

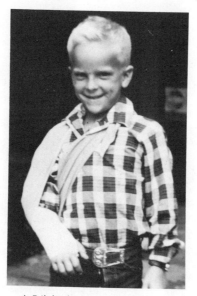

I, Erik broke his arm at daycamp.

J, Like so many boys, he needs to practice his printing at age 8.

K, Ingrid at age 10 likes horses, as do many other girls her age.

Erik age 10–11.

L, Erik is always busy building . . .

M, . . . or climbing, either alone or with his boy friends.

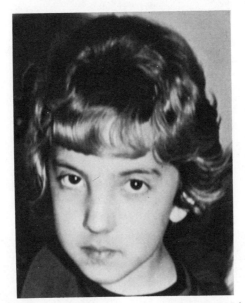

N, Ingrid is pensive nowadays—approaching adolescence at age 12 has brought on many changes. (Note maturation of facial features.)

LIFE SITUATION

Physical Development

The rates of growth in height and weight during the childhood years are undramatic compared to those in preceding and ensuing life periods, but height and weight constitute a summation of changes in many parts of the body. An appreciation of differential growth rate (Fig. 7–2) is needed to understand the variations found in physical characteristics during the childhood years. Growth of different tissues is discussed in detail in Chapter One.

Body Proportions.   One result of the variations in growth rate of different systems is a change in body proportions during childhood. The extremities grow relatively quickly compared to the trunk; the brain (and the skull) accomplishes 70 per cent of its growth by 2 and will reach almost adult size by 5; subcutaneous adipose tissue shows a relative decrease in growth during the early part of this period; muscle mass increases slowly but steadily. As a result, though the 2-year-old appears chubby, with relatively short legs and large head, he turns into

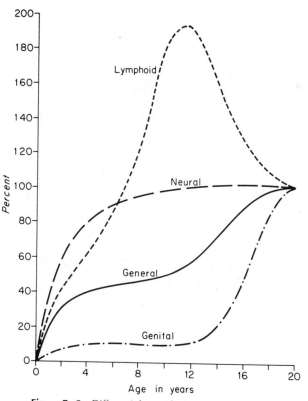

Figure 7–2   Differential growth rate of some tissues.

a slender, lithe 5-year-old, who insidiously becomes a long-legged and increasingly sturdier school-age child. (Fig. 7–1; compare the boy in *E, F,* and *M.*)

Posture. Posture also changes with growth. The toddler has a marked lumbar lordosis and a protruding abdomen. Posture is transformed as the earlier forward tilt of the pelvis is straightened and the abdominal muscles become better developed. The convex curvature of the thoracic spine finally develops during the early school years, but the full adult posture is not assumed until after the increased muscular growth during adolescence.

Lower Extremities. Great variations in the appearance of the lower extremities are found among children; most of these are of no functional concern, but are a cause of worry to parents for cosmetic reasons. Some of these variations reflect normal growth as, for example, toeing-out and toeing-in. The relatively top-heavy 2-year-old has a wide stance and his feet usually point out (Fig. 7–1, *E*), as there is a normal outward rotation of the legs at the hip. Growth and functional stresses subsequently contribute to an inward rotation of the hips (in the older child the hip allows approximately 30 degree rotation inwards and 60 degrees rotation outwards), which results in the disappearance of the typically everted feet in early childhood (Fig. 7–1, *F*). Instead, the older preschooler might be pigeon-toed. This toeing-in may occur if inward rotation of the lower legs (tibial torsion), which is normal in early infancy (Fig. 7–1, *B*), is still present. It might also occur if the legs are straight but the forefoot turns inward. A more severe form of this so-called metatarsus adductus is an abnormal congenital condition which merits treatment in early infancy. Finally, in-toeing might be due to excessive inward rotation of the hip beyond the neutral position called femoral anteversion. Most instances of these conditions, tibial torsion, mild metatarsus adductus, and femoral anteversion, disappear whether treated or not. Corrective shoes or appliances, which create stress that influences the direction of growth of the bones, can be prescribed. However, most children will grow out of a toeing-in condition. Professional intervention may be essential only for the occasional older preadolescent child in whom spontaneous correction has not taken place.

Other normal growth phenomena which often cause parental concern about the appearance of the legs include the presence of a fat pad in the instep of most toddlers, which makes them appear flat-footed, and a mild degree of knock-kneedness, which is frequently present during the late preschool years (Fig. 7–1; compare the girl in *D* and *G*). Both these conditions are usually temporary.

Face. Facial appearance shows characteristic changes during childhood. The toddler's face appears small compared to the skull, the mandible is small, the eyes appear relatively far apart, and the nasal bridge is low. As a result, the young child might appear mildly cross-eyed, demonstrating the so-called pseudostrabismus (Fig. 7–1, *A*). As the child ages, the face seems to grow out from under the skull. This stems from the relatively rapid growth of the maxilla and the mandible. The sequential replacement of the primary teeth by the larger, more yellowish permanent teeth (see Appendix) has an additional profound effect on the facial appearance of the school-age child (Fig. 7–1, *H*). The complicated differential growth process of the facial structures frequently results in maladaptive development, not all temporary. A large percentage of children ideally require professional supervision by dental specialists during this growth phase to allow for satisfactory development of the lower part of the face in terms of bite occlusion as well as for cosmetic reasons (Fig. 7–1, *N*).

Physiologic Development

Physiologic measurements change with age as a result of the complex interplay of growth, maturation, and aging. It is therefore common to refer to normative data collected for different ages when evaluating blood pressure, heart and respiratory rate, and blood count. (See Appendix.) Changes in some of these measurements are significant during childhood. For example, the differential white blood cell count changes from relatively more lymphocytes in early childhood to a greater per cent of leucocytes in the older child.

When assessing certain physiologic processes in childhood it is sometimes important to correct given norms for physical size. There are great variations in height and weight of normal children of the same age, as evident in the growth charts in the Appendix. Hence it is generally preferable to consider nutritional requirements and drug dosage in relation to height and weight rather than in terms of age. Surface area, estimated from height and weight measurements, is used when a most exact correction for size is necessary.

Gastrointestinal and Urinary Tracts. Most body systems are functionally mature at the onset of this biologic age. The kidneys are well differentiated, and specific gravity and other urine findings are now similar to those of an adult. The toddler's gastrointestinal tract can handle most adult foods, but children's nutritional requirements change with age and are given in the Appendix. The neurophysiologic pathways necessary for the voluntary control of the sphincters which regulate the elimination from these two body systems have matured. However, there is considerable individual variability, and the achievement of this control, usually accomplished during the third year of life, may be interfered with by complicating psychosocial factors (see section on Problems of Behavior in this chapter).

Immunologic System. The immunologic system reaches functional maturity early and allows for adequate response to challenges from infectious agents during childhood. The child builds up immunity to common pathogens as he is exposed to them. The young child, therefore, easily succumbs to colds, intestinal infections, the common contagious diseases, and other infections prevalent in the community. Again, social factors may influence immunity. The first and only child often experiences frequent infections upon entering nursery school, kindergarten, or first grade, when he first broadens his social contacts. A child with siblings a few years older often experiences infections at an earlier age.

Circulation and Respiration. Physiology of circulation and respiration, of course, has been operating since birth, but their functions are influenced by physical size. Heart murmurs in the growing child, resulting from the passage of blood through normal heart valves, are often heard. Soft, so-called physiologic or functional murmurs, of no medical consequence are present in as many as 50 per cent of children at some time because of the thinness of the chest wall and the changing relations between the chest and the inner organs due to growth. The diameter of the upper respiratory tract of a young child is small compared to that of the adult. Disastrous effects from obstruction of the critical upper airway can be caused in small children by swelling from inflammation or by inhalation of even tiny foreign bodies.

Reproductive and Endocrine Systems. The reproductive and endocrine systems change little until late in childhood, when the profound changes of adolescence are heralded by an initially slow and then rapidly increasing change in endocrine functions. Of course, the endocrine system with its many interrelating hormones has a profound effect during childhood as it affects and is affected by almost all aspects of physical growth and development. Its influence is probably best appreciated when studying the "experiments of nature" afforded by the appearance of abnormal endocrinologic states in childhood (see Chapter One).

Central Nervous System and Sensory Organs. In contrast to most other systems, neurophysiologic maturation continues throughout childhood and is of far-reaching importance. Sequential maturation of the central nervous system allows the growing child to perform increasingly complex tasks requiring coordination of gross and fine motor control. At 3 years of age he can ride a tricycle, by 7 he can probably ride a bike. At 4 years of age he can cut with scissors and button his coat, by 9 most children can sew or build models. There are great individual variations in maturation of coordination skills, which should be considered when planning programs for a child, such as participation in competitive athletics or playing a musical instrument. Neurophysiologic changes pave the way for language, learning, and behavioral development. Indirect observations of these processes are made by behavioral scientists studying intellectual, social, and emotional growth and development, as discussed in the next section.

Of the specialized sensory organs, the physiologic changes in the eye during childhood are of most practical importance (Fig. 7–3). The young child's eye is normally hyperopic, that is, the image of an object at a distance falls behind the retina. This condition is of no consequence, however, as children easily accommodate by increasing the power of their malleable lens to refract the light waves. In fact, most children's power of accommodation is so great that they can see clearly an object only a few inches from their noses. As the eye grows in length and changes during childhood, most children become emmetropic, that is, the image of a distant object will fall on the retina without accommodation (continued mild hyperopia is common in adults). If the eye becomes too long, the child becomes myopic, that is, the image of the distant object will be focused in front of the retina

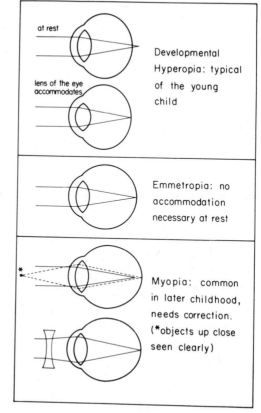

at rest

lens of the eye
accommodates

Developmental
Hyperopia: typical
of the young
child

Emmetropia: no
accommodation
necessary at rest

*

Myopia: common
in later childhood,
needs correction.
(*objects up close
seen clearly)

Figure 7–3 Changes of the eye during childhood.

and appear blurred. This situation is common, often familial, and should be corrected by glasses. It is important to appreciate that the myopic (nearsighted) child does not complain of poor vision, he knows nothing else. Astigmatism, uneven refraction through the different meridians of the eye, is another variation of eye growth. If marked, it needs correction, especially in the older child, as it might distort the image of letters and numbers enough to blur them and confuse the child. Vision, as it can be measured, seems to improve up to about 5 years of age, when most normal children have a measured vision of 20/20 (Table 7–1). This apparent improvement in vision is due to behavioral and neurologic maturation, not to changes in the eye *per se*.

A similar observation can be made about hearing. A satisfactory hearing screen by conventional means can usually not be obtained until a normal child is 4 to 5 years of age. Responses on audiologic testing of younger children have to be interpreted with a background knowledge of how children typically behave during hearing testing at different ages. Children in whom hearing problems are suspected, therefore, have to be evaluated by specially trained audiologists. Significant hearing loss is one of the most commonly overlooked serious handicaps in young children.

TABLE 7-1 DEVELOPMENT OF VISUAL ACUITY*

Age	Visual Acuity
1	20/200
2	20/40
3	20/30
4	20/25
5	20/20

*L. B. Holt, Pediatric Ophthalmology, Philadelphia, Lea & Febiger, 1964, p. 15.

Psychosocial Development

To understand behavioral development in childhood one needs a general view of what the normal child does at certain ages as a guide. It is well recognized that personality in adulthood is intimately related to experiences in childhood. There are several theoretical models available to guide the clinician's approach to social-emotional development, three of which will be outlined.

Normative Developmental Data

The determination of what normal children do at certain ages requires minute observations and sophisticated testing of intellectual and social behavior. Two of the best examples of observers of the normal child are Arnold Gesell and Jean Piaget. Gesell's works are well known in the United States, and during the last few years Piaget's studies of cognitive development have been receiving increased recognition. Numerous testing instruments, standardized on supposedly normal children are also available and clinically useful as an aid in detecting the deviant child. The Denver Developmental Screening Test is an example of a frequently used text. (Appendix.)

LANGUAGE. Development of expressive language is eagerly awaited by parents as an indication of normality in the young child. As in other areas of development there are great variations of what is normal. For example, at age 2 one child may use only a few words and another may have a vocabulary of 2000 words. The child should at least make some novel two-word combinations like "Daddy byebye."

The beginning of speech at the onset of this life period is a dramatic event, preceded by many months of developing communication skills. During the preschool years there is an almost explosive development of language skills, with the typical 5-year-old using syntactically complex sentences. The non-appearance of normal language development is often the first signal of serious problems. Language is the most complex task for which the human brain has been programmed, and thus vulnerable to many types of interference. Lack of development of normal language is not just a symptom of hearing loss but may be seen in environmental deprivation, and is a symptom of general intellectual retardation of the type associated with many disorders linked with abnormal development or function of the brain. It is frequently found in children who are labeled psychotic. The importance of the early childhood years for language development is illustrated by the observation that, if language has not developed by age 7, the likelihood that language ever will be used by that individual for meaningful communication is almost nil.

The Traditional View of Emotional Development in Childhood— Erikson

Freud contributed a number of observations on the human condition which are the basis for his theoretical system of emotional development. Erik Erikson has presented an expansion of these views and is best known for his theory of the stages of emotional development.

Erikson's first stages of emotional development coincide roughly with Freud's psychosexual stages of development. In each of Erikson's stages the individual must face and master a central problem which becomes dominant. He would assume that the normally maturing preschool child already has achieved a basic sense of trust in the world around him, and that to acquire a healthy "sense of autonomy" is the main emotional task in the early preschool years. During this time the child's urge for self-expression tends to be frustrated by his environment, often for his own safety, and some consistent limits have to be set to his behavior in consideration of others. This is an age of tantrums, but slowly the child learns self-control, and with wise guidance he learns it without loss of self-esteem. This process continues all the way through childhood.

During the later preschool and early school years, from the age of about 4 to 7, the appearance of another emotional stage of development overshadows the "sense of autonomy." At this time, Erikson says the child is acquiring a "sense of initiative"; he moves out farther in his social environment, he associates with other children his own age, increasingly experiences himself as a boy or girl, and in his imaginary play tries out many roles and ideas. This is a time for dress up and pretend, for fantasies and creativity. Through his inquisitiveness the child finds out about himself. He makes tentative decisions about what kind of adult person he wants to be. He finds out about others and how to relate to a variety of people outside of his home. He finds out about society and its standards and values. The optimum environment during this period encourages the child's creativity and does not belittle the imperfect results. This environment helps him relate his fantasies to reality and guides him when his ideas take him out of bounds, without making him feel guilt about his foolishness.

These interactions between the child and his environment continue, but during the later childhood years the importance of the child's interaction with his family and other adults is overshadowed by his close relationship with his peers. Erikson calls this stage one of acquiring a "sense of industry." The child directs his boundless energy toward mastering a wide variety of skills in which he compares himself to others of his age group, usually children of his own gender. These skills might include either school-type learning tasks or activities unacceptable to adult society. Most likely they include activities like climbing, building, swimming, bicycling, and organized group games. The peer group serves as a measuring stick for success, and in competition the child may experience either success or failure. Again during this stage, the child needs his home and his family to encourage him, to support him, and to take an interest in his activities.

The Social Psychological View of Emotional Development—Dreikurs

Alfred Adler is perhaps the earliest representative of the social view of child development. This social approach stresses the influence of membership in groups, rather than intrapsychic drives, as the important element in individual development. Man is seen as goal-directed and his acts are considered purposeful. Adler's theories have been adopted and expanded by several well-known social theorists, among them Rudolf Dreikurs. Dreikurs, too, stresses the importance of interaction between the child and his family group. This interaction determines the goals he moves toward as he develops his life style or life plan. This plan, once established, guides his future actions. The birth order position helps the child develop his role in the family group. In addition, family atmosphere and methods of training set by the parents are said to either encourage or discourage the child. Dreikurs suggests that in our society, with its emphasis on perfection, status, and competition, it is hard to avoid feelings of social inferiority. If the child feels worth less than other members of the family group he may seek one of four compensating goals. He may strive to overcome his inferiority feelings by forcing those around him to pay more *attention* to him through cuteness, laziness, or annoying behavior. If he still feels inferior or becomes yet more discouraged he may strive for the goal of *power*. At this level the child may try to defeat those about him by rebelliousness or being stubborn. As discouragement increases, a still more forceful goal is that of hurting others by *seeking revenge* for what seems to the child as others trying to hurt him. If the child fails to gain at least some involvement he may *give up* altogether and assume some passive role, in which he is not forced to compete at all. In Dreikurs' theory, if the child interacts in the family where he is accepted as equal in worth, where focus is on cooperation rather than competition, and where discipline is a logical consequence of misbehavior, the child will be motivated toward interest rather than status or power and will choose to cooperate rather than compete. If a child lives in such an equality-oriented atmosphere his life style will allow for a positive approach to peer and societal groups later in life. He will then be prepared to meet and solve life's three major tasks—love, work, and friendship.

The Behavioral View—Skinner

The newest model for emotional development of the child is that which stems from the work of B. F. Skinner. Behaviorists tend to avoid theoretical statements and instead attempt to use the scientific method in developing data on human behavior which is rigidly observed and recorded. The data are then used as a base from which to change behavior. A record, often a graph, of the rate of change is used as the basis of statement about effect of treatment or training.

The child's behavior is seen mainly as a function of antecedents or cues that precede his responses and the positive or negative consequences applied following his behavior. What a child becomes depends on how the environment surrounding the child's actions is structured and arranged. For example, in the area of compliance, a child who receives clear cues in terms of what his parents expect, and who receives positive reinforcement following each appropriate response, will tend to mind in the future. The child who receives mixed messages from his parents, and who may be punished when he responds too slowly or makes minor mistakes, will be less likely to mind in the future, according to the research findings of the behaviorist. The behaviorist deals only with observable behavior and would handle symptoms rather than look for underlying psychic problems when he works with the emotions of the child. He would tend to handle a temper tantrum by removal of the child to his room so that he is unable to receive any interaction positively or negatively from anyone for his behavior. In return, only behavior that is incompatible with a temper tantrum, such as cooperation, would be reinforced by word or act from the parent. Behavior theories have useful practical implications for child rearing. In addition, the behavior modifiers, as they are often called, have been especially effective in training the handicapped child.

Preventive Health Measures

Preventive health measures for the childhood years include immunizations and screening procedures to detect asymptomatic but potentially curable disorders and developmental deviations.

Immunizations. "Booster shots" of the initial immunizations, which have usually been given in infancy, are needed periodically during the childhood years. Up-to-date recommendations are published by the American Academy of Pediatrics and additional suggestions are available from local health departments. These recommendations cover the age at which immunizations should be given, time intervals between boosters, and which diseases to immunize against. At the present time, it is most important to provide booster innoculations against diphtheria, tetanus, and poliomyelitis during the childhood years. However, with advances in medical knowledge, recommendations for immunizations can be expected to change periodically. Some children do not receive preventive immunizations in infancy, the percentage varying greatly depending on socioeconomic conditions. Immunization programs in schools (with parental permission) are an effective way of providing this health care for unprotected children. They are also an efficient way of halting community epidemics, as communicable diseases are quickly transmitted among children in school. Two-thirds of the states, as of 1971, had laws requiring immunizations for school entry.

Screening Procedures. Following is a list of the most common screening procedures used for children at the present time by physicians and nurses in private offices, public health departments and schools.

VISION SCREENING. Approximately 25 per cent of all children will eventually need glasses, at least part time, to correct for myopia or astigmatism. A surprising number of these children have no complaints and will only be found through routine screening. Many discover how much they previously have missed only after their visual deficit has been corrected. Periodic reevaluations of visual acuity for both asymptomatic children and those who wear corrective lenses are recommended until growth ceases in adolescence. Because of the importance of good vision for education, annual screening, starting in kindergarten, is provided in most schools.

HEARING SCREENING. Children with language delay or possible hearing loss should have hearing tests by a competent professional person as soon as a problem is suspected. In addition, all children need periodic hearing screening, which is done regularly in most school systems. Over 5 per cent of school children will not pass the usual hearing screen, but in many the decrease in hearing acuity is mild and due to a temporary upper respiratory tract infection. However, long term collection of sterile fluid in the middle ears (serous otitis media) is a relatively common occurrence, especially prevalent around 4 to 7 years of age. Allergies might be a contributing etiology, but frequently there are no associated symptoms. Long-standing serous otitis media and chronic infectious otitis media (usually associated with earaches and drainage) are accompanied by fluctuating hearing losses. Untreated, these conditions might lead to permanent conductive hearing loss. There is also evidence that periodic mild hearing loss, even fluctuating, has an adverse effect upon learning, another impetus for routine hearing screening in public schools.

HEIGHT AND WEIGHT MEASUREMENTS. Nutritional deviations (most commonly obesity), chronic illnesses, and endocrine disorders are just a few examples of important conditions which will be discovered when adequate height and weight measurements are obtained. The importance of collecting these data over a period of time and comparing them to population and family standards has been discussed in Chapter One, Growth, but needs to be emphasized again. Many schools keep height and weight records on their pupils.

SCREENING FOR TUBERCULOSIS (TUBERCULIN TESTS). The aim of tuberculin skin testing is to find the individuals who convert from a negative to a positive test, indicating recent exposure to someone with active tuberculosis. At the present time, the child with a positive reaction is usually treated with antituberculosis drugs, even though he is typically asymptomatic, to prevent the occurrence of symptomatic tuberculosis later. A secondary gain from tuberculosis screening in children is that the source of infection usually is found among the child's immediate adult contacts, and so this person can be treated before spreading the infection further in society. Tuberculin testing programs are sometimes carried out in schools. The yield of routine screening is 1 to 2 per cent, higher in some racial groups and in low socio-economic populations.

URINE ANALYSIS. Routine urine analysis is customary in most medical settings. The main purpose is to find and treat silent urinary tract infections, common in girls (approximately 1 per cent of school girls have active urinary tract infections, many without symptoms). Chronic renal disease, which is a serious health hazard to the adult female, probably has its onset in childhood. The presence of a urinary tract infection is usually suspected on a microscopic evaluation of the urine or on urine culture, the latter now sometimes also done routinely. Other abnormal urine findings such as the presence of sugar (glycosuria) or protein (proteinuria) are less helpful for screening. They might indicate serious disease, but the conditions they reflect (juvenile diabetes, nephrosis, glomerulonephritis) are seldom if ever asymptomatic. Instead, these latter findings, especially proteinuria, are sometimes present without significant disease.

BLOOD TESTS. Hemoglobin or hematocrit determinations are frequently included in routine medical screening of children. They might disclose the presence of iron deficiency anemia, a common asymptomatic problem in several groups of children such as young preschoolers, children from economically depressed areas, and menstruating girls.

DENTAL AND PHYSICAL EXAMINATIONS. The need for early detection and treatment of dental caries is obvious. Caries can develop rapidly in young children, and checkups once or twice a year are recommended. Many communities have flouridated water but topical fluoride treatment provides additional protection against caries for young children. The prevalence of dental caries is 80 per cent during childhood. Fluoridation of water has cut this figure in half in some communities.

Routine physical examinations are usually recommended at yearly intervals. Few additional significant unsuspected physical conditions will be found in older children if the above screening tests have been performed. An example would be elevated blood pressure, a very unusual but highly significant finding in a child, another would be scoliosis (abnormal sideways curvature of the spine). Routine physical examinations serve mainly to reassure the child and his family regarding the degree of significance of minor physical deviations and as a way to provide health education.

DEVELOPMENTAL ASSESSMENT. The Denver Developmental Screening Test, DDST (see Appendix), is the most commonly used tool to assess development in the preschooler, but other tests, such as the Goodenough Draw-a-Man Test or Peabody Picture Vocabulary Test, can also be used. Developmental delays are common, but some that are environmental rather than inherent in the child may be remediable. More and more communities are developing rehabilitation programs for the young developmentally deviant child, thus early recognition becomes important. In the older child the school takes on the task of developmental screening, comparing the child's achievement to that of age mates. The child who, after being observed and screened, shows suspected or apparent deviation in development may need to be referred to specialty clinics, to school psychologists, or to other professionals for further evaluation.

Inquiry about problems of behavior of concern to parents or teachers is also part of the developmental assessment. If present, behavior problems could indicate significant adjustment difficulties needing professional intervention in order to prevent later mental health problems, remembering that some worries about childhood behaviors are unjustified and reflect a lack of knowledge of normal variations of child development.

The listed preventive health measures needed during childhood can be provided in many ways—by personal dentists, dental hygienists, physicians, and other specially trained health aides. Some new professionals, such as pediatric nurse practitioners, are being developed for this purpose. In some areas the school serves as the dispenser of a large part of this needed health care.

COMMON PROBLEMS

As can be seen in Figure 7–4, the death rate (mortality) of children 1 to 4 years of age is more than twice as high as for children 5 to 14 years of age, 0.9 per 1000 versus 0.4 per 1000. The incidence of disease (morbidity) figures for ages 5 to 14 is presented in Figure 7–5. Age-significant differences, when present, will be alluded to in the text.

Accidents

Accidents are the main cause of death during childhood. Some 15,000 children die in accidents in the United States every year, three times as many are permanently disabled. Three out of 10 children under 15 years of age sustain some kind of injury within any one year (Fig. 7–1, I). Five per cent of school absenteeism is caused by accidents, and 15 per cent of the visits to the physician's office are because of injuries. Forty per cent of accident-related deaths at all ages in childhood are secondary to motor vehicle accidents.

Accident Prevention. The most effective accident prevention for the very young child is supervision and environmental control of potential hazards. As the child gets older, the parents' teaching and discipline in relation to dangers are internalized. In the preadolescent child, as in the adult, accident prevention is largely a matter of self-discipline. However, there is always room for safety precautions. For example, to put poisonous substances in pop bottles is potentially homicidal, regardless of the age of the members in the household. The growing child is most vulnerable to accidents when participating in

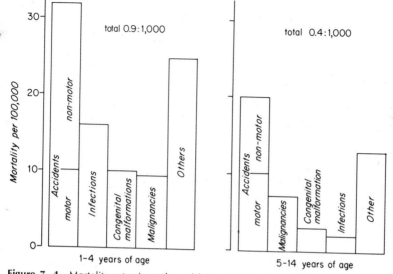

Figure 7–4 Mortality rates in early and later childhood, U.S.A., 1965. (Adapted from the Public Health Service, National Vital Statistics Division.)

newly learned activities and when exercising newly won freedom in his forever expanding world. For example the 3-year-old can play unsupervised in his backyard, but does not know which berries might be poisonous. The 4-year-old can walk to a nearby friend's house, but might forget and run out in the street to retrieve a ball. By age 6 most children can cross even busy streets and 8- and 9-year-olds bicycle

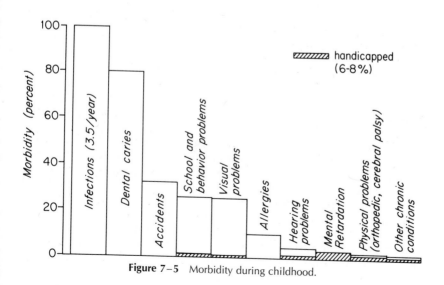

Figure 7–5 Morbidity during childhood.

around their neighborhood, both hazardous undertakings. In the expanding world of the older child new dangers are found in the home, such as burns from cooking. Parental guidance and tactful supervision —not nagging—are needed as the child learns new skills. Modeling of safe behavior by adults is most effective in teaching accident prevention to children.

Accident prevention is also a public health matter. Laws prescribing that children's night clothes cannot be manufactured from flammable material, that dangerous medicines must be sold in containers which are childproof, and that poisonous products must be clearly labeled as such are examples of ways in which society can be made less hazardous for children.

The Accident Prone Child. He might be a poison repeater or he might experience an excessive number of cuts and fractures. He is a well known figure in emergency rooms and physicians' offices. This child deserves careful professional evaluation and treatment of psychosocial factors influencing his behavior. Maybe he is a daredevil. If so, why does he have to show off? Maybe he cannot be controlled in any situation. If so, how can his parents learn to be more effective disciplinarians? Maybe he does not care about his own safety. If so, how can he be helped to feel that he is a worthwhile person?

Infections

Morbidity from infections of some kind or another is an almost universal occurrence. The average school-age child has 3.5 episodes of infectious disease during any one year. Seventy-one per cent of school absences are caused by infections and they contribute to 25 per cent of the visits to physicians' offices by young children. Not only are nonserious infections such as colds and gastrointestinal upsets more common in younger children, but potentially lethal illnesses such as pneumonia and meningitis are also more frequent. As can be seen on the mortality graph, infection is the second killer in the younger child, but ranks fourth in the older child. The decrease in incidence and seriousness of infections during the childhood years is related to immunological factors and exposure as previously discussed, but increase in physical size also plays a role. For example, the smaller the child, the more devastating might be the effects of dehydration from gastroenteritis.

Epidemiologic Aspects. Certain diseases common in one part of the country are unheard of in another. For the practicing health professional it is imperative to have up-to-date information from local health departments regarding diseases prevalent in a community at any one time. The so-called common childhood diseases constitute a group of contagious or communicable disorders of viral or bacterial origin which occur in epidemics typically affecting children. Those accompanied by a rash, such as scarlet fever, measles, rubella, and chicken pox may cause some problems in differential diagnosis within the group, but current public health information helps. Immunizations have now all but eradicated some of the more serious communicable diseases such as pertussis, diphtheria, and poliomyelitis. More diligent use of measles (rubeola) immunization could wipe out this potentially serious disease; vaccines are also available for mumps and rubella. Many of the previously common childhood diseases are no longer an inevitable part of growing up. However, there are some infections still common in childhood or peculiar to this age group which will be discussed.

OTITIS MEDIA. Acute middle-ear infection is a common complication of upper respiratory tract infection in infancy and early childhood. It is one of the most frequent illnesses of childhood due to the common occurrence of colds in this age group, coupled with anatomic factors. The eustachian tube is short and wide in the young child, and large amounts of lymphoid tissue (adenoids) may encroach upon its orifice as the child gets older. The first stage of middle-ear infection is blockage of the eustachian tube from inflamed tissue in the nasopharynx (Fig. 7–6). Secretions are trapped in the middle ear, and organisms which are present there multiply. Otitis media is accompanied by pain, fever and, if not treated, often by rupture of the ear drum and drainage. Adequate antibiotic therapy is at least partially based upon the knowledge of the most likely infective agent relative to the age of the child. If the infection is bacterial, which it is about half the time, it most likely is due to penicillin-sensitive pneumococcus infection; but it might be due to *Haemophilus influenzae* organisms, not

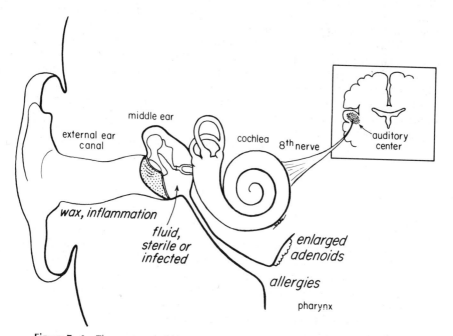

Figure 7–6 The anatomy of hearing, indicating common sources of interference with air conduction.

sensitive to penicillin, in the child under six years of age. Adequate treatment includes nasal decongestants to strive to maintain patency of the eustachian tubes and a followup appointment to inspect the eardrum to ensure complete resolution of the infection and drainage of the fluid from the middle ear. Inadequate treatment of acute middle-ear infection might be a contributing factor to serous otitis media, a nonpainful collection of fluid in the middle ear which is common during childhood (see section on Hearing Screening). Another reason for vigorous treatment of acute otitis media is to prevent complications such as mastoiditis and, rarely, meningitis. Recurrent and chronic middle-ear infections sometimes occur. As these might cause destruction of tissue in the middle ear and permanent hearing loss, they require intensive medical intervention. (See section on hearing handicaps.)

STREPTOCOCCAL INFECTIONS. Infections caused by streptococcus bacteria are common in childhood during the winter and spring months in temperate climates. These infections illustrate age variability in the host response to a given agent. Before 3 years of age, it is often a long, drawn out, nonspecific disease with relatively mild symptoms. After this age acute tonsillitis and pharyngitis often result from streptococcal infections with sudden onset of fever, malaise, pain on swallowing, often headaches, and sometimes vomiting. For poorly understood reasons, some children (about 20 per cent) show little or no symptoms with a streptococcal pharyngitis, but contribute to the spread of epidemics. In addition, streptococci cause other infections in childhood: they are one of the agents causing otitis media in older children; they also cause impetigo, a common, superficial contagious skin infection. One of the streptococcal strains is the cause of scarlet fever (scarlatina), which in essence is a pharyngitis accompanied by a characteristic rash. In childhood it is important to recognize diseases caused by streptococcal infections since they respond to antibiotics (the penicillins). Two serious complications of streptococcal infections occur in susceptible older children: rheumatic fever, an important cause of lifelong crippling heart disease, and acute glomerulonephritis, a usually self-limiting but sometimes life-threatening kidney disorder. Eradication of streptococci by antibiotics appears to prevent these complications. Prophylactic treatment wards off recurrences of rheumatic fever, which previously were common.

Malignancies

Neoplasms rank second in the older child and fourth in the younger child as a cause of death, contributing a total of 15 per cent to mortality in childhood. Both the site of predilection and the tumor type are different in children, most of the common adult malignancies being extremely rare.

Common Childhood Malignancies. Many brain tumors in childhood show particularly malignant cellular patterns and are most commonly located in the deeper part of the brain, close to areas controlling vital processes. As a result, surgical removal, with a few exceptions, is difficult and seldom curative. Leukemia is most common between 2 to 5 years of age, when it constitutes almost half of all the childhood malignancies. Childhood leukemias have been universally fatal and show an explosive course, even though new treatment methods now allow a progressively longer survival than the average 8-week course of untreated leukemia. A variety of neoplasms of bone, some benign, some malignant, occur in later childhood. The presenting complaint is usually pain, frequently blamed on trauma, which is so common in that age group; fortunately roentgenograms usually reveal the presence of bone tumors. Soft tissue tumors (different forms of sarcomas) are another example of a group of tumors peculiar to childhood. Some childhood malignancies seem to be of developmental-congenital origin, but the basic reasons for the distinctiveness of childhood tumors are not entirely clear.

The Effects of Malignant Disease on the Child. Even though malignancy figures high on the mortality list in childhood, it is not a major factor in morbidity. In spite of the fact that it affects a small number of children, malignancy contributes significantly to hospitalizations in childhood. It is difficult to explain the need for hospitalizations and painful procedures to a child, who usually equates them with punishment. It is especially important to handle this problem tactfully when dealing with children who have malignant disease.

The concept of death is not understood by young children. The most important need of a hospitalized child with a fatal disorder is to have the professional listen to him and talk to him honestly without discussing the eventual outcome of his disease.

Allergies

About 15 per cent of the childhood population is "atopic," that is, sensitive to substances that do not cause symptoms in the normal population. The manifestation of atopy, the allergic symptoms, changes with age. Allergic eczema commonly has its onset in infancy and usually improves during the preschool years. At this age it is encountered as a localized skin condition, commonly in the flexure area of the arms and the legs and is not particularly responsive to removal of either foods or inhalants. The most common allergic symptoms in childhood are respiratory: a chronically stuffy nose, frequent colds, nose picking, coughing, serous otitis, and later sinusitis. Seasonal hay fever in response to pollen is unusual in the younger child (in contrast to non-seasonal hay fever) but may occur in later childhood. Allergic asthma frequently has its onset after three years of age, seldom after ten years of age, and usually improves at puberty. True gastrointestinal allergies are extremely rare during childhood. In contrast, nonspecific vomiting and diarrhea are common, as is abdominal pain as a psychosomatic symptom. The child with a stomach-ache every school-day morning does not need an allergic workup or other medical tests. What he does need is to be listened to in an attempt to assess what really is bothering him.

Nutritional and Metabolic Disorders

Obesity. A common problem in adolescents (see Chapter Eight), obesity often has its onset in childhood. Some children never lose their "baby fat," continue to be chubby through childhood, and almost imperceptibly develop into fat adults. In some children obesity has its onset in the early school age years, but most commonly it starts in preadolescence, when there is a physiologic increase in the accumulation of adipose tissue prior to the adolescent growth spurt. At this time boys frequently accumulate fat around the mammary region, enough to suggest breast development. This phenomenon is more common in boys who are outright obese. It is a temporary condition of great embarrassment to the boy, who can be reassured about its innocence. Successful prevention of obesity in childhood would go a long way toward solving a major health problem in adults.

Malnutrition. Caloric and vitamin deficiencies are seldom seen in children in the United States. However, it is important to recognize that some children exposed to serious environmental deprivation are actually underfed—a form of child battering. These children may present as growth failures, with weight more affected than height. A clue to the reason for poor growth often is to be found in a history of bizarre eating habits, such as rifling garbage cans. They will gain in height and weight when offered food and tender loving care in a hospital or a foster home, the ultimate diagnostic test. Iron deficiency anemia still occurs during the preschool years, and more subtle forms of nutritional disturbances are common. An adequate amount of calories, vitamins, protein, and iron (see Appendix), is probably available in the average American diet, but as a result of ignorance and for convenience, satisfactory nutrition is by no means universal during the childhood years. Snacking on high carbohydrate foods and consumption of "empty calories" (pop and potato chips, for example) is common in children in our society.

Diabetes. About 5 to 8 per cent of all cases of diabetes mellitus (sugar diabetes) have their onset during childhood. The presenting symptom in children may be diabetic coma, but the classical symptoms of malaise, thirst, excessive urination, and weight loss are also seen. Management of childhood diabetes, like other chronic illnesses in childhood, is complicated by the fact that a child is in a varying stage of dependency, and that growing up means becoming increasingly independent. When special diet, regulated activity, and daily medications are part of a child's life, the growing up process is complicated. Professionals dealing with chronically ill children and their families should be particularly sensitive to social and emotional aspects of child development in order to be able to guide the family in letting the child assume an increasingly greater responsibility for the management of his own disease.

Handicapping Conditions

Handicapping conditions are those which have a significant detrimental effect on a child's entire life style, such as mental retardation, sensory handicaps, and cerebral palsy. Approximately 6 to 8 per cent of the childhood population are so afflicted. The etiologies of these conditions are varied. Some are of genetic origin, due to chromosomal abnormalities or prenatal factors, while others are caused by birth trauma or serious disorders later in life. Sometimes purely social and environmental factors result in a truly handicapping condition such as mental retardation. Several etiological factors may contribute to the handicap in one child, and environmental factors often add to organic injuries. Frequently, it is impossible to pinpoint the basic etiology of the handicap in an individual child.

Most of these conditions are static, and the child and family have to learn to work with and around his handicap. Some are correctable by surgery (physical malformations) and some may improve by proper environmental changes; for example, with physical or speech therapy. A few of these conditions cause progressive deterioration, as in the case of metabolic disorders affecting the central nervous system. Conditions associated with physical defects are usually diagnosed at birth. Conditions with mainly central nervous system manifestations only become apparent as the brain matures and the child grows older.

It is important to realize that the most commonly used classifications of handicapping conditions (to be used below) constitute a list of significant symptoms with no relation to basic etiology. The prevalence of handicapping conditions are presented in Table 7–2. Many children

TABLE 7–2 HANDICAPPING CONDITIONS IN CHILDHOOD*

	Prevalence per 1000
Mental retardation (MR)	30
I.Q. below 50	
Moderate MR	1.8
Severe MR	0.9
Profound MR	0.3
Hearing handicaps	15
Deaf	1
Visual handicaps	0.5
(legally blind)	
Totally blind	0.1
Light perception only	0.05
Congenital malformations	15
Congenital heart disease	2.0
Club foot	1.5
Down's syndrome	1.3
Neural tube malformation	
(meningomyelocele)	1
Cleft lip and palate	1
Polydactyly	0.5
Anal and rectal malformations	0.2
Cerebral palsy	5
Epilepsy	10
Childhood psychosis	?
Total	More than 75 per 1000

*From a variety of sources, see bibliography.

exhibit more than one symptom, and a more realistic picture would be represented by a series of overlapping circles. Many known etiologies of handicapping conditions affect multiple organs. For example, the child exposed to rubella in the first trimester of pregnancy might be deaf, blind, mentally retarded, cerebral palsied, and have seizures, or have any one of these symptoms singly or in combination. Similarly, many children, in whom it has not been possible to diagnose the basic etiology for their condition, exhibit a combination of handicapping symptoms.

Mental Retardation. This condition is frequently arbitrarily defined as having an intelligence quotient more than two standard deviations below the mean on a standardized psychological test, usually an IQ of less than 70. Three per cent of school-age children fall in this category. A child's response on psychological testing is fairly predictive of academic achievement, and most children thus identified as "retarded" do need special consideration for school programming. It needs to be emphasized, however, that a large percentage (almost 90 per cent) of these children are functionally retarded because of socioeconomic and environmental causes, and that the degree of their impairment is mild. They have the potential to function as fully contributing members of society as adults. Most children with a more severe degree of retardation (IQ less than 50) function this poorly because of some specific disorder which has resulted in inadequate development or deterioration of the brain. In this group other associated handicaps are common.

Hearing Handicap. Most hearing losses found on routine screening in children are temporary, mild, and amenable to medical treatment. Conditions muffling the air waves through the external ear canal, tympanic membranes, and middle ear cause so-called conductive hearing loss. (See Figure 7–6.) These conditions are common in children, but fortunately only rarely result in permanent middle ear destruction and handicap. Sensorineural hearing loss is caused by conditions affecting the cochlea, the eighth nerve, and the neurologic pathways relaying hearing impulses to the cerebral cortex. Most congenital hearing losses are of the sensorineural type. They are not medically remediable but may improve with hearing aids; they are of varying degree and are rarely progressive. Approximately 1.5 per cent of the childhood population has enough hearing loss of either type that it can be considered a handicap. Most of these children are "hard of hearing." They can be taught in regular school programs with the use of hearing aids, preferential seating, speech therapy, and special attention to their educational needs. Only one child per 1000 or less has nonfunctional hearing even with hearing aid and should be considered deaf. Total deafness, the inability to perceive sound of any intensity, is extremely rare even in the deaf population.

Visual Handicap. Blindness is usually defined as a visual acuity of 20/200 or less in the better eye with the best possible correction. Although visual problems are very common in childhood (Fig. 7–5), only rarely is a child visually handicapped using this definition, less than 0.5 per 1000. Of these, less than one-third are totally blind. Some legally blind children have sufficient vision to read large print and can move around in society like a sighted person. Most children who are visually handicapped need special education training in sight saving classes, or, if more severely impaired, the training to read Braille.

Congenital Malformations. Extensive examinations of infants and young children will reveal as high an incidence of congenital malformation as 4 to 5 per cent. However, many have single and remediable malformations of no serious consequence. Severe malformations contribute substantially to mortality during the first few years of life, and kill more children than infections in the 5 to 14-year-old age group (Fig. 7–4). Significant congenital malformations probably affect from 1 to 2 per cent of the childhood population, but only a small percentage of these children are seriously handicapped. About one tenth of that number (1.5 per 1000) attend classes for "crippling conditions." These classes also include youngsters with crippling physical symptoms caused by neurologic disorders, arthritis, and a variety of other conditions.

Cerebral Palsy. Under this heading is commonly grouped a variety of symptoms of motor dysfunction (increased or decreased muscle tone, incoordination, involuntary movements) due to a lesion or disorder of the central nervous system. Even though most lesions are static, the child's symptoms change over the years because of brain maturation. The degree of disability varies from clumsiness to complete nonambulance. Additional handicaps are common in more severely affected children, of whom about 15 per cent have visual disorders, 50 per cent have speech defects, and 35 per cent have general mental retardation. Even if they can handle a regular school program, many children with cerebral palsy need additional services, such as physical and speech therapy, in order to reach their potential for functioning.

Epilepsy. Convulsions are relatively common in children, especially at a young age, and are associated with a variety of underlying causes, as, for example, breath holding and fever. Convulsions are frequently encountered in children with other symptoms of abnormal brain function (cerebral palsy and mental retardation). Epilepsy, defined as convulsions of basically unknown etiology, afflicts approximately 0.5 per cent of the childhood population. Some forms of seizures are peculiar to the childhood years. Petit mal seizures or absence spells, consisting of brief episodes of staring, often with rhythmic blinking, and accompanied by specific changes on the electroencephalogram (brain wave test) are a seizure disorder with onset most commonly between 3 and 5 years of age. A variety of other seizures are also encountered in childhood. Daily medication keeps most epileptic children free of seizures. Epilepsy constitutes a true handicap only when control is difficult. Sudden loss of consciousness would be dangerous when the child participates in physical activities such as swimming.

Childhood Psychosis. Behavior and learning problems are common in childhood (Fig. 7–5) and are discussed in the next section. A small number of children, sometimes called psychotic or emotionally disturbed, have serious and handicapping deviance of social development, often associated with abnormal language development. They exhibit a constellation of frequently bizarre behavioral characteristics, tip-toe walking, hand waving, stereotyped play behavior with preoccupation with strings, shiny or spinning objects, and an aloofness toward other human beings. These actions set them apart from other children even though often no physical or neurologic abnormalities may be demonstrated. Many of these children function in the retarded range on intelligence tests. The understanding of the etiology of these conditions is incomplete at the present time and therapeutic approaches are controversial. There is even confusion about what criteria to apply to the diagnostic labels, such as autism, childhood schizophrenia, and symbiosis, which are used to describe these disturbed youngsters. Therefore no meaningful prevalent figures of these conditions can be given, though they are rare. Most of these children are truly handicapped for life.

Chronic Illness. Cystic fibrosis of the pancreas, rheumatic heart disease, diabetes mellitus, rheumatoid arthritis, and muscular dystrophy are just a few of the many, fortunately rare, conditions contributing to chronic disability in childhood. Asthma is the most common chronic illness in children. A few youngsters are so severely afflicted by their chronic illness that they have to be considered handicapped.

The presence of a handicapped child in a family creates similar kinds of problems regardless of the nature of the child's handicap. Strong emotions in the parents, such as guilt, anger, frustration, and depression, are frequently encountered. The family's child-rearing practices are often distorted with respect to their handicapped child, creating a variety of behavioral complications. Any remedial program, whether medical or educational, should take parental feelings into consideration. Handicapping conditions influence all aspects of the child's development. They might provide a distorted sensory input or cause lack of normal social experiences; the child often has to learn to live with pain and discomfort. The child's own reaction to the handicap varies with the type and degree of limitation, but almost invariably the older child's sense of self-worth is shaken. In addition to its cost in human resources, the care of handicapped children is a great financial burden which is usually beyond the average family's means and so it must be carried by society.

Problems of Behavior

Problems in the behavior of children are confounded by the interrelationships of physical and motivational factors. The possibility of a physical base for any behavioral problem must first be considered. What remains in the absence of a physical disorder may be described as motivational. A young child essentially must do as his parents ask if he is to be considered to be developing properly. He must generally eat what is provided him, eliminate in a certain place, and go to sleep on a schedule determined by his parents. If the parents have resolved their method of training so that the child chooses to cooperate in self-help care, social, and academic areas, few problems result.

Unfortunately, this ideal situation is not always realized and the behavior problems common to childhood are numerous. A partial list would include aggressiveness, destructiveness, disobedience, eating problems, encopresis, enuresis, fire setting, hyperactivity, immaturity, language delay, lying, poor manners, not minding, poor peer adjustment, reading problems, school phobia, lack of school readiness, sibling rivalry, sleep problems, stealing, and thumb sucking. Since each child is unique and is affected by different environmental conditions at different ages, it is beyond the scope of this chapter to discuss all these behavior problems and their alternate forms. However, there are some general strategies for solving behavior problems which can be used when guiding parents, and several problems will be discussed in the light of these suggested strategies.

If the parents use their time effectively with the child, his motivation is enhanced. Three aspects of the use of time seem important. First is the positive use of time. The wise parent concentrates on what the child does well rather than on mistakes. In this way he uses his time to encourage the child and not to point out failure. As the parent uses more time in a positive way, associated with the child's cooperative behavior and the small steps of improvement shown, the child learns that he does many things well even though he still may not have mastery over a particular skill. The second aspect of use of parent time is involved in the area of limit setting or discipline. Each child must learn order, and thus time must be spent in discipline. However, if the parent spends a great deal of time in criticism, lecturing, fault finding and spanking, no purpose is served. Research indicates that the child soon begins to involve the parent ever more in this negative behavior. Parents can be helped to decide on fair, firm, efficient discipline, and exercise it with a minimum of words and action. Finally, parents must understand that changing behavior takes time.

There would be fewer behavioral problems in childhood if parents spent more than half their time with their children positively, using words of encouragement or physical reinforcers such as hugging or touching, and the rest of their time only as necessary in fair, noncorporal limit-setting which involves a minimum of talk and action.

Disobedience. Many of the problems of childhood can be loosely grouped under the general complaint that the child "does not obey." Typically, parents often spend a great deal of time verbally trying to make the child mind without following through on their demands. If the child is asked to mind once and he does not, some logical consequence such as spending a few moments in his room should follow his disobedience. Handling the situation this way tends to decrease the amount of noncompliance. Of course, it is critical that cooperative behavior be reinforced by parents with comments on the improvement the child shows.

Reading Problems. A special problem sometimes occurs in the area of reading in children, most frequently in boys, who otherwise have developed normally. Some of these youngsters show minimal neurologic deficits on medical or psychological evaluation. In recent years the concept that a reading problem is a medical condition has been challenged by educators. It is their view that most of the time the child must be motivated through educational means to overcome whatever physical disability he has. The parent can help with reading problems by focusing on what the child does well rather than on his mistakes or errors. With proper educational treatment, most of these youngsters eventually learn to read, but it is important to attempt to reduce the amount of discouragement and frustration they experience before mastering this skill.

Hyperactivity. Poor attention span, inability to attend to tasks, and many forms of annoying activity are generally loosely referred to by the term "hyperactivity." There is great controversy surrounding appropriate therapy for the child with this problem. This constellation of symptoms has a physiologic base in some children, but is the result of anxiety and other environmentally caused factors in others. A great many potent medications have been offered as therapy for hyper-activity. Long-term side effects of most of these drugs are not known, however, and they should be used only for children in whom objective evidence of the drug's efficacy has been obtained. It would seem prudent to attempt to control the hyperactive child through a combination of positive reinforcement for calm behavior, plus limit-setting in a clear, efficient, and firm way when activity is inappropriate.

Peer Adjustment. A child must learn to get along with others in his peer group. The parent must provide a model and help the child by encouraging him to find his own way. Early emphasis on cooperative acts with family members and other group activities is a step toward helping the child. The parent can be of most help by encouraging the child to think through current peer difficulties and point out alternatives for the child to consider while focusing comments on what the child does do well. Too frequently parents assume control over the child and what he is doing. If the parent intervenes in areas beyond health and safety considerations, he may find himself excluded entirely from the process of adjustment to peers. Parents should be encouraged not to interfere in interpersonal tasks, where the child best learns without someone to blame if things go wrong. Yet a child needs someone to support his attempts in this difficult and important area of adjustment to life.

Sexual Development and Sex Education. Overt manifestations of abnormalities in sexual development (mainly significant gender confusion) are rare in children. However, misinterpretations by parents of expressions of normal childhood development in this area are common. At about 4 years of age, when most children become increasingly aware of the differences between sexes, mutual visual inspection of sex organs is common. In their role-playing, young children may play doctor and undress each other or even pretend to perform the sex act. Masturbation continues all through childhood. In older children it is more common in boys and is usually done in privacy. In preadolescence, children often have "crushes" on persons of their own sex. These activities are frequently labeled deviant by adults, a sad commentary on our failure in sex education. People learn about sex during childhood, whether it is formally taught or not, thus sex education is a childhood problem with far-reaching implications.

The education of children about sex has not kept pace with social changes, which now allow new openness about sex in the public media. Teaching about sex in public schools still remains controversial, and in most communities the parents retain this responsibility with precious little support. To properly educate a child about sex one needs both knowledge of the anatomy and physiology of the sex organs and an understanding of the psychology of human sexuality. Facts about sex are becoming more accessible from a variety of sources, including physicians and related health professionals. Of equal, if not greater, importance for proper sex education of children and adults is an understanding of the highly cooperative nature of sexuality. Problems occur when competition rather than cooperation is present in the personal interaction of partners. If parents are to adequately educate their children about sex, they must agree on their own approach to sexuality and understand some of the psychology of sex. Finally, parents must be comfortable in answering children's questions about sex honestly and openly. The parent need not be concerned that he will tell the child more than is good or proper for him to know, for the child will screen out what he needs to know. Parents who are happy with their own sexuality usually have few problems in handling their children's questions about sex adequately, if they are provided with accurate information. It seems important for health professionals to advocate factual sex education in schools and to encourage the availability of proper material about sex for parents and children, in order to break the vicious circle of misinformation about sex being handed down from generation to generation. The ultimate result of improper sex education in childhood is sexual suffering in adolescence and adulthood.

REFERENCES

General

American Academy of Pediatrics, Committee on School Health: School Health: A Guide for Physicians. Evanston, Ill., American Academy of Pediatrics, 1972.
American Academy of Pediatrics, Committee on Standards of Child Health Care: Standards of Child Health Care. 2nd ed. Evanston, Ill., American Academy of Pediatrics, 1972.
Green, M., and Haggerty, R. J. (Eds.): Ambulatory Pediatrics. Philadelphia, W. B. Saunders Co., 1968.
Whipple, D. V.: Dynamics of Development: Euthenic Pediatrics. New York, McGraw-Hill Book Company, Inc., 1966.

Handicaps and Chronic Illness

Kennedy, W. P.: Epidemiologic Aspect of the Problem of Congenital Malformations. Birth Defects Original Article Series, Vol. III, No. 2, December, 1967. The National Foundation-March of Dimes.
MR 67. President's Committee on Mental Retardation. Washington, D.C., U.S. Government Printing Office, 1967.

Pless, I. B., and Douglas, J. W. B.: Chronic illness in childhood: Part I. Epidemiological and clinical characteristics. Pediat., 47:405–414, 1971.
Richardson, W. P., and Higgins, A. D.: A survey of handicapping conditions and handicapped children in Alamance County, North Carolina. Amer. J. Pub. Health, 54: 1817–30, 1964.

Psychosocial Development

Dreikurs, R.: Children: The Challenge. New York, Duell, Sloan and Pearce, 1964.
Holland, J. G., and Skinner, B. F.: The Analysis of Behavior. New York, McGraw-Hill Book Company, Inc., 1961.
Ilg, L. M., and Ames, L. B.: The Gesell Institute's Child Behavior. New York, Dell Publishing Company, 1955.
Maier, H. W.: Three Theories of Child Development. New York, Harper and Row Publishers, 1965.
McIntire, R.: For Love of Children. Delmar, California, Communications/Research/Machines, Inc., 1970.
Patterson, G. R.: Families. Champaign, Ill., Research Press Company, 1971.
Piaget, J.: Psychology of Intelligence. Totowa, N.J., Littlefield, Adams and Company, 1963.

CHAPTER EIGHT

ADOLESCENCE

S. L. HAMMAR

J. W. M. OWENS

During the period of adolescence, sexual maturity and the ability to reproduce is achieved. Adolescence in girls spans the years from 10 to 18 years, in boys from 12 to 20. Puberty is a period when many physical, psychological, and psychosocial changes occur. It is difficult to evaluate adolescents by their chronological age because of the wide range of individual variations and the differences in the ages at which puberty is reached. Each adolescent must be considered individually in terms of his own biological age and stage of maturation.

PHYSICAL CHANGES

The appearance of testosterone in the male and estrogen in the female triggers a sequence of changes. At puberty, there is a marked change in the growth rate, resulting in an increase in body size, a change in body shape, and rapid development of the gonads. The mechanisms which initiate puberty are not entirely understood. Gonadotropins (FSH and LH), although secreted in small amounts by the pituitary during early childhood, increase markedly two to three years before puberty, stimulating an increased production of sex hormones. Pubertal changes are the result of increased secretions of these sex hormones by the gonads and the adrenal cortex.

While the timing of the adolescent growth spurt is variable, the sequence of events once it occurs is fairly predictable. Nearly every muscular and skeletal dimension of the body takes part and exhibits a characteristic pattern of growth. The average boy begins his growth spurt around 12 years of age, reaching his maximum velocity in height growth at about 14 years of age. At this time he will be growing at nearly twice his childhood or preadolescent rate. Girls begin puberty approximately two years earlier (8 to 10 years) and will reach maximum velocity in their height growth around 12 years of age. The maximum rate of growth for the girl will be somewhat less than that exhibited by the boy. Although children have been getting progressively taller and heavier and maturing earlier over the years, this two-year difference between the sexes in the timing of the adolescent growth spurt has remained unchanged.

Figure 8–1 shows the "typical" individual velocity curves. Velocity is defined as the rate of growth per year. The velocity curve of human growth illustrates that even though the child is making significant gains from birth through childhood, his rate of growth is decelerating until he reaches puberty. The greater adult height in the male has been attributed to the longer period of preadolescent growth and the greater velocity rate during the adolescent spurt. The growth pattern for body weight is similar.

Although we are most aware of the growth changes in height and weight during puberty, a similar growth spurt can be seen in other body parameters, such as pelvic and shoulder diameters, hand and foot length, and head circumference.

The pubertal spurt in height and weight is accompanied by rapid development of the reproductive organs and the appearance of the

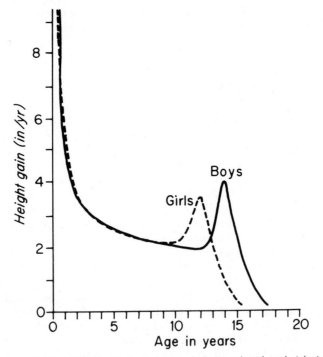

Figure 8–1 Typical-individual velocity curves for supine length or height in boys and girls. (From Tanner, J. M.: Growth at Adolescence. Oxford, Blackwell Scientific Publications, 2nd ed., 1962.)

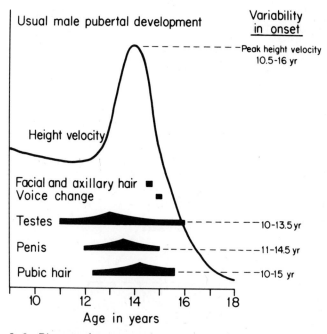

Figure 8–2 Diagram of sequence of events at adolescence in boys. (Adapted from Hammar S. L.: Adolescence. *In* Kelley, V. C. (ed.): Brenneman's Practice of Pediatrics. Hagerstown, Maryland, Harper & Row, Publishers, Inc., Vol. I, Chapter 6, 1970.)

secondary sexual characteristics. The sequence of events, as well as the average age of occurrence of these changes in the male, is shown in Figure 8–2. The first sign of the onset of puberty is the appearance of axillary sweating, increased testicular sensitivity to pressure, an enlargement of the testes, and reddening and stippling of the scrotum. An increase in the length of the penis occurs about the time the spurt in height begins. Axillary hair, facial hair, and voice changes are later manifestations of puberty and appear after the peak growth in height has passed. The first ejaculations of seminal fluid generally occur about a year after the penis has begun the adolescent spurt in growth. Nocturnal emissions usually begin at about age 14.

Most of the secondary sexual characteristics in the male are completed within two years after the onset of puberty, though shape changes, growth of body hair, and muscle development may continue at a slower rate until age 19 to 28. Although the greater part of the growth in stature for most North American males is complete by 18 to 19 years of age, an additional 1 to 2 cm in height can be expected during the third decade of life through continued growth of the vertebral column.

The sequence of pubertal changes in the girl is shown in Figure 8–3. The appearance of the breast bud occurs in the average female at about age 10, coinciding with the onset of the height spurt. Menarche occurs about 9 to 12 months after the peak height velocity has

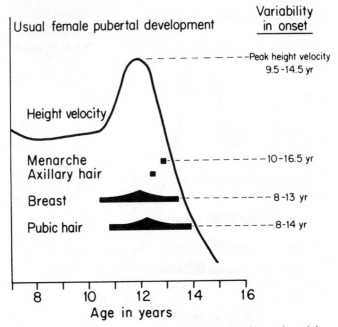

Figure 8–3 Sequence of events at adolescence in females. (Adapted from Hammar, S. L.: Adolescence. *In* Kelley, V. C. (ed.): Brenneman's Practice of Pediatrics. Hagerstown, Maryland, Harper & Row, Publishers, Inc., Vol. I, Chapter 6, 1970.)

been achieved. For the average North American girl this will take place around 12.8 years of age. Although achievement of the menarche represents a mature stage of uterine development, it does not signify full reproductive capacity, since the earlier ovarian cycles are usually anovulatory. This period of adolescent sterility may last for 12 to 18 months after menarche.

PHYSIOLOGIC CHANGES

Also as a consequence of the appearance of sex hormones, many physiologic as well as physical parameters change. Knowledge of these changes helps us to understand some of the common disorders found in this age group. One important change to note is the rise in gastric acidity. One of the most common complaints in adolescents is abdominal pain. Occasionally, frank ulcer symptoms appear; these may well relate not only to the life stresses and concerns of the patient but to this physiologic rise in gastric acidity.

The apocrine glands in the skin begin to produce large amounts of thick sebum resulting in plugging of hair follicles and the picture of acne. Some of the reasons for acne may lie in the adolescent's life style, one in which hectic activity prevents frequent skin cleansing. Nevertheless, the physiologic fact of the excessive sebum must be considered.

Red cell mass and hemoglobin rise during late adolescence, in the male under the effects of testosterone. In girls, these changes are less striking; a mild decrease in hemoglobin and red cell mass usually occurs several years after menarche, which persists until menopause.

CARDIOVASCULAR CHANGES

Pulse Rate.   The pulse rate drops persistently from birth until 10 years of age. The pulse rate decreases in both boys and girls during the adolescent period, more in the male than in the female; this sex difference becoming apparent during the late preadolescent period.

Blood Pressure.   The systolic blood pressure rises during the adolescent period in both sexes. Girls experience their rise in systolic blood pressure earlier, but adolescent boys exhibit a greater rise than that of girls. This sex difference becomes established at adolescence. Accompanying the rise in systolic blood pressure is a rise in the pulse pressure. The diastolic pressures show little change during adolescence and no sex difference.

Heart Size.   The heart size increases during childhood. From 12 years on, boys have larger values for the transverse cardiac diameters. In most girls an increase in cardiac size is closely related to the time of menarche.

Pulmonary Function.   The increase in vital capacity is fairly constant during childhood, but increases rapidly during adolescence. The vital capacity of the lungs is constantly greater in boys than in girls, even when corrected for differences in body size and surface area. This sex difference increases rapidly from ages 13 through 19 years. In contrast to other parameters, the respiratory rate under basal conditions decreases steadily throughout childhood and continues to do so during puberty, but no sex difference is apparent.

SOCIAL AND BEHAVIORAL CHANGES OF PUBERTY

The physical and physiologic changes of adolescence described above act as a catalyst for the psychologic maturation that occurs during this period. As in the case of the physical-physiologic changes, the timing and rate of these developmental changes are somewhat variable.

During this decade of life, the adolescent is expected to complete at least four major developmental tasks. These are (1) achieving a stable identity or self-image; (2) adjusting to an adult sexual role; (3) establishing independence from the family unit; and (4) making a vocational or career choice.

Achieving a Stable Self-image. During this period of rapid physical change, achieving a stable self-image and establishing one's identity become critically important for making a satisfactory adult adjustment. Adolescents become preoccupied with their bodies; appearance, physique, and physical prowess become very important assets. When an adolescent differs significantly from his peers in his rate of growth and pubertal development, he often shows excessive concern and may develop behavioral problems and adjustment difficulties.

Studies of the effects of early and late maturation on psychological adjustment have indicated that the early maturing male tends to show fewer adjustment problems, to be more self-assured and secure, to be better accepted by his peers, to excel at sports, and often to be a better student than the late maturing male. The latter, in contrast, has been found to be less secure and to show more body concerns. Acceptance by his peers is often poorer, and he is apt to be more emotionally labile and unstable. The late maturing male oftentimes appears to compensate for his "handicap" either by passively withdrawing from his peers or by "acting out" and engaging in unacceptable and attention-getting delinquent activities.

In contrast, the late maturing girl appears to have an easier time of adolescence, and gets along better with her peers. The early maturing girl tends to become more serious, more adultlike in her behavior, and tends to gravitate toward an older peer group for more satisfying relationships. In so doing, she temporarily becomes alienated from her age-mates.

Acceptance of these deviations in pubertal development often requires professional help with meaningful interpretation and reassurance.

Adjusting to an Adult Sexual Role. Much of the ease of accepting the sexual changes and the accompanying sexual drives of adolescence is determined by the previous preparation. Although sexual identification becomes firmly established during adolescence, early childhood, around 3 to 4 years, is probably a more critical period. Successful identification appears to be the result of a combination of conditioning and reinforcement by the parents through the manner in which they handle the child, and by the role models which they, or other significant adults, provide for emulation.

Adolescents are sexually active, a fact which tends to be disturbing to parents; sexual activity such as masturbation, heterosexual experimentation, and sometimes homosexual experience is common. Boys usually become more sexually experienced than girls during adolescence, partially due to the achievement of higher sex drives during late adolescence and to the fact that sexual activity in the male is more socially acceptable. Generally, boys are also less closely supervised and have more opportunity for sexual experiences than girls. Another important factor is that boys feel that other boys are having more sexual experiences, a feeling which covertly tends to foster their own sexual activity. Teenagers usually channel these drives into their studies, sports, and hobbies as a means of handling some of their anxieties about their developing sexuality. Most adolescents learn to accept their sexuality, becoming well identified and able to form meaningful heterosexual relationships.

Others, who withdraw from their peers, become preoccupied, exhibit excessive modesty, or deny their sexual changes, often have a more difficult time accepting a mature sexual role. Gravitation toward a younger, more immature and, therefore, less threatening peer group often characterizes their behavior. These adolescents frequently require professional attention.

It should be emphasized that earlier maturation in addition to changes in our cultural attitudes toward sex may be producing a significant change in sexual behavior in this age group. The constant emphasis on "romantic sex" in mass communications media and advertising, changes in censorship codes, liberalizing of sex in the arts, widespread awareness of "the pill," and the drive for sexual freedom appear to be important influences. Previous attitudes held toward adolescent sexual behavior need to be reevaluated in light of these social changes.

Establishing Independence. By age 15, most adolescents should be showing signs of emancipating themselves from their parents. Limits and restrictions on activities must be decreased as the adolescent matures, or at least be commensurate with his stage of emotional maturity. During this period there is customarily a growing away of the teenager from the nuclear family. He seeks to put distance between himself and his parents in a variety of ways, such as by becoming involved in extra-family activities, sometimes selecting a different religion and different political orientation. He usually prefers to be with his peers rather than his family, and to choose his own friends. Communication between the adolescent and his parents often breaks down; the teenager may choose other adults, with whom he has fewer emotional ties, in sharing his confidence and his ideas or in seeking advice. During this period, the adolescent needs more privacy and, above all, needs to be respected as a worthwhile young adult. Learning to drive and obtaining the driver's license, in our culture, is very important to the adolescent, important to his social life and for obtaining peer respect and status.

Because this maturing process is at times painful and unsettling, periods of transient depression are not uncommon and may seriously affect the adolescent's functioning. Many parents feel uncertain and threatened by the developing independence of the adolescent and may respond by trying to establish tighter limits and firmer controls. Such a response may elicit rebellion on the part of the adolescent rather than dutiful compliance.

Making a Vocational or Career Choice. During the adolescent period, the teenager should begin to think about his future. Pressures in our society unfortunately are requiring teenagers to commit themselves and to make these decisions progressively earlier. In spite of these pressures, adolescence is still a period of "role-testing," and there may be great vacillation with frequent goal changes. The adolescent should not be "goofing off" in school. He need not be a neurotic overachiever, but he should be performing consistently within his potential.

He should be taking his job seriously and be able to see some relevance in his educational programming to his future plans.

MORBIDITY AND MORTALITY DURING ADOLESCENCE

The major causes of death in the adolescent age group are traumatic, with motor vehicle accidents leading. (See Figure 8–4.) Suicides increase markedly after age 14. Adolescent girls make more suicidal gestures than boys, but the adolescent male is more successful in his suicidal attempts and is less likely to give warnings.

The leading nontraumatic causes of death during adolescence are malignant neoplasms and cardiovascular disorders.

Accurate morbidity data on the adolescent age group are very difficult to obtain. College Health Service or Boarding School Health Service statistics may be most representative. However, most services close for the summer and, therefore, data are available only for the fall, winter, and spring months.

In such services the most common complaints are upper respiratory tract infections, various types of traumatic disorders, gastrointestinal disorders, and emotional upsets.

In special medical referral facilities for adolescents, the most common problems seen are: school underachievement, obesity, behavior disorders, growth and metabolic disorders, seizures, infectious diseases, and mental retardation. Obviously, patients seen in these clinics represent a select population, but they reflect areas in which physicians dealing with this age group need to develop expertise.

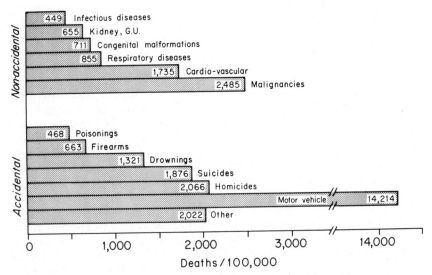

Figure 8–4 Causes of death in the United States in the 15- to 24-year age group, based on World Health Organization statistics.

DISORDERS COMMON TO ADOLESCENCE

Infectious Diseases

The incidence of the usual childhood infections such as measles, mumps, and chicken pox, tends to decline rapidly during adolescence, though some cases still occur in the 10 to 14 year age group. The incidence of pulmonary tuberculosis tends to increase during adolescence. Though adolescents are susceptible to all types of bacterial and viral infections, only two will be discussed.

Infectious Mononucleosis. Infectious mononucleosis is an acute infectious disease most commonly seen in older children, adolescents, and young adults. It is generally felt to be related to the Ebstein-Barr virus, though the exact etiological mechanisms are still unclear. Generally, it is a disease of low communicability. The peak incidence occurs in the spring and autumn; the incubation period is generally from 4 to 14 days, with the onset being acute or gradual.

This disease often is characterized by chronic fatigue or generalized malaise, and should always be considered in a teenager who complains of feeling tired and listless, even though obvious emotional reasons for these symptoms may be present. The cardinal signs are fever, sore throat, enlarged lymph nodes, and splenomegaly. The febrile phase is variable, lasting one to three weeks. The pharyngitis may appear as a late rather than an early manifestation and may be characterized by the presence of an exudate and a thick, white, shaggy membrane.

The lymphadenopathy usually makes its appearance during the febrile stage, beginning with the cervical nodes and gradually becoming generalized. The enlarged nodes are usually tender, discrete, and firm, rarely becoming suppurative. Splenomegaly occurs in about 50 per cent of cases. Other findings may include hepatitis, skin eruptions, central nervous system involvement, and pneumonitis. Hepatitis is relatively frequent, with abnormal liver function tests present in about 80 per cent of patients. Skin rashes, which occur in 10 to 15 per cent of cases, typically appear as an erythematous maculopapular eruption similar to that of rubella, and often are present from the fourth to the tenth day.

Central nervous system involvement may occur early or late in the course of the disease, and such suggestive symptoms as stiff neck, blurred vision, mental confusion, weakness of the extremities, and depressed reflexes may be present.

The blood smear usually shows an absolute increase of greater than 20 per cent atypical lymphocytes peaking, in most cases, around the seventh to the tenth day of the illness. A positive Monospot test and a rise in serum heterophile antibody titer depend upon the phase of the illness. The serum heterophile antibody titer usually rises by the end of the first week or early in the second week, but may subsequently fall rapidly, making it easy to miss a positive titer.

Venereal Disease. Once thought to be conquered, venereal disease has again become a major health problem. Since 1957, the incidence of gonorrhea has continued to rise at an alarming rate and has reached pandemic proportions. At best, the reported cases represent only a small portion of the actual number, since many patients are treated by private doctors. Because of the social stigma involved and concern for secrecy, many cases are unreported. Over half of the cases reported in this country and in Western Europe involve the 15 to 24 year age group. The increased incidence appears to be directly related to changing sexual mores and behavior among young adults and is not peculiar to any particular social class or stratum. The apparent increase in male homosexuality is also of significance in the spread of venereal disease among older adolescents and young adults. Male homosexuals appear to have several times as many contacts as heterosexuals in a shorter period of time. The confirmed adult homosexual poses the greatest public health threat because of his mobility and transient encounters, often with a multiplicity of unknown partners, which make an epidemiological approach to case finding extremely difficult.

Serological tests for syphilis are routinely performed in many hospitals, clinics, and physicians' offices. However, gonorrhea poses a greater threat to this age group in many more ways than syphilis because of the difficulty of diagnosis, particularly in the female. In adolescent girls the diagnosis is easily missed since girls seldom complain of pain, discharge, or other symptoms until the infection spreads to the uterus and fallopian tubes, and pelvic inflammation develops.

Acute gonorrhea in the male generally appears as a urethritis or urethral discharge and is diagnosed by culture or by finding organisms in a smear of the exudate. When prostatitis develops in males, homosexual practices should be suspected.

Because of difficulties in diagnosis, all sex partners of males who have gonorrhea should be treated regardless of culture or smear.

Chronic Diseases

Juvenile Obesity. Obesity is a major problem of the adolescent. Between 10 to 16 per cent of the 10 to 19 year age group are found to be more than 20 per cent above ideal body weight. In many cases, the obesity is long-standing, dating from the early childhood years. In those cases where the weight problem is long-standing, not only does the patient have a greater body weight for age, but often an advanced height age, slightly accelerated bone maturation, and a greater lean body mass. These adolescents often develop pubertal changes slightly earlier than the non-obese. In 65 to 70 per cent of cases, one or both parents are also obese, indicating perhaps a strong genetic predisposition toward the development of obesity.

Ninety-five per cent of this population appear to have exogenous obesity; rarely can an endocrine cause be found. There is increasing evidence that metabolic and cellular differences may be present in obesity, but as yet it is unclear whether these differences are primary factors or secondary changes resulting from long-standing obesity and hypernutrition. In any event, the present methods of treatment are largely unsuccessful and usually fail to bring about a permanent reduction in body weight.

Obesity in the adolescent is complicated by social and psychological factors. In part, this may be due to soceity's attitude in viewing obesity as a moral defect rather than as a chronic disease.

The psychosocial characteristics of the obese adolescent are important and affect the success of any therapeutic efforts. Many obese teenagers feel socially ostracized, ugly, and unacceptable. Depression is frequent. Severe environmental stress and intra-family conflicts often potentiate the weight problem, since many obese patients tend to react to anxiety and stress by eating compulsively. Motivation for weight loss is frequently limited in the adolescent. His goals for weight reduction are often unrealistic. If weight loss is to be achieved and maintained by our present methods, careful attention must be given to emotional adjustments, self-image, sexual feelings, social adaptation, and activity patterns, as well as to the diet. Providing adequate nutritional education to the adolescent is extremely important. The group approach to managing obesity has also been successful in some cases. Organizations such as T.O.P.S. or Weight Watchers are often appropriate referral sources, providing they have special groups for teenagers. Every obese adolescent deserves a thorough medical and psychosocial evaluation as a part of an initial workup.

Seizure Disorders. The actual incidence of seizure disorders in the adolescent and young adult populations is difficult to establish because of the reluctance of families to reveal this affliction. It is often quoted that one in every 100 persons in the United States suffers from some type of seizure disorder. Most seizure patients are diagnosed, or experience their first seizure, before they are 20 years old. Grand mal is the most common type of seizure encountered in the adolescent. Petit mal epilepsy, although usually tending to disappear as puberty approaches, is also not uncommon in this age group. Temporal lobe (psychomotor seizures) epilepsy is often difficult to diagnose; the clinical picture is varied and may include automaton-like behavior, lip smacking, chewing movements, confused psychotic attacks, nocturnal fears, and sleepwalking. Seizures are only a symptom of a disease and not a disease in themselves; therefore, every adolescent with a seizure problem requires a thorough evaluation in order to rule out possible underlying disorders such as hypoglycemia, brain tumor, vascular anomaly, or atrophic lesions which may be treatable.

Seizures often become difficult to control at the time of puberty. Adolescent girls may experience seizures just before the onset of their menstrual period. This may be related to the complex hormonal changes that occur during the menstrual cycle or to the increased fluid retention which may irritate the central nervous system and lower the seizure threshold. Hyperventilation, water loading, sudden environmental changes, stressful and highly charged emotional situations, or family disruptions have been known to increase seizure activity.

The adolescent with seizures usually has many anxieties and concerns which require patience, understanding, and skillful handling.

Excessive restrictions are unnecessary, and the adolescent should be encouraged to become as self-sufficient and independent as possible. Physical activity and participation in sports should be encouraged, while some activities, such as mountain climbing, should be discouraged. Other activities, such as swimming and sailing, may be permitted in the company of others rather than as a solitary activity. Physical and peer group activities are important to the overall development of the teenager, and restrictions should be kept to a minimum.

In many cases, the epileptic adolescent must learn to conduct his life and social activities without the use of a car. This is usually upsetting to the adolescent boy, unless he is well prepared in advance. Many epileptic adolescents are concerned about the advisability of marriage. There is no contraindication to marriage for most seizure patients, provided they are otherwise able to assume the responsibilities which marriage involves. Girls are often concerned about the possible adverse effects of pregnancy upon their seizures. In some instances, seizures occur more frequently during pregnancy, particularly when complicated by fluid retention, excessive weight gain, or toxemia. Pregnancy may require a modification of the anticonvulsant medication in order to obtain the best possible seizure control. While inheritance of these disorders is dependent to some extent upon the etiology and type of seizure, epileptic patients need not, in general, be denied parenthood on the slim chance that their children may later develop seizures. The risk of this happening is only slightly greater than in the normal population. The teenager with epilepsy requires occupational counseling in order to steer him into an appropriate vocation. The seizure patient is undoubtedly best employed in a business or vocation of his own which allows him some flexibility. Workman's Compensation Laws and industrial insurance vary from state to state at the present time and may greatly limit occupational choices.

School Underachievement

Adolescents with school underachievement can be categorized roughly into three groups: (1) mentally subnormal adolescents who are depressed in all areas of intellectual functioning, (2) adolescents with specific learning disorders but with normal intelligence, and (3) psychogenic underachieving adolescents.

The Mentally Subnormal Adolescent. Most of these adolescents who present as school underachievers fall into the mild or borderline range of intelligence. With maturation and increased educational demands, their defects become more obvious, making school placement difficult. Problems regarding future vocational training, anxiety about their sexual development and behavior, and concern about future supervision and care require professional attention.

Specific Learning Problems. The adolescents with specific learning disabilities generally are delayed in their reading. A few may be reading at their appropriate level, but exhibit specific defects related to spelling, mathematics, and handwriting. Although of normal intelligence, evidence of visual-perceptual problems, soft neurological signs, or other findings suggestive of mild central nervous system dysfunction may be present. Poor memory retention, short attention span, distractibility, and impulsive behavior are frequent problems noted by their teachers. Behavior problems resulting from years of frustration, repeated school failures, and inadequate educational programming are common.

Psychogenic Underachievers. These adolescents comprise a group whose academic problems appear to be related to primary emotional disturbances and environmental factors. Preoccupation with, and reaction to, family stresses may interfere with scholastic efficiency and school progress. School refusal or inconsistent school attendance in an adolescent who is bright, sensitive, overanxious, and unable to cope with the school situation represents a more serious type of school problem and usually requires immediate psychiatric intervention. The parents are often ineffective and unable to cope with or set limits on the teenager's behavior without professional support. In some adolescents, school underachievement appears to be related to intense parental demands for scholastic achievement. The failure may be an effective passive-aggressive method of retaliation. In others, cultural expectations, peer group values, and familial patterns of underachievement may be largely responsible for the school failure.

Since the physician is usually the first professional to be consulted, he must be able to define the school problem and make the appropriate referrals for consultation and treatment.

Behavioral Disorders of Adolescence

Emotional problems are common in adolescence. Extreme mood swings are characteristic of the period. Transient depressions or acute emotional reactions are generally clearly related to events such as a death in the family, the injury of a friend, or a ruptured romance. Failure to achieve independence from parents, to make a mature sexual adjustment, or to resolve problems of identification may result in symptomatic behavioral reactions of varying intensity. Transient neurotic symptoms, antisocial behavior, or rebelliousness may be seen. If these reactions occur against a background of reasonably good previous adjustment, the prognosis is good. Severe obsessive-compulsive behavior, acute psychotic episodes, suicide attempts, and severe behavioral disorders are more commonly seen in teenagers who have established a pattern of maladjustment before adolescence.

Antisocial behavior in teenagers appears to be increasing. Partly because of overcrowding and urbanization, even minor infractions are more likely to come to the attention of the authorities than in years past. Referrals to the juvenile court system indicate that the antisocial boy is most frequently involved in car theft, running away, and stealing; girls usually are referred for sexual acting out or running away.

Drugs. The medical profession and the pharmaceutical industry must both share much of the blame for drug abuse today. The idea that every ill which besets man, every anxiety and worry, can be cured with a pill, and the over-prescription of potent pharmacologic agents as a substitute for spending time with the patient to find out what is really bothering him have both been factors in the increasing use and abuse of drugs in all age groups.

Drug use among teenagers and young adults has become an increasing health hazard and one of great concern to professionals. Those adolescents who use drugs are not necessarily alienated or in rebellion or even emotionally disturbed, though they may be. Many are "experience seekers"; some take drugs to prove their courage by risk-taking, to relieve loneliness, to provide an emotional experience, or to seek meaning in life.

Alcohol. For far too long the abuse of alcohol has been considered separately from other drug problems, although alcohol-related problems far exceed, perhaps as much as tenfold, the problems related to other drugs. Part of the unwillingness to accept the facts regarding alcohol has been our punitive rather than therapeutic approach to alcoholics. Another part of the problem is the widespread use of alcohol and the acceptance of the "drunk" as a comic character rather than someone whose life situation does not furnish him with enough reinforcement, making escape via alcohol abuse necessary. The problem is not the alcohol, but rather why an individual's life is so painful that he has to run away from it. This same principle applies to abuse of drugs. The chronic "pothead" who is unable to face reality or function in society is no sadder than the drunk sleeping it off in the doorway of some old building.

The use of alcohol among teenagers has shown a dramatic increase in recent years. One very carefully done study by Gilbert Sax in a suburban community showed that among high school students 82 per cent reported regular use of alcohol while only 40 per cent reported regular use of marijuana. In the middle school population in that community, the figures were 50 per cent for alcohol and 6 per cent for marijuana. Considering that the leading cause of death in the adolescent age group is traumatic, and that a high percentage of these deaths are alcohol-related traffic accidents, this subject is critical in any review of drug abuse.

Glue and Other Volatile Substances. In the younger adolescent, glue-sniffing is a common form of drug abuse. The chronic glue-sniffer most frequently has a history of emotional problems resulting from family disruption, and a number of these children have committed serious antisocial acts. Glue-sniffing initially produces a feeling of lightheadedness and exhilaration. Continued use results in slurred speech, unsteady gait, and even loss of contact with reality. Habituation appears to result in psychic dependence and increasing tolerance.

Barbiturates and Amphetamines. The effects of barbiturates (goof balls, red devils, etc.) and amphetamines (bennies, speed, etc.) are well known and are abused by adolescents in search of euphoria or relief from depression. Both may be taken orally (dropping) or intravenously (shooting). The dangerous practice of shooting drugs is complicated by the hazards of unsterile injections such as local abscesses, septicemia, hepatitis, and sclerosed veins.

Hallucinogenic Drugs. The synthetic hallucinogenic drugs (LSD, STP) are more potent. Some users have reported the occurrence of nausea, anorexia, vasomotor changes, headaches, palpitations, and tremors. Disturbances of the electroencephalogram and even grand mal seizures have occurred in some users.

Hallucinogens have great appeal for socially alienated young people who wish to escape unpleasant reality or who are attempting to understand themselves. There is little indication that the lives of such users have been improved with such use; however, there is evidence that the effects of these drugs upon the individual are largely conditioned by the environment or setting in which the drug is taken and by the psychological makeup of the user.

Marijuana. Smoking of marijuana has become a social activity (pot parties), with the users often experiencing freedom from anxiety, distortion of sensation and perception, release of inhibitions, and freedom from hunger. Some have felt that the danger in adolescent pot smoking is that marijuana may prove insufficient in its effects and lead to experimentation with other drugs for psychic relief of anxiety. Our society's attitudes and mores concerning the use of marijuana have undergone a drastic change in recent years. There is evidence that marijuana is widely used by adolescents and adults and should not be considered with the more dangerous drugs.

REFERENCES

Daniel, W. A., Jr.: The Adolescent Patient. St. Louis, C. V. Mosby Company, 1970.

Gardner, L. I. (Ed.): Endocrine and Genetic Diseases of Childhood. Philadelphia, W. B. Saunders Company, 1969.

Hammar, S. L.: Adolescence. *In* V. C. Kelley (ed.): Brennemann's Practice of Pediatrics. New York, Harper & Row Publishers, Inc., 1970, Vol. II, Chap. 6.

Sax, G., (Project Evaluator): Renton Area Youth Services, Project Evaluation, June, 1972. Personal communication.

Tanner, J. M.: Growth at Adolescence. 2nd ed. Oxford, Blackwell Scientific Publications, 1962.

Usdin, G. L. (Ed.): Adolescence: Care and Counseling. Philadelphia, J. B. Lippincott Company, 1967.

CHAPTER NINE

ADULTHOOD, ESPECIALLY THE MIDDLE YEARS

EDWIN L. BIERMAN
WILLIAM R. HAZZARD

LIFE SITUATION

Physical

Following completion of growth, and attainment of mature adult stature, there is a gradual loss of musculoskeletal integrity. A progressive decrease in bone density (Fig. 9–1) and mass occurs, and gradual vertebral compression results in a decreasing ratio of body length to arm span. In addition, the limited regenerative capacity of articular cartilage, and the accumulated insults to joint surfaces, aggravated by excessive weight, make arthritic complaints progressively more common in middle age. With assumption of a sedentary way of life and continued intake of calories in excess of those expended, adipose tissues expand and weight increases (Fig. 9–2), despite a decrease in lean body mass. Acquired obesity, subtle or obvious, is a hallmark of life's middle years in developed cultures. Since such phenomena as "aches and pains" and the "middle-aged spread" are commonly accepted as inevitable consequences of aging and even worn with pride as badges of hard work and success, the distinction between "normal" and "abnormal" with regard to arthritis and obesity may become blurred.

Physiologic

The linear decrease in the functional capacities of various organ systems (see Chapter 2, Fig. 2–4) becomes more evident with each

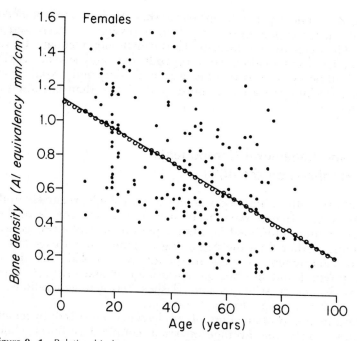

Figure 9–1   Relationship between age and bone density in females. Although the trend toward a decline with age is apparent, wide variation among women of comparable ages is also evident. (From Baylink, D. J., et al.: Two new methods for study of osteoporosis and other metabolic bone disease. Lahey Clinic Foundation Bulletin *13*:217, 1964.)

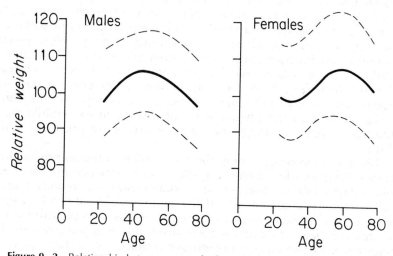

Figure 9–2   Relationship between age and relative body weight (ideal = 100) in males and females in an American community—Tecumseh, Michigan. Solid lines are 50th, dashed lines 20th (lower) and 80th (upper) percentiles. (From Epstein, F. H., et al.: Prevalence of chronic diseases and distribution of selected physiological variables in a total community —Tecumseh, Michigan. Am. J. Epidemiol. *81*:307, 1965.)

passing year. The capacity for physical work declines, and the decrease in basal energy expenditure (Fig. 2–5) necessitates a decreased food intake. The decrease in caloric intake is usually not adequate, however, to avoid fat accumulation. Peak reproductive and sexual activity in early adulthood gives way to a decrease in fertility and sexual function, the latter declining at a much more gradual rate than has often been suggested.

Social and Behavioral Components
(with Emphasis on the 40's)

Until recently, adulthood was viewed as a single, relatively uniform plateau of life. In our current Western civilization this is no longer the case. Young adulthood is often a period of prolonged education or training, rather than the beginning of independent existence. The delayed achievement of total independence, coupled with the ever-earlier physical and psychologic maturation characteristic of modern cultures, brings frustrations and clashes between generations, both adult, which are unique to the present era.

Despite the prolongation of adolescence enforced by extensive education, today the average married couple has fewer children, grouped closer together, and at an earlier age than ever before. Hence, by their mid-40's a couple enters a new phase of adulthood which will occupy one-half of their married life span. The departure of their children provides a critical challenge to their adaptive faculties, giving an opportunity for new or reclaimed intimacy or increasing distance and chronic loneliness. At the same time, the current urban living pattern whereby adults interact but little with the departed children or their own parents and siblings places an even greater demand for intimacy and dependence upon the marital partner. Paradoxically, this requirement occurs at a time when cultural patterns allow greater autonomy and independence to both men and women. This shift in middle life to an isolated married pair, both members being subjected to forces which they do not share in common, represents a major challenge to the stability of the marriage bond in contemporary life. Small wonder, then, that the phenomenon of divorce in the middle years, often after a relatively long marriage, has become so prevalent in our culture.

Divorce, of course, is only the most visible consequence of these stresses. Couples who remain together also experience the same turmoil. Adaptations in interpersonal relationships are required in all families. The same parents who thrive on the rearing of children when they are tiny and totally dependent may be unable to cope with them as the children begin to express their needs for independence during adolescence. Just when parent-teenager conflicts reach their apex, the retired grandparents may begin to place emotional and financial demands upon the parents. Both younger and older generations may evoke conflicts over the issues of dependence and independence, responsibility and nonresponsibility, which may go unresolved. As a result, the parents may feel less like the "middle generation" than the "generation in the middle."

On a more personal level, changes also occur in personality and in its sexual expression throughout adulthood. During young adulthood men usually manifest the stronger sexual drives, whereas women most often experience their greatest sexual drive and satisfaction during the middle years of marriage. As a result, the opportunity is afforded for an optimal sexual relationship in middle life when husband and wife share equally in the intimacy and satisfaction of their sexual lives. However, the strong emphasis on youthful sexual attractiveness and performance in contemporary culture may provoke doubts over sexual adequacy in the middle-aged person. Because of this, the doubting adult may trade his sense of poise, self-respect, and acceptance of the aging process for the usually vain attempt to recapture the vigor of youth through extramarital sexual exploits or the acquisition of a new, youthful marriage partner.

Other personality changes also occur in middle life. Men often become less aggressive and thus more nurturing, more concerned with the feelings and needs of others, less domineering and less consumed with the conquest of their world. Their wives, on the other hand, become freer as their children become less dependent. Often this results in women becoming more aggressive, demanding, and self-generated.

In our present cultural environment all these forces and conflicts reach their peak in the years between ages forty and fifty. During these years, particularly for the business and professional man, this may be the decade of greatest opportunity and productivity. It is also the time for crucial decisions: promotion or stagnation, leader or perpetual also-ran; realization of youthful ambition or of dwindling mediocrity. For the woman, her career as nursemaid and mother completed, this age is often one of searching for a new identity through a new career or style of living. For both man and woman this decade is therefore one of continual adjustment to change.

Individual and family development may be viewed in terms of recurrent cycles of change and stabilization. It has been likened to a spiral staircase in which the successful ascent of each step provides the base upon which to cope with the next so that life has its platforms of rest: latency, ages 6–12; young adulthood, 25–40; and middle age, 50–65. But the years between forty and fifty represent a major step up, involving changes in personality, marriage, family, and vocation, all taking place in the whirlwind of twentieth century social change. This decade represents one of the critical periods of human development. Success or failure at this step determines the course of the second half of one's life.

PREVENTIVE MEASURES FOR HEALTH MAINTENANCE

Possible preventive measures for health maintenance entail the personal rejection of most aspects of a way of life which is still enthusiastically accepted by the vast majority of society. Furthermore, given the complex, often subtle association between a risk factor such as tobacco smoking and its attendant disease, *e.g.*, cancer of the lung, it becomes very difficult to prove a causal relationship between the two. It is even more difficult, but not impossible in this case, to demonstrate conclusively that the correction of the risk factor will prevent the associated disease. Considerations both of personal freedom of choice and of a lack of conclusive proof of cause and effect, as well as powerful economic forces, leave the burden of the reversal of a popular way of life upon the individual. If he chooses to attempt that reversal, he can expect to be subjected to powerful social and economic pressures to conform to contemporary living patterns. The problems of preventive health maintenance in middle age appear to have been largely identified. The means of their correction, except at a very high price of personal sacrifice and determination, have not.

Most disorders of middle age, such as osteoarthritis and obesity, are both common and chronic. They are so common that they are often accepted as the price of having achieved middle age and are therefore not even considered abnormal. Furthermore, it is unusual for such disorders to have a single obvious cause. The response of a given individual to a certain set of circumstances usually reflects a complex interaction between environmental forces and his unique genetic makeup. Most often, these common disorders are designated as "multifactorial" in origin and are looked upon as the consequence of our way of life. As such, they are associated with its most obvious characteristics: a sedentary existence, high economic productivity, psychologic stress, high caloric intake—especially of foods derived from animal sources—the consumption of alcohol, tobacco, and drugs, and chronic exposure to environmental pollutants including radiation and the emission from internal combustion engines.

Obesity is the single most common preventable factor associated with excess mortality and morbidity in this age group. Excess mortality in men who are 30 per cent overweight exceeds 40 per cent and is due mainly to atherosclerosis, hypertension, and the complications of diabetes. Morbidity is also excessive among the obese from disorders of the digestive system (gallstones and hepatic dysfunction), respiratory system (hypoventilation syndromes), and musculoskeletal system (osteoarthritis). An enormous proportion of adult Americans are overweight: 20 per cent of men are more than 10 per cent overweight and 5 per cent of men are at least 20 per cent above average; corresponding proportions for women are somewhat higher, 25 per cent being more than 10 per cent above average, and 12 per cent at least 20 per cent above average. Furthermore, the "ideal" or "best" weight for lowest mortality and health maintenance may lie below the present average weight of the population. This problem is probably totally amenable to preventive measures which simply involve reduction of caloric intake. But this restriction must take place in the face of increasing availability and attractiveness of food. Alternatively, a solution could be found through an increase in energy expenditure by regular exercise.

However, this would have to occur in spite of progressive automation and availability of labor-saving devices.

Other preventive dietary measures for minimizing the risk of atherosclerosis through decreased cholesterol and saturated fat intake, and of osteoporosis through adequate calcium and protein intake, may also be warranted. The intake of particular foodstuffs may produce conflicts in the achievement of certain goals in adults. For example, though milk is a rich source of calcium and protein, it is also high in saturated fat and calories. Modified foodstuffs, such as skim milk for the foregoing situation, may provide appropriate compromises.

Regular exercise may improve cardiovascular status to the extent that the risk factor of sedentariness associated with coronary artery disease (see below) is significantly reduced. Furthermore, such exercise may increase cardiovascular efficiency and allow the individual with a limited cardiovascular capacity to function adequately in his daily activities.

The adverse health consequences of chronic cigarette smoking, and, to a lesser degree, cigar and pipe smoking, become manifest during this phase of life. Well-documented excess morbidity and mortality stem from lung cancer, oral cancers, chronic bronchopulmonary diseases (commonly diagnosed as chronic bronchitis or pulmonary emphysema) and cardiovascular disease, particularly coronary heart disease. Cigarette smoking is the most important cause of chronic bronchopulmonary diseases in the United States; even younger smokers have demonstrable reduction in ventilatory function. The ratio of overall death rate of smokers to that of nonsmokers is highest during the age decade from 45 to 55, more than a twofold increase. Furthermore, cessation or appreciable reduction of cigarette smoking has been shown to decrease excess morbidity and mortality.

Excessive exposure to external radiation is usually preventable, since, barring a nuclear catastrophe, exposure from diagnostic and therapeutic radiology constitutes the major source of radiation in the environment. In these disciplines, efforts are made to minimize risks of morbidity, and maximal permissible levels of exposure are rarely reached. Other environmental hazards not controllable by the single individual appear to be under ever-increasing public surveillance and control due to the collective efforts of concerned citizens.

The health problems related to chronic excessive intake of alcohol are multifaceted (psychologic, sociologic, medical) and constitute a major concern during this age span. In the United States there are currently at least four million alcoholics, where alcoholism is defined as a dependence on alcohol to a degree sufficient to interfere with health, interpersonal relations, and social and economic positions. The secondary effects of chronic excessive alcohol intake in terms of decreased productivity, accidents, crime, mental and physical disease, and disruption of family life, are also preventable through efforts to curb alcohol abuse.

The consequences of drug addiction (narcotics) and drug dependence (tranquilizers and stimulants) assume increasing importance during this age, not only through effects upon the middleaged addict or habitué, but through influence upon other, usually younger family members.

COMMON PROBLEMS OF THE MIDDLE YEARS

Behavioral

Emotional and behavioral disorders which are prevalent during the middle years include: neurotic depression; manic-depressive disorders; paranoia; sexual conflicts; and somatization of anxiety. Associated with the marital, vocational and other life stresses, various forms of depressive disorders commonly develop in mid-life. In the older years, a more common pattern of depressive withdrawal is sometimes termed "involutional depression." During mid-life there may also occur appearances of either manic or depressive episodes that may spontaneously remit and reappear with little apparent life stress. Degrees of paranoid reactions are also frequently seen in middle-aged women. This appears to be related to increased marital strain in the middle years of a conflictual marriage.

As mid-life brings increased anxiety over sexual performance, the menopause, and the climacteric, both men and women may develop either hyposexual symptomatology (impotence, frigidity), or hypersexual symptomatology (interest in sexual experimentation, compulsive sexuality).

With increasing age and the gradual decrease in physical prowess, there may be added concern with bodily functions. This may take the form of minor hypochondriases, vague or generalized pain problems, and, more especially, the concern over adequacy of normal body functions. As old age approaches, this is reflected in the well-known preoccupation with food and bowel function.

Nutritional and Metabolic Disorders

These include obesity, gallbladder disease, and anemia. Obesity itself leads to morbidity because of its aggravating effect on a variety of other disorders such as hypertension, diabetes mellitus, atherosclerosis, varicose veins, hernia, gallstones, and osteoarthritis. A combination of obesity with these other disorders may appreciably compound the problem, as is evident in the increased mortality risk noted in the presence of *both* moderate overweight and slight elevation of blood pressure. Adiposity secondary to weight gain in adult life may have different implications from adiposity present since early childhood. Adult-onset obesity appears to be less chronic and therefore potentially more reversible. However, pound for pound, perhaps it may be more ominous insofar as cardiovascular risk is concerned.

The overweight patient undergoing surgery offers special problems, both to the anesthesiologist because of inadequate respiratory exchange, poor airway, and large anesthetic dosage requirements, and to the surgeon because of increased frequency of postoperative thromboembolism, infection, and wound breakdown. In addition, the overweight woman incurs an extra risk during pregnancy from toxemia and increased fetal mortality. Reduction of overweight in these circumstances has been clearly associated with reduction of morbidity.

Gallstones occur with gradually increasing frequency after age 30 and are particularly common in multiparous women; the overall female-male ratio below age 65 is 4 to 1. By age 75, one of every three persons will have gallstones, though symptoms of colicky pain and/or complications of infection, obstruction, liver damage or neoplasm may not necessarily follow. Although some gallstones are composed mainly of bile pigments and/or insoluble calcium salts, most contain at least 70 to 80 per cent cholesterol, which crystallizes in the gall bladder in the absence of adequate bile acids and/or phospholipids. The pharmacologic correction of this imbalance among biliary cholesterol, bile acids, and phospholipids as a means of preventing (or dissolving) gallstones is presently under evaluation.

Non-iron related nutritional anemias are not common among adults in the United States except in association with alcoholism. Females are particularly prone to develop iron deficiency anemia related to iron intake inadequate to compensate for chronic periodic blood loss associated with normal menses or excessive menstrual bleeding, which is common in the peri-menopausal years.

Chemical Agents

Alcohol is the most common toxic external agent involved in morbidity and mortality in this age span. In addition to cirrhosis of the liver, pancreatic dysfunction and neurologic disorders (such as peripheral neuropathy, cerebellar degeneration, and encephalopathy) are prominent. Mortality from alcoholic cirrhosis peaks in the fifth and sixth decade at 50 per 100,000 in the United States. It is markedly higher for males than females at all ages, and is higher for nonwhites below age 45.

Trauma

The mortality rate from all types of accidents is roughly comparable to that from alcohol. In addition, nonfatal, severe trauma affects a large segment of this group. On a more subtle but more universal level, chronic or acute trauma often causes musculoskeletal problems that occur as the initial clinical manifestations of aging in connective tissue.

Bone mass declines in a linear fashion during middle age (Fig. 9–1). "Pathologic" fractures, due to inapparent or minor trauma, are uncommon in this age group, but trauma which earlier in life would be insignificant, such as stepping off a curb or tripping on the front steps, may result in major osseous injuries. Whereas in the young adult injuries to joints frequently result in ligamentous disruption, similar injuries in middle age usually result in fractures.

Articular (arthritic) complaints are also progressively more common in the middle years. Growth of articular cartilage ceases at maturity while attrition continues. Articular cartilage has no inherent capacity to repair or renew itself. At maturity, mitotic activity ceases and, with aging, there is a steady decline in cell density. Attrition, however, continues throughout the life of the joint. The rate of such attrition appears to be influenced by the stress to which it is subjected, since optimal pressures seem to be necessary for normal cartilage nutrition. Areas of cartilage subjected to either too little or too much pressure degenerate, and, once the process has been initiated, it appears to be self-perpetuating.

The frequency of joint disease at all ages and its progressive increase with age illustrate the common problem of making the distinction between specific disease processes and physiologic aging. Arthritis of all types accounts for a significant proportion of the problems encountered in adult medical practice, afflicting an estimated 14 per cent of males and 23 per cent of females beyond the age of 45, and trailing only heart disease as the leading cause of restricted activity among adults. The social and economic burdens imposed by joint diseases therefore loom very large. The frequency of disorders of periarticular tissue (capsule ligaments and bursae) is readily apparent clinically, but the pathogenesis of these degenerative conditions is poorly understood. Repetitive trauma, as in a baseball pitcher's elbow, unusual activity, as in the shoulder of a week-end ceiling painter, or infrequent vigorous activity, as in the once-a-week squash player, may result in painful, inflammatory lesions of the periarticular structures. According to the site of involvement, these conditions are called tendonitis, fasciitis, bursitis, or capsulitis. Presumably the additive effect of unusual stress in the presence of preexisting degeneration produces an irritative inflammation that results in pain and limitation of motion.

Infection

Viral illness, particularly respiratory, is a common cause of intermittent, transient disability in this age span. Individuals of this age, unless disabled by coexistent heart or lung disease, are least likely to develop serious complications of viral agents, such as influenza. Viral exanthems are rare because of immunity developed during childhood; however, when they are contracted in adulthood, complications are more frequent and serious, and may include encephalitis, orchitis, pancreatitis, or myocarditis. Viral hepatitis of both infectious and serum varieties may affect adults throughout the age span.

Bacterial infection is a problem of lesser importance during adulthood. In those individuals whose host defense mechanisms have become impaired through a coexisting disorder, such as cancer or alcoholism, a bacterial infection may be disastrous. This is particularly true of tuberculosis, which remains an important cause of morbidity and mortality among the socioeconomically disadvantaged and immunologically vulnerable.

Immunology—Allergy

The allergies of childhood carry over into adulthood mainly as allergic rhinitis (hay fever) and bronchial asthma. Approximately half the cases of asthma are associated with hypersensitivity to specific environmental antigens and are referred to as extrinsic asthma; the remainder are called intrinsic asthma and are of unknown origin, but may result from repeated infections and hypersensitivity to bacterial products or pollutants. The latter frequently has its onset during the middle years, may become chronic, and is a common cause of disability. Persistent asthma from any cause may produce pulmonary emphysema and permanent ventilatory insufficiency.

An important, relatively recent phenomenon is the emergence of drug allergies among adult populations. The widespread, often indiscriminate use of pharmacologic agents, notably sedatives and antibiotics and especially penicillin, makes inquiry into past drug reactions an important part of the medical history and a critical determinant in the choice of treatment.

The rapid decrease in the incidence and severity of streptococcal infections coincident with improved socioeconomic conditions and the widespread use of antibiotics has led to a dramatic decline in the prevalence of two formerly very common immunologic disorders related to streptococcal antigens—rheumatic valvular heart disease and chronic glomerulonephritis. Although reparative valvular heart surgery and renal dialysis and transplantation have ameliorated early mortality risk in afflicted persons, morbidity related to these disorders still remains a major task for medical and paramedical personnel and family members, and is a large economic burden.

Neoplasm

Cancer accounts for one fourth to one third of the deaths during this age span (Fig. 9–3). The types of malignancies differ strikingly for males and females due to the high prevalence of breast and uterine cancer among the latter. Skin cancer, although frequent, has a high cure rate so that lung cancer is currently the leading cause of death from cancer in men.

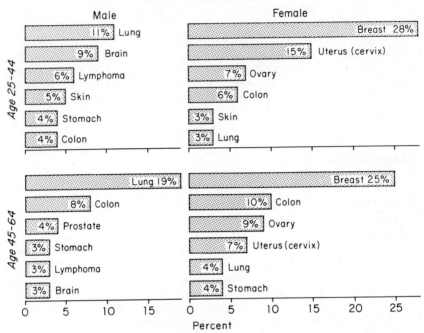

Figure 9–3 Death from various types of cancer as per cent of the total in younger and older middle-aged males and females. (Adapted from World Health Organization: Mortality from Malignant Neoplasms, 1955-1965. Part I. Geneva, Switzerland, 1970. pp. 78–101.)

Other Problems: Multifactorial Disorders

The most striking difference in types of disorders between youth and adulthood is the shift toward chronic diseases with advancing age. These diseases, such as coronary heart disease, hypertension, and peptic ulcer, tend to be common and either progressive or recurrent. Therefore the aim of medical treatment of these disorders is more often to arrest or control rather than to cure, and prevention remains the ultimate goal. Since these disorders are both common and time-related, it is not surprising that they are felt to be largely multifactorial in origin, the result of many interacting forces, both genetic and environmental. In the United States, more persons die from coronary heart disease (30 per cent of all deaths) than from any other single cause. The risk of death from this disorder dramatically increases with age—over age 45 the risks from one decade to the next double for males and triple for females (Fig. 9–4). Since males have a relatively higher incidence of this disorder earlier in middle age, the mortality differential between the sexes becomes less as age advances. This approximation of the female toward the male mortality curve in later life, however, may reflect more the earlier removal of many high-risk males than a true equivalence in risk between the sexes at advanced ages.

Coronary heart disease appears to be a "disease of affluence" and is appropriately considered a modern epidemic in the United States. Risk factors toward coronary disease that have been firmly identified include hypertension, cigarette smoking, and elevated blood levels of cholesterol-rich and triglyceride-rich lipoproteins. Less well-defined and -understood associated factors may include certain personality traits such as aggressiveness and conscientiousness, hyperglycemia,

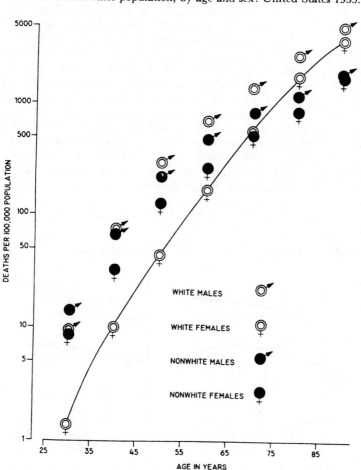

Death rates for coronary heart disease
White and non-white population, by age and sex: United States 1955.

Figure 9-4 Semilogarithmic plots of coronary artery disease mortality in white and nonwhite United States population in 1955. (From Furman, R. H., et al.: Gonadal hormones, blood lipids and ischemic heart disease. In Miras, C. J. (Ed.), et al.: Progress in Biochemical Pharmacology, Vol. 4 [Recent Advances in Atherosclerosis.], White Plains, N.Y., Phiebig, 1968, p. 334.)

certain dietary habits, possibly increased fat intake and sucrose intake, and decreased physical activity. It is not surprising that several of these risk factors—hypertension, hypercholesterolemia, hypertrigly-ceridemia, hyperglycemia and a sedentary existence—are most common in persons who are obese. Genetic predisposition to many of these risk factors has been demonstrated, and such propensities may underlie the well-known tendency of heart disease to run in families. Although preventive genetics may not be currently practicable, prevention of obesity and cigarette smoking may yield important advantages not only for the individual at special genetic risk but also for the entire affluent population in Western societies.

Just as routine body weight increases with age (Fig. 9–2), so do blood pressure (Fig. 9–5), serum cholesterol (Fig. 9–6) and blood glucose following an oral glucose challenge (Fig. 9–7). These age-related changes pose important diagnostic problems which are discussed in detail in Chapter 10. The epidemiologic implications of these changes are clear, but their importance in a given person remains largely conjectural. For example, according to insurance company statistics, approximately 10 per cent of the United States' population have blood pressures greater than 140 mm Hg systolic and 90 mm Hg diastolic by the age of 40 to 50. Some individuals with chronic blood pressure elevations develop hypertensive vascular disease, arteriosclerosis of the smallest arteries of the kidney, retina and brain and/or large vessels. However, many hypertensive individuals never develop significant ischemia and therefore remain asymptomatic. Thus, as with all risk factors, the significance of hypertension in the individual adult cannot be assessed with a high degree of precision.

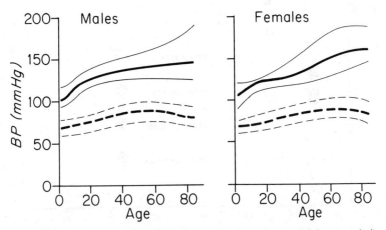

Figure 9–5 Relationship between age and systolic (upper, solid lines) and diastolic blood pressure (BP) (lower, dashed lines) in males and females in an American Community—Tecumseh, Michigan. Heavy lines are 50th percentile; lighter lines are 20th (lower) and 80th (upper) percentiles. (Adapted from Epstein, F. H., et al.: Prevalence of chronic diseases and distribution of selected physiological variables in a total community, Tecumseh, Michigan. Am. J. Epidemiol. 81:307, 1965.

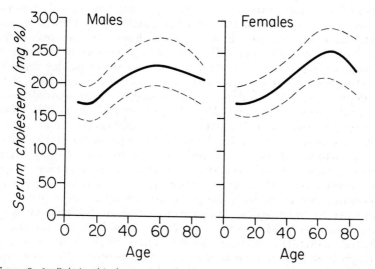

Figure 9–6 Relationship between age and serum cholesterol concentration in males and females in an American community—Tecumseh, Michigan. Solid lines are 50th percentiles; dashed lines are 20th (lower) and 80th (upper) percentiles. (Adapted from Epstein, F. H., *et al.*: Prevalence of chronic diseases and distribution of selected physiological variables in a total community, Tecumseh, Michigan. Am. J. Epidemiol. *81*:307, 1965.

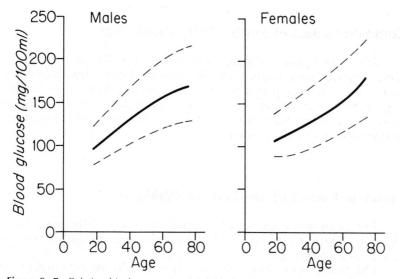

Figure 9–7 Relationship between age and blood glucose one hour following a 100 gm oral glucose challenge in males and females in an American community—Tecumseh, Michigan. Solid lines are 50th percentiles; dashed lines are 20th (lower) and 80th (upper) percentiles. (Adapted from Epstein, F. H., *et al.*: Prevalence of chronic diseases and distribution of selected physiological variables in a total community, Tecumseh, Michigan. Am. J. Epidemiol. *81*:307, 1965.

Primary hypertension, exclusive of renal disorders and other causes of secondary increases in blood pressure, remains a disorder of unknown etiology and is thus not yet preventable. However, exacerbating factors, such as obesity and perhaps chronic excessive salt intake are correctable. Regardless of etiology, treatment to lower blood pressure does appear to prevent untoward cardiovascular sequelae in hypertensive patient groups as demonstrated in recent clinical trials.

Peptic ulcer is a common, presumably multifactorial disorder which may affect as many as 10 to 15 per cent of adults. The disorder is more common in males than females and occurs at all ages; but symptoms most often develop between the ages of 20 to 40 and reach a peak incidence between 45 and 55. The disease is more frequent among people whose occupations involve administrative responsibility, competitive effort, and nervous tension. It is usually duodenal in location, though all sites along the human upper digestive tract are responsive to "ulcerogenic" influences that affect the balance between tissue resistance and secretory products, mainly acid and the acid-activated proteolytic enzyme, pepsin. There appears to be a genetic predisposition and an increased incidence in people with blood type O. The disorder occurs in association with practically all diseases except those characterized by complete absence of gastric acid, and is particularly frequent in patients with chronic pulmonary disease and chronic alcoholism.

Common Causes of Morbidity in Middle Age

Revealing figures relating to disorders peculiar to this age have been obtained from diagnoses made on ostensibly healthy patients who have come to a large prepayment medical group (Kaiser) for screening (Fig. 9-8). It can be appreciated from the figure that many of these disorders may produce no symptoms until a complication, usually cardiovascular in nature, occurs.

Common Causes of Mortality in Middle Age

The commonest causes of mortality in the middle years are depicted in Figure 9-9 and clearly reflect the shift toward chronic disease in this age group.

The health spectrum is broad in the middle years, ranging from individuals who are clearly free of both symptoms and risk factors to those who are gravely ill and dying. Since most of the causes of morbidity and mortality in this age group are intimately connected with processes which appear to be universal and age-related, the varied health of middleaged adults serves to emphasize the highly variable rate of aging in individuals who may share in common only their chronologic age.

DISORDERS OF MIDDLE AGE

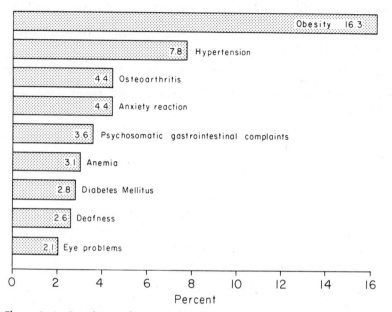

Figure 9-8 Prevalence of various disorders detected in screening examinations of ostensibly healthy middle-aged American members of a prepaid health care plan. (Adapted from Collen, M. F.: Automated Multiphasic Screening, Chapter 2, pp. 25-66. *In* Sharp, C. and Keen, H.: Presymptomatic Detection and Early Diagnosis. London, Pitman Medical Publication Company, Ltd., 1968.)

COMMON CAUSES OF DEATH IN MIDDLE AGE

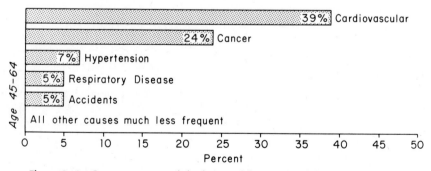

Figure 9-9 Common causes of death in middle age, as per cent of total deaths between ages 45 and 64. (Adapted from Vital Statistics of the United States, 1968. Vol. II, Part B: Mortality. Rockville, Maryland, United States Department of Health, Education and Welfare, 1971, pp. 114-126.

REFERENCES

Chilman, C. S.: Families in development at mid-stage of the family life cycle. Family Coordinator, *172*:297–310, 1968.

Erickson, E. H.: Identity and the Life Cycle. Psychological Issues, Monograph I, Vol. 1, No. 1, 1969.

Mayer, J.: Overweight: Causes, Cost and Control. Englewood Cliffs, New Jersey, Prentice-Hall, 1968.

Simon, A. W.: The New Years: A New Middle Age. New York, A. A. Knopf, 1968.

Society of Actuaries: Build and Blood Pressure Study. Metropolitan Life Insurance Company, 1959.

Stamler, J., and Epstein, F. N.: Coronary heart disease: Risk factors as guides to preventive action. Prev. Med., *1*:27–48, 1972.

CHAPTER TEN

OLD AGE, INCLUDING DEATH AND DYING

EDWIN L. BIERMAN
WILLIAM R. HAZZARD

LIFE SITUATION

Physical

All elderly people exhibit to some degree evidence of changes which have accumulated during "normal aging." Many also have one or more superimposed pathologic conditions which frequently result in impaired function and limitation of mobility. Figure 10–1 illustrates the sharp increase in the prevalence of chronic disease with age and the even sharper increase in functional disability. After age 65, more than 30 per cent of individuals have significant limitation in the ability to carry on their major activity. Such limitation has far-reaching consequences. The elderly person with severe functional limitations frequently suffers from physical and social isolation. Unable to maintain habitual environmental contacts, independence and sense of purpose in life, elderly persons become an economic burden to the community.

Age-related changes may occur in different individuals at varying chronologic ages. However, in all persons, increasing age is characterized by a decreasing capacity for adaptation and a decreasing ability to maintain homeostasis in the face of internal or external stress. As a result, the homeostatic balance in many elderly persons is very delicate, though their external appearance may give the impression of good health. All of us have known older individuals in whom the occurrence of a seemingly minor illness or injury precipitated a catastrophic chain of irreversible reactions. One is often in a quandary as to how to list the specific cause of death in such cases. Is death caused by the specific pathologic process which has ended life (usually cardiorespiratory arrest) or by the incident, often relatively minor, which triggered the terminal chain reaction? An argument could be

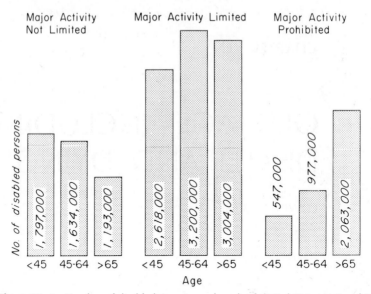

Figure 10–1 Number of disabled Americans, based on United States National Health Survey July, 1957 to June, 1958, grouped according to age and degree of functional disability. Persons over 65, comprising 10 per cent of the total population, account for a disproportionate amount of disability of all degrees, but especially of major disability. (Adapted from Limitation of Activity and Mobility Due to Chronic Conditions, July, 1957 to June, 1958, Selected Reports from the United States National Health Survey, United States Public Health Service Publication No. 584, series B, No. 11.

made for the latter, particularly since the tail of the human survival curve beyond age 92 (Fig. 10–2) resembles the semilogarithmic curve which describes the survival of water glasses in a cafeteria (Fig. 2–1, Chapter Two), suggesting that death in the aged may occur almost as a random event.

Physiologic

The general physiologic functional decline in organ systems has been discussed in the section on the Biology of Aging (Chapter Two) and summarized in Figure 2–4. The physiologic changes of aging are often indistinguishable in the aged from medical changes of disease. This poses a serious dilemma for the health professional who deals with geriatric patients, since the diagnosis of "disease" depends upon a separation of "abnormal" from "normal." Not only does the diseased population overlap the normal population with regard to the diagnostic characteristic measured so that the observed distribution fails to suggest two discrete populations (Fig. 10–3), but an age-related shift in that characteristic in the abnormal direction further increases the degree of overlap and blurs the distinction between normal aging and disease. This is well illustrated by measurements of diastolic blood pressure or blood glucose, which change with age in the same direction as

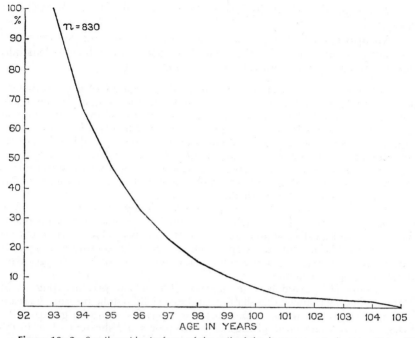

Figure 10-2 Semilogarithmic form of the tail of the human survival curve above 92 years of age. (From Ageing: The Biology of Senescence, by Alex Comfort. Copyright © 1956, 1964 by Alex Comfort. Reprinted by permission of Holt, Rinehart and Winston, Inc.)

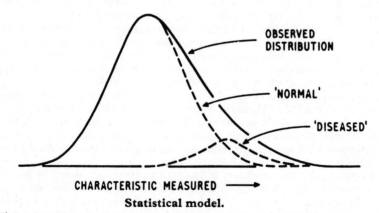

Statistical model.

Figure 10-3 Curve of the frequency distribution of a hypothetical quantitative characteristic, such as blood pressure, serum cholesterol, or post-oral glucose blood sugar levels. The asymmetrical upper tail of the curve may reflect the presence of two populations, one normal, the other diseased; however, the considerable overlap between the populations often makes the decision as to whether a given individual is diseased or normal highly arbitrary and subject to considerable error. Most such distributions become more widely spread and skewed in older populations, thus further blurring the distinction between normal and abnormal among aged persons.

alterations produced by hypertensive disease and diabetes mellitus, respectively.

An approach to the problem of aging, disease, and standards of normality is illustrated by the following discussion which is partially derived from a presentation by R. Andres.*

With the passage of time, anatomical-physiological-biochemical changes occur in the adult individual which we ascribe to the processes of aging. At the same time, other changes occur which we ascribe to the processes of disease. As health professionals, we are taught to seek out, identify and eradicate disease, almost as if it were a physical entity distinct from the patient. There are rules for its detection and we expect, if we follow the rules, to be able to say that disease is either present or absent. Disease then has come to be considered something foreign or abnormal; aging, on the other hand, has about it an aura of inevitability and even of normality.

Despite these philosophic concepts in which aging and disease seem to be mutually exclusive, a more searching examination of these ideas leads one to the realization that disease and nondisease are not as black is to white but are in fact more like a continuous spectrum of grays. Furthermore, our vision today may not permit us to differentiate the graying of disease changes from the graying of age changes.

Consider, for example, age differences in blood pressure [Fig. 9–5]. Many studies have shown that diastolic and especially systolic pressure increases with age. Yet we know that hypertension is a physical sign of a group of diseases and may be harmful, giving rise to symptoms and shortened life. In this instance, where quantitation of the physical measurement is simple and quite accurate, and where a profusion of effective therapeutic agents is available, it becomes of great importance to define the standards of normality and to know whether these standards should be adjusted for age. Is normal blood pressure that of healthy 20-year-old subjects? Is the increase in pressure simply a manifestation of aging *per se,* and therefore normal?

Blood pressure is only one of many examples of the principle that the change in organ function with age may be indistinguishable in magnitude, direction, and character from the change in function which occurs in well-defined disease states. Tests of pulmonary or renal function clearly demonstrate progressive decrements with increasing age which resemble the common chronic pulmonary and renal diseases. In these instances, however, where therapy is by no means as effective or as readily evaluated as in the hypertensive diseases and where the measurements themselves are not as simple to perform, the relation of age change to disease has not become as pressing a problem. If the fall in glomerular filtration rate (GFR) were as easy to document as the rise in blood pressure, and if medications were available to raise the GFR, then physicians would be as agitated by the problem of what to do about the low GFR as they are about what to do about elevated blood pressure in the aged.

Consider also the condition of prostatism. Here our ability to quantitate the change with age (or disease?) is poor indeed and the therapy, surgery, not one to be undertaken lightly. The physicians' solution here is duly to perform the ritual of palpating the prostate, but to pay no attention to it until symptoms become severe enough so that the patient seeks relief.

The point to be made by these examples is that the conditions of a par-

---

*After Andres, R.: Relation of physiologic changes in aging to medical change of disease in the aged. Mayo Clin. Proc. 42:413, 1967.

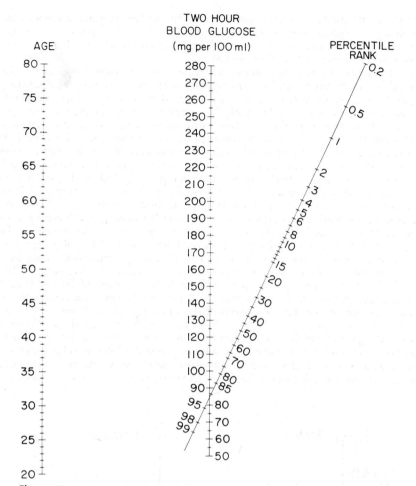

AGE

TWO HOUR
BLOOD GLUCOSE
(mg per 100 ml)

PERCENTILE
RANK

Figure 10–4 Nomogram for determining percentile rank of an individual's two-hour postprandial blood glucose level as a function of age. (From Andres, R.: Relation of physiological changes in aging to medical change of disease in the aged. Mayo Clinic. Proc. 42:679, 1967.)

ticular historical moment strongly influence the physician's view towards aging and disease. These conditions are: How easily can the age change or the disease state be identified and quantitated? How effective is therapy? What are the potential dangers of therapy? If the condition is readily detected and easily treated, then we tend to identify it as a disease. If detection is difficult and therapy hazardous, then we lean toward calling it the inevitable ravages of age and leave it alone.

A critical example is the relation between age changes in glucose tolerance and the diabetic state. A diagnostic hallmark of diabetes is a defect in glucose tolerance; yet, striking deteriorations of glucose tolerance occur with age. These changes with age are universal and not secondary to poor diet, inactivity, or the presence of other types of disease. Nor can they be attributed to "senility" —they are progressive, beginning as early as the fourth decade of life. Furthermore, one cannot escape the dilemma of age change versus disease by technical modifications of the test procedure. The decline in glucose homeostasis with age is evident whether glucose is given orally or intravenously, whether there is pre-test stressing with an adrenal corticosteroid, or whether a tolbutamide response test is administered.

To define the dilemma more clearly, it must be pointed out that if the standards in common use for the diagnosis of diabetes are uncompromisingly applied to all subjects regardless of their age, then over half of all apparently healthy older people must be labeled as "diabetic." Is this change in performance with age then truly the emergence with time of a vast number of diabetics, or is the basis of the change "physiologic aging?" At present this dilemma is unresolved. Yet physicians must continue to take care of patients and a *modus vivendi* for the present must be sought. A nomogram [Fig. 10–4] which permits an individual's performance to be compared quickly and easily to that of his age cohorts in terms of percentile ranking has proven very useful. This nomogram has been constructed from data obtained on volunteer subjects and is based upon statistical principles. Utilization of the nomogram, however, does not require knowledge of the technique of its construction. Reference to the figure will illustrate the principle. This nomogram is used to judge performance on an oral glucose tolerance test. A straight edge connecting the subject's age with his blood glucose concentration two hours after the ingestion of 100 g of glucose will intersect the percentile rank line. A rank of 50 per cent is an average performance, and a rank of 2 per cent is relatively poor, since it indicates that 98 per cent of subjects of the same age will perform better than that individual. What specific rank is to be considered diabetic at different ages? Prospective studies are needed to answer this. Only then will we be able to say which rank carries with it the increased hazards known to be associated with diabetes mellitus (the overt symptomatic diabetic state), the recognized late microvascular complications of diabetes, those disorders known to be associated

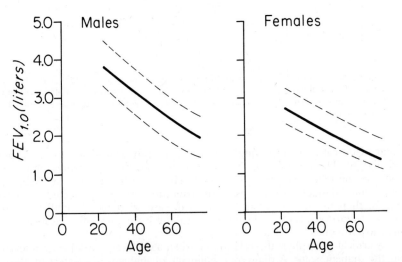

Figure 10–5 Relationship between age and 1 second forced expiratory volume (FEV$_{1.0}$) in males and females in an American community (Tecumseh, Michigan). The solid lines are 50th percentiles; the dashed lines are 20th (lower) and 80th (upper) percentiles. (Adapted from Epstein, F. H. *et al.*: Prevalence of chronic diseases and distribution of selected physiological variables in a total community, Tecumseh, Michigan. Amer. J. Epidemiol. *81*:307, 1965.)

with diabetes such as atherosclerosis, or indeed an increased mortality rate. The future may show that there will be no dividing line between black and white but that with diabetes, as with other age-associated disease, we must learn to think in terms of degrees of grayness.

Aging changes in bone, muscle, and the nervous system are of particular importance to function and thus their age-related decline in integrity presents a particular hazard to the aged person. Bones show a decreased mass with age (Fig. 9–1, Chapter Nine). The obtuse angle between the neck and the shaft of the femur of the young adult may shift to nearly a right angle. As a result, weight-bearing produces increased shearing stresses in this area and predisposes to fracture. Some bones, like the mandible, may change shape. Calcification within cartilage and ligaments occurs to some extent in almost all individuals. The spine may show kyphosis, scoliosis, and thinning of intervertebral discs. Lipping at the edge of the joint surfaces is frequent. Joints show loss of elasticity, with thinning and degenerative changes of joint cartilage.

There is a gradual, progressive decrease in muscle bulk. However, aging muscle is still capable of regeneration. Histologically, there is increased interstitial fat and the occurrence of large, round, lipid droplets in the muscle fibers themselves. Functionally, muscle strength decreases. Individual muscle strength in the 65-year-old is about 60 per cent of that found in the 25-year-old, with grip strength being 77 per cent. There is no agreement as to how much of this decrease in strength is due to decreased activity and disuse, and how much of it is due to aging, *per se*. Most authorities theorize that changes in muscle size and strength are secondary to decreased activity. However, atrophy and decreased strength of hand muscles have been consistently demonstrated; and it is hard to explain how disuse atrophy could occur in the hands, which are used regularly throughout life. In addition to loss of muscle strength, exercise experiments demonstrate decreased capacity for maximum oxygen uptake and pulmonary ventilation (Fig. 10–5) and decreased diffusing capacity of the lung.

Aging of the nervous system has been studied in great detail. Of prime importance is the fact that neurons are not capable of regeneration. With increasing age, there is a steady loss of these nonreproducing cells, with resulting so-called "normal changes" in neurologic signs. The pupils in the aged have a tendency to miosis with sluggish reaction to light and accommodation. A fine tremor and muscle wasting, especially of the small muscles of the hand, are frequently noted. There is a tendency for reflexes to be hypoactive or absent, especially the ankle jerks and abdominal reflexes. Plantar responses may be equivocal and hard to interpret.

There are also well-documented sensory decrements and deficiencies in higher perceptual functioning. Diminution in visual and auditory acuity are well-known phenomena. There is also some decrease in perception of light touch, vibration and temperature, and an increased pain threshold. Proprioception, especially from the soles of the feet, is impaired. The perception of the position of one's body in space and of the true vertical may be distorted. Balance and coordination may be impaired. Psychomotor responses are generally slowed, reaction time doubling between ages 30 and 70. This is apparently due to slowing of higher integrative functions. Therefore, the more complex the response, the more markedly it is slowed.

The typical posture of the aged is one of flexion. The head and neck are flexed, with eyes downcast. There is a mild dorsal kyphosis and loss of normal lumbar lordosis, with slight flexion at knees and hips. As a result, the antigravity muscles are under constant strain and may become tight. This contrasts with the posture of a younger person, with hips and knees extended, in whom the largest burden of maintaining the upright position falls on the joint ligaments, while the antigravity muscles are relaxed. In the aged, the posture of flexion persists during ambulation. The gait becomes one of small, shuffling steps with feet barely clearing the ground. This is probably due to a combination of factors: the loss of ability to balance safely and recover quickly, the distortion of gravitational forces produced by flexed posture, and the need to watch the ground and use visual cues as a substitute for proprioceptive cues from the feet. There is limited or absent arm swing. Speed of gait is slowed.

Social and Behavioral Components

Attitudes and practices with respect to the aged, the ill, and the weak appear to be determined largely by the society's survival needs and its idiosyncratic cultural traditions. In nomadic hunting societies, where survival depended upon rapid, efficient movement of small groups from one seasonal hunting ground to another, drastic methods of relieving the group's burden of aged persons were adopted. Industrialized Western societies deal with the aged in ways which are less obviously cruel.

A chronologically aged healthy person usually has needs and behavior patterns that do not differ greatly from those of younger persons. However, given the prevailing preoccupation with youth and its attendant physical activity and attractiveness, and the severely economically disadvantaged position of the elderly in Western societies, different theories have emerged as to the best means of adapting to old age: *Disengagement*—retirement from usual activities into a sedentary and slower pace of living, to the ghetto of a retirement community where economically feasible. *Maintenance of activity*—based on the premise that the best old age is the most middle-aged behavior possible, no special age segregation and no planned changed behavior associated with aging are contemplated. *Maintenance of utility*—effective functioning is based, in large part, on the conviction of one's usefulness; when no contribution is possible, living has little or no meaning.

Consideration of these three alternatives makes it obvious that none represents the optimal, realistic approach to old age and stresses the imperfect attitudes toward old age which prevail in our civilization.

Family and Interpersonal Relationships. As people grow older their families and friends become preoccupied with their own problems, change jobs, move, become ill, age, or die. Often older people find it difficult to maintain interpersonal ties as change is required to adapt to new situations. A distinction can be made between the aged isolate —one who can live alone in pleasure and comfort—and the aged desolate—one, who having lost family or friends, remains inconsolable or desperately in need of replacements.

Socioeconomic Factors. The importance of socioeconomic factors cannot be underestimated. The socioeconomically deprived appear to be less well prepared to tolerate the adversities and changes of old age than those with more nurturant, educational and occupational advantages. Economic security is an important factor in the maintenance of good morale in old age. Money is an effective preventive of some of the psychologic and social misery of old age.

Sexual Behavior. In both men and women, change in appearance and loss of sexual value pose serious problems. Men are often seriously worried about loss of potency, not only as a source of pleasure, but as a symbol of masculinity and worth as a person. For the female, loss of sexual attractiveness may threaten her security in the marital relationship, and for this reason she may welcome a diminishing of sexual interest on the part of her mate. The decline of sexual interest and activity in both men and women appears to be directly related to early sexual practices; for example, the timid, prudish and inhibited tend to welcome loss of sexual powers and interest. However, for some older persons, sexual activity can continue into the seventies and eighties.

PREVENTIVE MEASURES FOR HEALTH MAINTENANCE

In the face of the imposing array of age-linked changes and the consequent high risk of the aged to hazards which would be trivial in a younger person, how can health best be maintained in the geriatric patient?

Exercise

Neurophysiologic studies have shown that retention of capacities may depend upon their use and exercise. For most people such use requires being out of bed, engaged in purposeful activity which provides constant interaction with the environment, in pursuit of a goal which seems worthwhile. A recent study of the effect of physical conditioning on older individuals demonstrated overall improvement of aerobic metabolism. It appears that, despite the common findings of structural change and functional decrement, appropriate exercise and training can improve functional level regardless of age.

While the importance of exercise is well recognized, the question of what kind and how much for the individual elderly person may be perplexing. Any exercise undertaken should help to maintain normal posture, correct joint alignment, prevent contractures, preserve strength for ambulation, stimulate circulation and metabolism, and provide emotional satisfaction. Certainly, an individual's previous exercise history must be considered. If a man has been accustomed to playing 18 holes of golf three times weekly and demonstrates no symptoms of cardiovascular or musculoskeletal distress, there is no reason why he should not continue, regardless of chronologic age. On the other hand, one would hardly prescribe such a regime for the person who regularly becomes short of breath climbing stairs.

It is equally important to maintain a form of exercise which is appropriate to the person's interests. Most elderly people dislike busy-work. Many of them are convinced that the best way to get stronger is by resting. Therefore, prescribed exercise which involves purposeful activity, such as walking to the grocery store or working in the garden, is more likely to be successful than a program of calisthenics. Regardless of the nature of the exercise, it is important that it be performed on a regular basis, preferably daily.

Accident Prevention

The environment should be evaluated to determine what alterations are necessary to make it easier for the elderly to function and to remove hazards which are a threat to safety. Accidents are a major cause of disability in the aged. In one study, 73 per cent of accidents occurring in the home were found to involve patients over 65; one-third of falls occurred on stairs, either due to poor illumination or because the last step was misjudged. Such measures as housing on one floor, stairs well-lighted and with strong, easily grasped railings on both sides, night lights in bedrooms, bath, and hallways, and grab-rails beside tub, shower, and toilet in bathrooms are obvious precautions and their use should be more commonplace.

Diet

There are no specific dietary requirements unique to the aged, but it must be recognized that many people eat less as they grow older. In addition, economic circumstances, depression, or loneliness may lead to deficient diets, lacking especially in proteins, vitamins, and minerals, though overt clinical malnutrition may not be common. Dental status and the possibility of malabsorption in this age group also need to be considered. The elderly person who must exist on a meager diet, cook for one, and dine alone often eats poorly, resulting in a negative nitrogen balance and possibly mild ketosis. Since this in turn produces anorexia, a vicious cycle may be set up which can culminate in severe physical and mental breakdown. Since the elderly population is no longer obese (Chapter Nine, Fig. 9–2), perhaps as a result of the earlier death of obese individuals, who are subject to a higher mortality risk, regular, adequate, balanced, easily assimilable caloric intake needs to be encouraged despite the fact that older people have about only 80 per cent of the caloric requirements of 25-year olds to maintain a constant weight.

Prevention of Major Catastrophes Triggered by Minor Disruptions

Minor illness or injury in elderly people can cause serious pathophysiologic reactions in multiple systems because of the very delicate balance of homeostatic mechanisms in these individuals.

Prevention of such chain reactions requires the taking of a comprehensive history, which includes not only pertinent medical data but also information about the patient's level of activity, his personality, interpersonal relations, living conditions, and economic status. Failure to obtain such a history and prescription of a therapeutic regimen inappropriate for the age of the individual, even in seemingly trivial circumstances, can lead to disastrous results, as is illustrated by the following example: A 70-year-old woman appeared in the emergency room with a simple dislocation of the shoulder. The emergency room physician reduced the dislocation, strapped the shoulder, and sent her home with instructions not to use her arm for two weeks. What he failed to ascertain was that she lived alone and had no one to care for her. She was unable to sit up in bed or get out of a chair except by gripping with both arms to pull herself up. Furthermore, she had had a colostomy for twenty years, which she irrigated and dressed regularly herself, using both hands. The outcome was that the patient's situation soon became acute and within 48 hours she had to be admitted to the hospital as an emergency. A relatively minor injury had become a major crisis, not because of improper care, but because of ignorance of other pertinent physical and social factors necessary to maintain the patient's capacity to function.

Maintenance of Function

Consideration should be given to the total energy demands of the environment as the individual goes through his usual daily routine. Many modifications such as shopping twice weekly instead of daily, decreasing garden size, simplifying cleaning and laundry routines, and arranging kitchen utensils more efficiently, can be made without significantly altering total life-style. In general, energy expenditure should be channeled to the most productive and satisfying activities. Development of schedules and regular routines will also conserve energy and help compensate for slowed psychomotor performance and memory deficits.

It is interesting that most elderly people view themselves as healthy so long as they can do what they want and need to do, and maintain a state of physical, psychologic, and social harmony with their environment. Studies have repeatedly shown that, capable of adequate functioning, individuals do not regard the presence of known disease as reason to consider themselves in poor health. Therefore, a plan for each individual should be developed based on a comparison of the person's existing functional level with his potential. The approach should be two-pronged: correcting remediable deficits in the individual on the one hand, and providing compensatory mechanisms in his environment to substitute for irretrievably lost function on the other. Specific diseases, of course, will require appropriate treatment. Whether or not the individual in this age span has a significant disease, the importance of adequate diet and exercise should be stressed as a means by which he can maintain or improve his own ability to function and his sense of well-being.

A major goal of preventive geriatric medicine, then, is maintenance of a level of function which will permit satisfying interaction with the environment despite the presence of disease or age-associated changes. In addition to identification and treatment of specific disease, the achievement of this goal requires: knowledge of alterations in structure and function common to all aging individuals; a preventive and therapeutic program designed to minimize the effect of such changes; and a thorough understanding of the interactions between the individual and his environment, so that where necessary environmental alterations can be used to help compensate for declining function.

COMMON PROBLEMS

Behavioral and Emotional Disorders

The aged appear to be at a particularly high risk for mental disorders, but statistics relating to this risk are difficult to evaluate. Regarding serious mental disorders, a study in Baltimore revealed a weighted rate of 28 per 1000 for persons above 65 years of age, as compared to 6 per 1000 for those 35 to 64 years. On the other hand, it has been stated that the frequency of the psychoneuroses changes little beyond maturity. However, deviant behavior among older people appears to be well tolerated by the broader culture and perhaps accepted as normal until, without early intervention, the problems result in destructive behavior, and the older patient is brought into the mental health system. When this occurs, the patient is often hospitalized, frequently under full custodial care and for prolonged periods. Ambulatory or preventive care of the mental health of the aged is often neglected with only 2 per cent of all psychiatric and mental health center outpatients being in the 65 and older group. In contrast, approximately half of nursing home occupants have at least one psychiatric diagnosis, and two-thirds receive psychotropic medication. This all-or-none approach to mental disease in the elderly which involves little or no preventive or outpatient attention and then total care, results in neglect of the lesser but important emotional needs of those still able to care for themselves and excessively comprehensive care for those who come to medical attention. Currently, approximately 4 per cent of the age group over 65 are under custodial care. If proper support were available, it is estimated that one-third of these people could live in the community.

The etiology of behavioral and emotional disorders is often complex in the elderly person. In the past there was a tendency to overestimate the role of brain dysfunction and damage to the exclusion of the social, psychologic, and economic factors. Brain changes do occur with aging, attributable to degenerative processes in the brain cells, atherosclerotic cerebral vascular disease, or a combination of both factors. However, when careful attention is paid to rehabilitation and therapy, the response of the aged patient may be highly gratifying. This requires careful attention not only to the correction, where possible, of coexistent physical disorders such as congestive heart failure, cardiac arrhythmias, anemia, or urinary tract infection, but also to the economic and psychosocial stresses which may have precipitated the overt mental disturbance.

Specific behavioral disorders in the aged are often qualitatively similar to those of younger age groups. They include:

Depression. Depressive reactions are very common in old age, while manic reactions are less common. Depression may be found in association with organic mental syndromes as well as in relatively pure form. One such form which initially appears in the aged has been termed involutional psychotic reaction. This is characterized by depression, hypochondriasis, low self-esteem, guilt (especially about sexual behavior), and often florid paranoid ideation. Depression in the aged may be reactive to loss of spouse, friends, home, income, or social status, but may persist for long periods. It not infrequently leads to suicide, which is increasingly common with age among males: The base rate for white males aged 15 to 24 is 7.4 per 100,000; this climbs to 45.5 per 100,000 for ages 65 to 74 and to 54.5 for those above age 75. For females the rate is lower at all ages, plateaus at 55 years, and drops beyond age 74.

Schizophrenic Disorders. The incidence of schizophrenia increases with age. Whether this represents age-related expression of a lifelong predisposition or a specific effect of the aging process is undetermined.

Alcoholism. This is more common among the younger of the older age group. As with coronary artery disease, its declining prevalence in the aged may reflect the effect of selective early mortality among younger alcoholics, or, less likely, an actual decrease in alcohol consumption and dependence with the approach of old age.

Acute Brain Syndrome. Persons with acute brain syndrome show transient but severe mental impairment including confusion, memory loss, disorientation, and disordered thinking. This is often at least a partially reversible condition and is usually related to acute febrile, debilitating, or exhausting illness.

Chronic Brain Syndrome. This condition describes persons with relatively uncomplicated but irreversible mental impairment who often require institutional care. Single episodes of cerebral thrombosis, hemorrhage, or embolism give rise to focal rather than diffuse damage unless there is cardiovascular, pulmonary, or other system disease. Senile brain changes (a descriptive, largely nonspecific term) are presumed to be etiological when there are no focal neurological signs and when there is no history of stroke. Controversy currently exists as to whether senile dementia is a single disorder which is part of a continuum with Alzheimer's disease (pre-senile dementia, occurring before age 65) with a common viral etiology or a descriptive syndrome encompassing several specific disease entities.

Metabolic and Nutritional Disorders

Gallstones (see Chapter Nine). The frequent detection of gallstones in the asymptomatic elderly patient poses a particular dilemma for the physician. Should a cholecystectomy be performed on an elective basis under optimal surgical conditions, so as to prevent acute cholecystitis and the necessity for emergency surgery with its inherently greater risk? Or should one ignore the condition until symptoms arise which the patient cannot tolerate? This question is not resolved, but recent trends in medical practice, tempered by physicians' increasing awareness of the particular susceptibility of the aged patient to the stress of hospitalization and even minor surgery, have swung toward more conservative "wait-and-see" management.

Diabetes Mellitus. The incidence of symptomatic diabetes rises steadily with age. This syndrome is more than twice as prevalent at age 70 than at age 50. The true incidence of the disease is unknown, in part because of the difficulties in establishing the diagnosis with certainty in the presymptomatic state, in the face of age-related changes in glucose homeostasis (see above). Estimates place the prevalence at 2 per cent of the population, affecting more than 3 million persons in the United States. High risk groups include relatives of known diabetics and the chronically obese. The microvascular changes associated with diabetes increase with the duration of the disorder and, together with the macrovascular atherosclerotic changes which are more widespread and severe in the diabetic, account for most of the excess mortality and morbidity of the disease. For example, diabetes is the third leading cause of blindness. Unfortunately, apart from the prevention of ketoacidosis (rare in the obese patient) or the syndrome of nonketotic, hyperosmolar coma (a particular hazard in the elderly patient because of decreased mobility and access to oral fluid, the loss of which underlies the syndrome), the means of preventing both micro- and macrovascular complications have not been discovered. Consequently, major attention in the elderly diabetic should be directed toward avoidance of accidents such as trauma to the feet, and other stresses such as infection and dehydration which can trigger a rapid progression to major clinical problems including gangrene, septicemia, stroke, and often death.

Chemical Agents. Drug overdose is common and frequently iatrogenic, resulting from the failure of the physician to reduce doses to adjust for the age-associated decline in hepatic and renal function.

This is particularly true with regard to central nervous system-active agents such as barbiturates and stimulants and may also reflect increased sensitivity to these agents in the aged patients.

Trauma, Including Suicide

Accidents are a serious menace to the life and limb in older people. More than three million persons in the United States age 65 and over, or nearly 20 per cent of this age group, receive medical attention because of accidental injury, most often occurring in and around the home. Falls are common, and fracture of the vulnerable neck of the femur is a frequent cause of hospitalization and surgical repair, particularly in individuals over the age of 75.

Suicide rates progressively increase with age, reaching a high incidence above age 75. It has been estimated that there are two million persons in the United States who have attempted suicide at least once. Suicide has become a medical and social problem of major dimensions. The reasons for the high rate in the aged include not only the increased incidence of serious mental disorders, notably depression, in this age group but also the reaction of the aged person to the common loss of function, self-esteem, and comradeship of spouse and peers, the prospect of lingering, often painful disease such as cancer, and the pervasive feeling of rejection by society. Whereas many of these feelings may be avoided by changes in the immediate environment of the patient or the attitudes of society toward its aged members, consideration must inevitably be given to the right of the individual to choose his own time and means of death and to passive (negative) and even active (positive) euthanasia. Recognition of the need to preserve the dying patient's dignity and to resist the impulse to sustain life by unnatural means when considerations of the feelings of the patient and his family do not justify such heroic measures reflects recent changes in the attitude of physicians toward death, changes reinforced by the counsel of clergymen of many faiths.

Infectious Disorders

Viral Illnesses. The respiratory tract is the primary site of serious involvement; influenza may be particularly virulent in this age span.

Bacterial Illnesses. Bacterial pneumonitis is prevalent among the elderly and, in fact, has been referred to as "the old man's friend." Often this type of infection is superimposed on other debilitating disorders, and bronchopneumonia may be the terminal event.

Tuberculosis. Although the prevalence of this disease has declined, the pattern of its distribution shows a shift in the peak of mortality from the younger to the older age groups. In the United States, tuberculosis has become predominantly a disease of older males. Diabetes mellitus, more common in the elderly, predisposes to tuberculosis, which is often of a more florid type when superimposed upon diabetes or conditions of immune deficiency (see below).

Immunologic Disorders

Autoimmune Disorders. Many of the diseases which increase in incidence with age, such as pernicious anemia, Addison's disease, and chronic thyroiditis, are associated with demonstrable circulating autoantibodies to the tissue from which the deficient chemical principle is normally secreted, but etiologic relationships have yet to be firmly established.

Immune Deficiency States. Immune mechanisms appear to deteriorate with age. Evidence of immune response to past tubercular infection (a positive tuberculin skin test) is less prevalent in older age groups, perhaps reflecting an immune deficiency state which may allow reinfection or reactivation of latent infection and account for the increased incidence of clinical tuberculosis in the aged. Neoplastic disorders, particularly of the immune tissues themselves (multiple myeloma, lymphoma) may also impair resistance to infections. Moreover, the treatment of many malignancies or autoimmune disorders frequently involves the use of immunosuppressive agents, producing an iatrogenic susceptibility to infection processes.

Neoplastic Disorders. The incidence of most cancers increases with age (Fig. 10–6). Approximately half of all cancer deaths occur over age 65. The myeloproliferative disorders, such as the chronic leukemias and multiple myeloma, appear with increased frequency in the elderly. In men, hyperplasia of the prostate with age is almost universal, and histologic findings of neoplasia are common at necropsy, though widespread dissemination is less frequent.

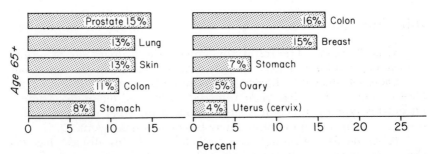

Figure 10–6 Death from various types of cancer as per cent of the total in males (left) and females (right) above age 65. (Adapted from Mortality from Malignant Neoplasms, 1955-1965, Part I. Geneva, Switzerland, World Health Organization, 1970, pp. 78–101.)

Common Causes of Morbidity

Degenerative and Structural Disorders. Common causes of morbidity are various degenerative and structural disorders, including visual and auditory impairment, osteoporosis, osteoarthritis, fracture of femur, diverticulitis, and hernia. These common disorders result from age-linked changes which occur throughout the life span, culminating in impaired function in the elderly.

Although deafness is commonly ascribed to a decrease in functioning neurones, blindness is more commonly the result of senile cataract or glaucoma. The former is therefore best approached by individualized supportive measures such as hearing aids, whereas the latter may be responsive to surgical or medical treatment.

As noted previously, the musculoskeletal system is particularly vulnerable to age-related degeneration. Osteoporosis (decreased bone mass) severe enough to predispose to fracture may occur in as many as 30 per cent of persons over the age of 65 and is four times more common in women than in men. Although etiologic factors are obscure, a chronic low intake of dietary calcium during adult life may be a factor which is superimposed on age-associated changes to produce the clinical disease. Compression fractures of the lumbar spine and fractures of the femoral neck are the common sites that give way to trauma. Osteoarthritis is another common cause of disability with increasing age.

Diverticula of the colon are extremely common in the elderly, presumably resulting from connective tissue changes in the bowel wall. They are so frequently seen in roentgenograms of the large intestine that radiologists often refer to them as "gray hairs of the colon." Despite the fact that the inflammatory process of diverticulitis occurs in only a fraction of individuals with diverticula, it represents a common cause of intra-abdominal disease in the elderly. Direct inguinal hernia may be a manifestation of degeneration of supporting tissues of the abdominal wall and can occasionally lead to acute intestinal obstruction. However, as with "silent" gallstones, most physicians do not regard the presence of asymptomatic, easily reducible hernias in the aged patient as a major indication for surgery.

Multifactorial Disorders. These include generalized atherosclerosis with features of coronary artery disease, cerebrovascular disease or peripheral vascular disease, hypertensive disease, and pulmonary emphysema.

In addition to coronary artery disease (see section in Chapter 9), other manifestations of the atherosclerotic process, such as cerebrovascular disease, become predominant in the old age group. The marked prevalence of stroke (cerebrovascular accident) in older populations reflects the accumulation of arterial changes secondary to both atherosclerotic and hypertensive disease. Strokes are often fatal, resulting in 200,000 deaths per year in the United States, with 80 per cent in individuals over age 65. For those eight out of ten who survive, there may be serious impairments such as paralysis and loss of speech. At least two million people now alive in the United States have suffered a stroke; many live in a chronically disabled condition, imposing an economic burden on both family and community. Hopefully, earlier detection and treatment of hypertension, now shown to reduce the incidence of strokes, will serve to reduce the prevalence and impact of cerebrovascular disease in the future.

Although not a significant factor in mortality, peripheral vascular disease, mainly arterial insufficiency of the lower extremities, is a frequent cause of disability in the elderly. Overall, atherosclerotic lesions in the large arteries of the brain, heart, and kidney, directly or indirectly constitute the most common cause of death in older people in Westernized societies.

The progressive changes associated with chronic hypertensive disease culminate in this age group with congestive heart failure (secondary to left ventricular changes), myocardial infarction, stroke and nephrosclerosis. Onset of the disease in the elderly is uncommon, although blood pressure changes with age occur (see section on the diagnosis of disease in the aged).

Chronic obstructive pulmonary disease, manifested as chronic bronchitis, fibrosis, and emphysema, is a very common cause of disability and death in this age span and is four times more common in men than in women. Predisposing factors include cigarette smoking, urban air pollution, and dusty working environments. The disease involves a breakdown of the normal connective tissue framework of the lung, presumably a combination of age-related changes and chronic insults which promote inflammatory changes. The disorder is a source of great discomfort and limitation of activity. Progressive changes lead to death from superimposed bacterial infections, right ventricular heart failure and/or severe hypoxia.

Common Causes of Death in Old Age (65+)

Death in this age group represents the high prevalence of serious disorders and the particular susceptibility of the aged. Major causes of death are depicted in Figure 10–7.

DEATH AND DYING

Discussion of this topic has often been limited by the fear that younger people have about the negative effects of such discussion upon older people. The frequency with which old people actually do talk about death, and, apparently, at times welcome such discussion, does not support this belief. Most older persons derive considerable support from a realistic evaluation of their life position. It often appears to be the living and not the dying who fear death and therefore isolate the dying physically and psychologically.

The question of physical versus social death raises enormous com-

COMMON CAUSES OF DEATH IN OLD AGE

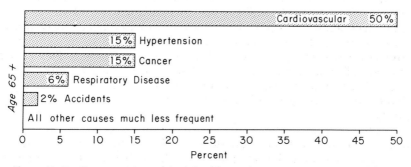

Figure 10–7   Common causes of death in old age (above age 65) as per cent of the total. (Adapted from Vital Statistics of the United States, 1968. Vol. II, Mortality, Part B. Rockville, Maryland, United States Department of Health, Education and Welfare, 1971, pp. 114–126.)

plexities. Positive and negative euthanasia must be considered and discussed if one is responsive to patient and societal needs. What responsibility does the dying person have concerning the manner in which he dies? How much power and responsibility should the relatives and the physician have? What is a meaningful definition of death, considering the efficiency of life-assisting systems?

These issues may be for the present largely imponderable. A more immediate problem is the special role of the health professional, especially the physician, in the case of the dying patient. Conflicts generated in those who serve and care for dying patients can be intense. The tendency to avoid interaction and to withdraw emotional or physical support from such a patient and his loved ones is an understandably human failing, but grievous because communication at that time is desperately needed. Kubler-Ross identifies dying as a process with stages ranging from the initial denial and isolation, progressing to anger, to bargaining, to depression, and finally to acceptance. She regards the persistence of hope as a necessary condition to the accomplishment of the work of mourning one's own or another's death. Hope, she claims, may be different for the dying than for the living. For the dying, hope may not necessarily be the expectation that the dying process will be reversed but rather that this process will not erode one's dignity, and that the suffering will be bearable.

In the experience of dying vicariously with their patients, health professionals must set aside what has been called "the satisfaction of rescue fantasies," which often influence the choice of medicine as a vocation in the first place. In attending dying and death, health professionals must also cope with their own death fears and the deaths of their loved ones. Justification for avoiding dying patients is that they have too little time left to warrant the health professional's attention and energies. A logically more tenable argument could be made that precisely because so little time remains, the dying patients should have their days and hours as enriched and peaceful as possible.

Arguments are currently voiced that expecting physicians to fill the dual roles of curing and caring for patients is simply unrealistic, and that these two roles will become subspecialties in all fields of medicine. Technologic progress will continue to extend the dying process with dubious justification either in patients' comfort or in the expense entailed. Concerning the ethical issues of euthanasia, Dr. George Maddox of Duke University claims that physicians are no more knowledgeable about such issues than anyone else in society and the responsibility for resolving conflicts in this area should not be relegated to physicians alone.

Experienced witnesses of death maintain that the shadow of death is more awesome than death itself. If the work of mourning one's own loss and the acceptance of death has been accomplished, death is often the only appropriate and merciful event, and is accomplished with serenity.

Physicians vary widely in whether or how they communicate probable terminality to patients and their families. Some state categorically, "I never tell my patients they are going to die," while others invariably confront the patient and everyone concerned with the possibility at least that the condition may be fatal. In our experience, as well as that of others, the issue does not become an either/or question at all, if one takes one's cues from the patients. By their questions and comments, by their verbal and nonverbal actions they will tell us when, how, and what they need to know about their immediate or remote futures. If, for example, a diagnosis is made clear to a patient and the patient does not indicate in any way his concerns about his prognosis or his future, one can be reasonably sure he is not yet ready to speculate about it realistically. However, this initial reaction should not make the physician insensitive to other or later cues which indicate that the patient has become ready to look at his future and discuss it honestly with his physician and his family.

REFERENCES

Andres, R.: Relation of physiologic changes in aging to medical change of disease in the aged. Mayo Clin. Proc., 42:413, 1967.

Beeson, P. B. and McDermott, W. (eds.): Cecil-Loeb Textbook of Medicine. 13th ed. Philadelphia, W. B. Saunders Company, 1971.

Birren, James E.: The Psychology of Aging. Englewood Cliffs, New Jersey, Prentice-Hall, Inc., 1964.

Chinn, A. B. (ed.): Working with Older People, A Guide to Practice. Vols. I to IV. Washington, D. C., United States Department of Health, Education and Welfare, Public Health Service, United States Government Printing Office, 1971.

Haynor, N. S., et al.: Carbohydrate tolerance and diabetes in a total community, Tecumseh, Michigan. Diabetes, 14:413, 1965.

Kubler-Ross, E.: On Death and Dying. New York, Macmillan Company, 1969.

The President's Commission on Heart Disease, Cancer and Stroke. Vol. I. Washington, D. C., United States Government Printing Office, 1964.

Rossman, I. (ed.): Clinical Geriatrics. Philadelphia, J. B. Lippincott Company, 1971.

APPENDIX

INTRAUTERINE GROWTH, BOTH SEXES

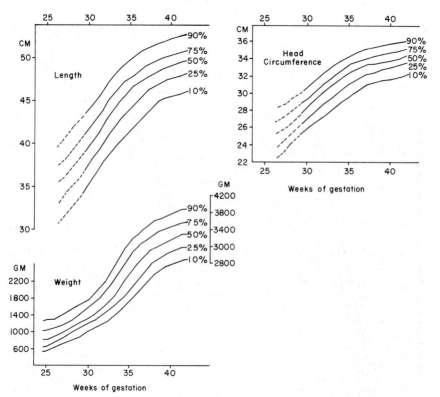

FROM LUBCHENCO, L.O., ET. AL.: PEDIATRICS 37:403, 1966

PERCENTILE CHARTS FOR MEASUREMENTS OF CHILDREN

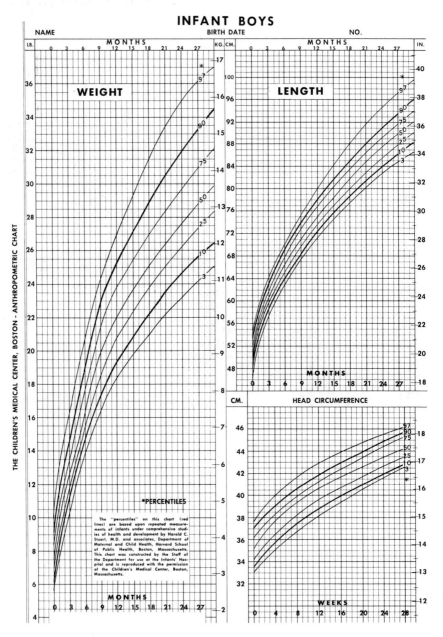

THE CHILDREN'S MEDICAL CENTER, BOSTON - ANTHROPOMETRIC CHART

INFANT BOYS

NAME   BIRTH DATE   NO.

WEIGHT

LENGTH

HEAD CIRCUMFERENCE

*PERCENTILES

The "percentiles" on this chart (red lines) are based upon repeated measurements of infants under comprehensive studies of health and development by Harold C. Stuart, M.D. and associates, Department of Maternal and Child Health, Harvard School of Public Health, Boston, Massachusetts. This chart was constructed by the Staff of the Department for use at the Infants' Hospital and is reproduced with the permission of the Children's Medical Center, Boston, Massachusetts.

PERCENTILE CHARTS FOR MEASUREMENTS OF CHILDREN (Continued)

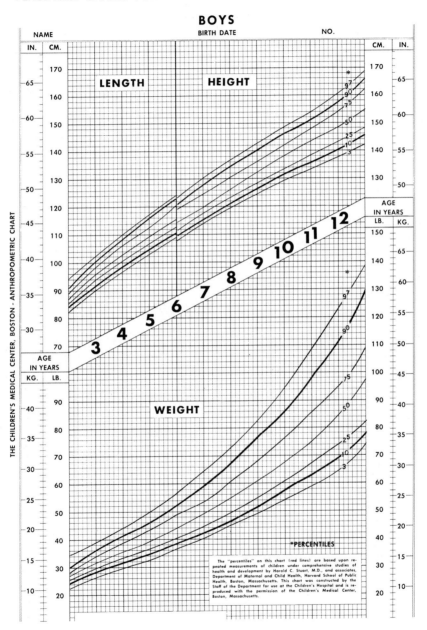

BOYS

NAME · BIRTH DATE · NO.

LENGTH · HEIGHT

WEIGHT

AGE IN YEARS

THE CHILDREN'S MEDICAL CENTER, BOSTON · ANTHROPOMETRIC CHART

*PERCENTILES

The "percentiles" on this chart (red lines) are based upon repeated measurements of children under comprehensive studies of health and development by Harold C. Stuart, M.D., and associates, Department of Maternal and Child Health, Harvard School of Public Health, Boston, Massachusetts. This chart was constructed by the Staff of the Department for use at the Children's Hospital and is reproduced with the permission of the Children's Medical Center, Boston, Massachusetts.

PERCENTILE CHARTS FOR MEASUREMENTS OF CHILDREN (Continued)

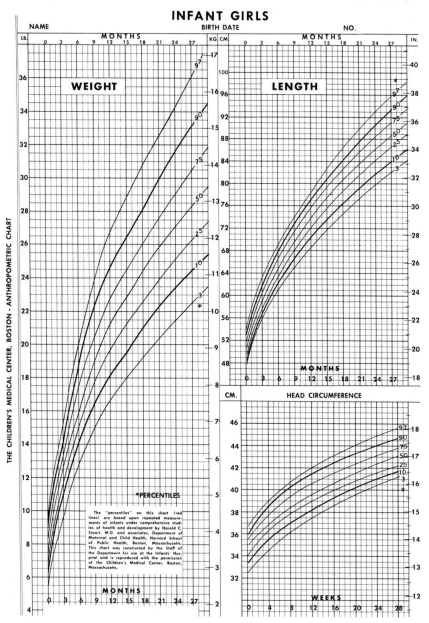

INFANT GIRLS

WEIGHT

LENGTH

HEAD CIRCUMFERENCE

*PERCENTILES

The "percentiles" on this chart (red lines) are based upon repeated measurements of infants under comprehensive studies of health and development by Harold C. Stuart, M.D. and associates, Department of Maternal and Child Health, Harvard School of Public Health, Boston, Massachusetts. This chart was constructed by the Staff of the Department for use at the Infants' Hospital and is reproduced with the permission of the Children's Medical Center, Boston, Massachusetts.

THE CHILDREN'S MEDICAL CENTER, BOSTON - ANTHROPOMETRIC CHART

PERCENTILE CHARTS FOR MEASUREMENTS OF CHILDREN (Continued)

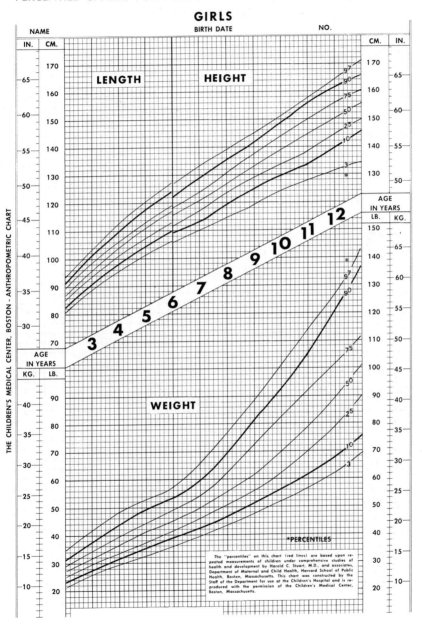

GIRLS

NAME

BIRTH DATE

NO.

THE CHILDREN'S MEDICAL CENTER, BOSTON - ANTHROPOMETRIC CHART

LENGTH   HEIGHT

WEIGHT

AGE IN YEARS

*PERCENTILES

The "percentiles" on this chart (red lines) are based upon repeated measurements of children under comprehensive studies of health and development by Harold C. Stuart, M.D., and associates, Department of Maternal and Child Health, Harvard School of Public Health, Boston, Massachusetts. This chart was constructed by the Staff of the Department for use at the Children's Hospital and is reproduced with the permission of the Children's Medical Center, Boston, Massachusetts.

HEAD CIRCUMFERENCE

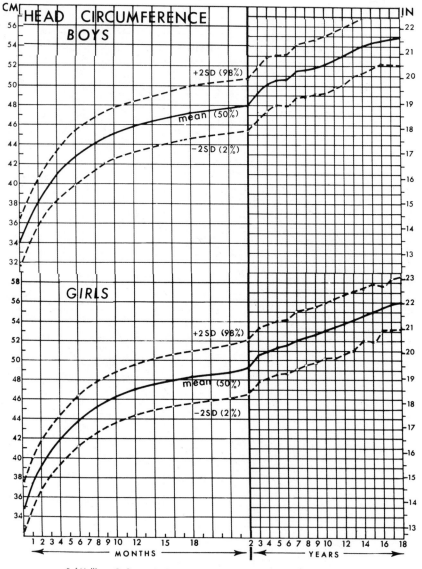

Ref:Nellhaus,G.,Composite International & Interracial Graphs,PEDIATRICS 41:106,1968.

FACE AND SKULL

Maxillary growth sites. The primary centers of growth contributing to the downward and forward direction of the maxilla are:

A, Growth at the spheno-occipital and sphenoethmoidal junctions.

B, Growth of the nasal cartilaginous septum. The following sutures are considered secondary or accommodating growth sites for the primary centers of growth:

Frontomaxillary suture.
Zygomaticomaxillary suture.
Zygomaticotemporal suture.
Pyramidal process of palatal bone.
Alveolar process.

Zygomatico-temporal suture
Frontomaxillary suture
Zygomatico-maxillary suture
Pyramidal process of palatal bone
Alveolar process
DENSE FIBROUS CONNECTIVE TISSUE
CARTILAGE
BONE

Mandibular growth sites. Growth in the condyle increases the anterior-posterior (downward and forward pattern of growth) dimension of the mandible. Anterior-posterior dimension of the mandible is also increased by resorption of bone on the anterior border of the ramus and apposition of bone on the posterior border of the ramus. Appositional growth of alveolar bone increases the superior-inferior dimension of the mandible. (From Graber, T. M.: *Orthodontics,* 2nd ed., Philadelphia, W. B. Saunders Company, 1966, p. 60.)

B 2019 ♂
3-0-0
8-0-0

Tracing of superimposed films of head showing the normal downward and forward facial growth pattern. Ages 6 months, 3 years, and 8 years.

DECIDUOUS DENTITION

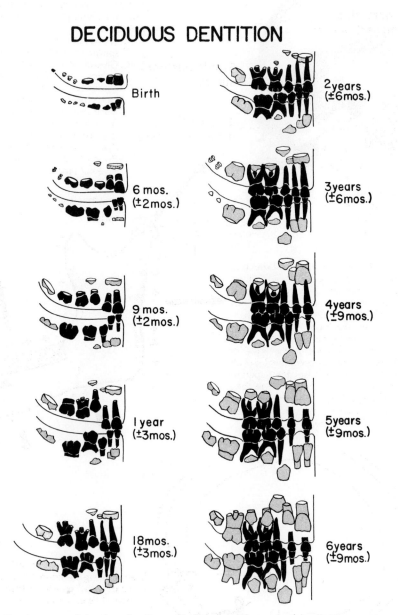

Development of human dentition. Black = deciduous teeth: gray = permanent teeth. (From Schour et al.: *Atlas of the Mouth*. Copyright by the American Dental Association. Reprinted by permission. Modified by Graber, T. M.)

MIXED DENTITION   PERMANENT DENTITION

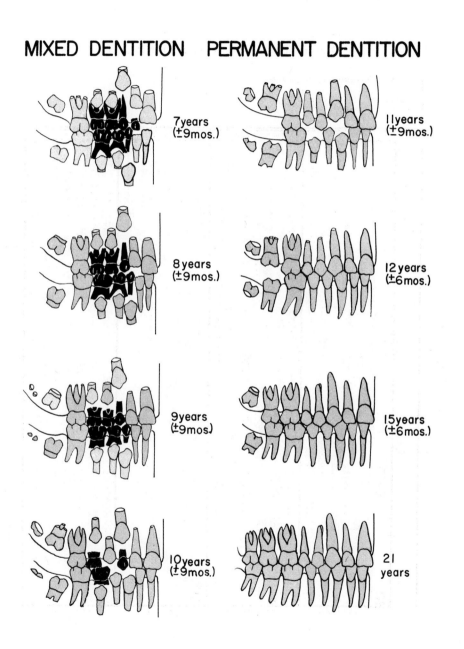

7years
(±9mos.)

8years
(±9mos.)

9years
(±9mos.)

10years
(±9mos.)

11years
(±9mos.)

12years
(±6mos.)

15years
(±6mos.)

21
years

DENVER DEVELOPMENTAL SCREENING TEST

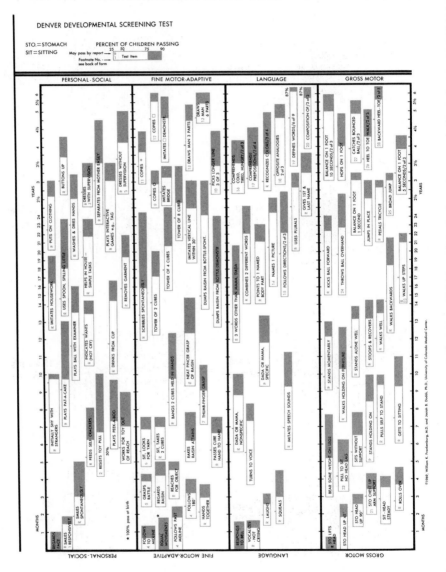

DENVER DEVELOPMENTAL SCREENING TEST

The screening chart at the left depicts the age ranges of normal performance for each test item. The beginning of each bar represents the age when 25 per cent of children can perform or demonstrate this item and the shaded area of each bar denotes the age range by which 75 to 90 per cent of children have this capability. A total testing, to maximal levels of performance for each category, can be assessed in terms of *developmental age*. Developmental age, divided by chronologic age, times 100 gives the *developmental quotient*. Below are directions, pertinent to the numbers to the right of the bars on the opposite page.

1. Try to get child to smile by smiling, talking or waving to him. Do not touch him.
2. When child is playing with toy, pull it away from him. Pass if he resists.
3. Child does not have to be able to tie shoes or button in the back.
4. Move yarn slowly in an arc from one side to the other, about 6" above child's face. Pass if eyes follow 90° to midline. (Past midline; 180°)
5. Pass if child grasps rattle when it is touched to the backs or tips of fingers.
6. Pass if child continues to look where yarn disappeared or tries to see where it went. Yarn should be dropped quickly from sight from tester's hand without arm movement.
7. Pass if child picks up raisin with any part of thumb and a finger.
8. Pass if child picks up raisin with the ends of thumb and index finger using an over hand approach.

9. Pass any enclosed form. Fail continuous round motions.
10. Which line is longer? (Not bigger.) Turn paper upside down and repeat. (3/3 or 5/6)
11. Pass any crossing lines.
12. Have child copy first. If failed, demonstrate

When giving items 9, 11 and 12, do not name the forms. Do not demonstrate 9 and 11.

13. When scoring, each pair (2 arms, 2 legs, etc.) counts as one part.
14. Point to picture and have child name it. (No credit is given for sounds only.)

15. Tell child to: Give block to Mommie; put block on table; put block on floor. Pass 2 of 3. (Do not help child by pointing, moving head or eyes.)
16. Ask child: What do you do when you are cold? ..hungry? ..tired? Pass 2 of 3.
17. Tell child to: Put block on table; under table; in front of chair, behind chair. Pass 3 of 4. (Do not help child by pointing, moving head or eyes.)
18. Ask child: If fire is hot, ice is ?; Mother is a woman, Dad is a ?; a horse is big, a mouse is ?. Pass 2 of 3.
19. Ask child: What is a ball? ..lake? ..desk? ..house? ..banana? ..curtain? ..ceiling? ..hedge? ..pavement? Pass if defined in terms of use, shape, what it is made of or general category (such as banana is fruit, not just yellow). Pass 6 of 9.
20. Ask child: What is a spoon made of? ..a shoe made of? ..a door made of? (No other objects may be substituted.) Pass 3 of 3.
21. When placed on stomach, child lifts chest off table with support of forearms and/or hands.
22. When child is on back, grasp his hands and pull him to sitting. Pass if head does not hang back.
23. Child may use wall or rail only, not crawl. May not crawl.
24. Child must throw ball overhand 3 feet to within arm's reach of tester.
25. Child must perform standing broad jump over width of test sheet. (8-1/2 inches)
26. Tell child to walk forward, ⟨⟩ heel within 1 inch of toe. Tester may demonstrate. Child must walk 4 consecutive steps, 2 out of 3 trials.
27. Bounce ball to child who should stand 3 feet away from tester. Child must catch ball with hands, not arms, 2 out of 3 trials.
28. Tell child to walk backward, ⟨⟩ toe within 1 inch of heel. Tester may demonstrate. Child must walk 4 consecutive steps, 2 out of 3 trials.

DATE AND BEHAVIORAL OBSERVATIONS (how child feels at time of test, relation to tester, attention span, verbal behavior, self-confidence, etc,):

RECOMMENDED DAILY DIETARY ALLOWANCES,[1] REVISED 1968

Designed for the Maintenance of Good Nutrition of Practically All Healthy Persons in the U.S.A.
(Allowances are intended for persons normally active in a temperate climate)
Food and Nutrition Board, National Academy of Sciences—National Research Council

Age[b]		Weight		Height		Kilocalories	Protein	Fat-Soluble Vitamins			Water-Soluble Vitamins							Minerals				
From-Up to								A activity	D	E activity	Ascorbic acid	Folacin	Niacin	Riboflavin	Thiamine	Vitamin B₆	Vitamin B₁₂	Calcium	Phosphorus	Iodine	Iron	Magnesium
years		kg (lb)		cm (in)		gm	gm	IU	IU	IU	mg	mg	mg equiv[e]	mg	mg	mg	mcg	gm	gm	μg	mg	mg
Infants																						
Birth–1/6		4	(9)	55	(22)	kg.×120[c]	kg.×2.2	1,500	400	5	35	0.05	5	0.4	0.2	0.2	1.0	0.4	0.2	25	6	40
1/6–1/2		7	(15)	63	(25)	kg.×110[c]	kg.×2.0	1,500	400	5	35	0.05	7	0.5	0.4	0.3	1.5	0.5	0.4	40	10	60
1/2–1		9	(20)	72	(28)	kg.×100[c]	kg.×1.8	1,500	400	5	35	0.1	8	0.6	0.5	0.4	2.0	0.6	0.5	45	15	70
Children																						
1 – 2		12	(26)	81	(32)	1,100	25	2,000	400	10	40	0.1	8	0.6	0.6	0.5	2.0	0.7	0.7	55	15	100
2 – 3		14	(31)	91	(36)	1,250	25	2,000	400	10	40	0.2	8	0.7	0.6	0.6	2.5	0.8	0.8	60	15	150
3 – 4		16	(35)	100	(39)	1,400	30	2,500	400	10	40	0.2	9	0.8	0.7	0.7	3	0.8	0.8	70	10	200
4 – 6		19	(42)	110	(43)	1,600	30	2,500	400	10	40	0.2	11	0.9	0.8	0.9	4	0.8	0.8	80	10	200
6 – 8		23	(51)	121	(48)	2,000	35	3,500	400	15	40	0.2	13	1.1	1.0	1.0	4	0.9	0.9	100	10	250
8 – 10		28	(62)	131	(52)	2,200	40	3,500	400	15	40	0.3	15	1.2	1.1	1.2	5	1.0	1.0	110	10	250
Males																						
10 – 12		35	(77)	140	(55)	2,500	45	4,500	400	20	40	0.4	17	1.3	1.3	1.4	5	1.2	1.2	125	10	300
12 – 14		43	(95)	151	(59)	2,700	50	5,000	400	20	45	0.4	18	1.4	1.4	1.6	5	1.4	1.4	135	18	350
14 – 18		59	(130)	170	(67)	3,000	60	5,000	400	25	55	0.4	20	1.5	1.5	1.8	5	1.4	1.4	150	18	400
18 – 22		67	(147)	175	(69)	2,800	60	5,000	400	30	60	0.4	18	1.6	1.4	2.0	5	0.8	0.8	140	10	400
22 – 35		70	(154)	175	(69)	2,800	65	5,000	—	30	60	0.4	18	1.7	1.4	2.0	5	0.8	0.8	140	10	350
35 – 55		70	(154)	173	(68)	2,600	65	5,000	—	30	60	0.4	17	1.7	1.3	2.0	5	0.8	0.8	125	10	350
55 – 75+		70	(154)	171	(67)	2,400	65	5,000	—	30	60	0.4	14	1.7	1.2	2.0	6	0.8	0.8	110	10	350
Females																						
10 – 12		35	(77)	142	(56)	2,250	50	4,500	400	20	40	0.4	15	1.3	1.1	1.4	5	1.2	1.2	110	18	300
12 – 14		44	(97)	154	(61)	2,300	50	5,000	400	20	45	0.4	15	1.4	1.2	1.6	5	1.3	1.3	115	18	350
14 – 16		52	(114)	157	(62)	2,400	55	5,000	400	25	50	0.4	16	1.4	1.2	1.8	5	1.3	1.3	120	18	350
16 – 18		54	(119)	160	(63)	2,300	55	5,000	400	25	50	0.4	15	1.5	1.2	2.0	5	1.3	1.3	115	18	350
18 – 22		58	(128)	163	(64)	2,000	55	5,000	400	25	55	0.4	13	1.5	1.0	2.0	5	0.8	0.8	100	18	350
22 – 35		58	(128)	163	(64)	2,000	55	5,000	—	25	55	0.4	13	1.5	1.0	2.0	5	0.8	0.8	100	18	300
35 – 55		58	(128)	160	(63)	1,850	55	5,000	—	25	55	0.4	13	1.5	1.0	2.0	5	0.8	0.8	90	18	300
55 – 75+		58	(128)	157	(62)	1,700	55	5,000	—	25	55	0.4	13	1.5	1.0	2.0	6	0.8	0.8	80	10	300
Pregnancy						+ 200	65	6,000	400	30	60	0.8	15	1.8	+0.1	2.5	8	+0.4	+0.4	125	18	450
Lactation						+1,000	75	8,000	400	30	60	0.5	20	2.0	+0.5	2.5	6	+0.5	+0.5	150	18	450

[a]The allowance levels are intended to cover individual variations among most normal persons as they live in the United States under usual environmental stresses. The recommended allowances can be attained with a variety of common foods providing other nutrients for which human requirements have been less well defined.

[b]Entries on lines for age range 22-35 years represent the reference man and woman at age 22. All other entries represent allowances for the midpoint of the specified age range.

[c]The folacin allowances refer to dietary sources as determined by *Lactobacillus casei* assay. Pure forms of folacin may be effective in doses less than 1/4 of the RDA.

[d]Niacin equivalents include dietary sources of the vitamin itself plus 1 mg equivalent for each 60 mg of dietary tryptophan.

[e]... not available to human milk. For proteins not 100% utilized, factors should be increased proportionately.

INDEX

Page numbers in *italic type* refer to illustrations and tables.

Abuse, physical, of infants and children, 103–104
Accident prone child, 126
Accidents
  in adulthood, 161
  in childhood, 124–126
  in infancy, 101–103
  in old age, 185–186
    prevention of, 180
Acute brain syndrome, 183
Adaptive behavior, changes in, in infancy, 92
Adipose tissue, growth and, 10
Adolescence, 139–153
  adjustment to adult sexual role in, 144
  alcohol abuse in, 152
  barbiturate and amphetamine abuse in, 152
  behavioral disorders of, 151–153
  blood pressure in, 143
  cardiovascular changes in, 143
  chronic diseases of, 148–150
  disorders common to, 147–153
  drug abuse in, 151–153
  emotional problems in, 151
  establishment of independence in, 145
  glue-sniffing in, 152
  growth spurt in, 139, *140*
  hallucinogenic drugs and, 153
  heart size in, 143
  infectious diseases in, 147–148
  marijuana and, 153
  morbidity and mortality during, 146, *146*
  obesity in, 148
  physical changes in, 139–142, *140–142*
    sequence of, 141, *141, 142*
  physiologic changes in, 142–143
  pulmonary function in, 143
  pulse rate in, 143
  school underachievement in, 150–151
  seizure disorders in, 149
  self-image in, 144

Adolescence (*Continued*)
  social and behavioral changes of, 143–146
  vocational or career choice in, 145
Adrenal gland, in pregnancy, 55
Adult progeria, 24
Adulthood, 154–167
  alcohol abuse in, 159, 161
  allergies in, 163
  anemias in, 161
  arthritic complaints in, 162
  behavioral disorders in, 160
  blood glucose changes in, 166, *167*
  bone density decrease in, 154, *155*
  cancer in, 163, *164*
  common problems of, 160–169
  coronary heart disease in, 164, *165*
  gallstones in, 161
  health maintenance in, preventive measures for, 157–160
  hypertension in, 166, *166,* 168
  immunology in, 163
  infection in, 162–163
  joint disease in, 162
  life situation of, 154–157, *155*
  middle, marriage stresses in, 156
  morbidity and mortality in, 168, *169*
  multifactorial disorders in, 164–168, *165–167*
  nutritional and metabolic disorders in, 160–161
  obesity in, 158, 160
  peptic ulcer in, 168
  personality changes during, 157
  physical aspects of, 154, *155*
  physiologic aspects of, 154–156
  serum cholesterol concentration in, 166, *167*
  sexual expression in, changes in, 157
  smoking in, hazards of, 159
  social and behavioral components of, 156–157

Adulthood (*Continued*)
 trauma in, 161–162
 weight changes in, 154, *155*
Age
 biologic, 1
  estimation of, skeletal tissues in, 6, *8*
 "bone," 6, *8*
 height, 7
 maternal and paternal, as factors in
  reproduction, 27, *30*
 old, 171–190. See also *Old age.*
"Age pigment," 21
Aging
 alteration of, experiment and disease,
  23–24
 as autoimmune process, 22
 biology of, 17–25
 general factors affecting, 22–23
 hormonal imbalance theory of, 22
 molecular, 22
 "normal," 171
 organ and organ system, 20–21, *20*
 physiologic, 20, *20*
 process of, 17–25
 subcellular, 22
 tissue and cellular, 21–22
Alcohol abuse
 in adolescence, 152
 in adulthood, 159, 161
 in old age, 183
 maternal, as factor in reproduction, 28
Allergies
 in adulthood, 163
 in childhood, 129
Amniotic cavity, fetus and, 45
Amniotic fluid, meconium staining of, 78
Amphetamine abuse, 152
Amyloid, cellular aging and, 21
Anemia(s)
 in adulthood, 161
 in infancy, iron deficiency, 101
  physiologic, 76
Apgar score, 80, *80*
Appendicitis, in pregnancy, 53, *55*
Articular complaints, in adulthood, 162
Asphyxia, fetal, 77–81
Astigmatism, 117
Atherosclerosis, 187
Autism, 134
Autoimmune disorders, in old age, 186

Bacterial pneumonitis, in old age, 185
Barbiturate abuse, 152
Battered child syndrome, 103–104
Behavior
 adaptive, changes in, in infancy, 92
 changes of, in adolescence, 143–146
 development of, in infancy, 90–94

Behavior (*Continued*)
 disorders of, in adolescence, 151–153
  in adulthood, 160
  in childhood, 134–137
  in infancy, 99–100
  in old age, 182–184
 patterns of, in old age, 178
Behavioral components, fetal, 45
Bilirubinemia, perinatal, 76
Biologic age, 1
 estimation of, skeletal tissues in, 6, *8*
Birth control, means of, 26, *28*
Birth weight, low, vs. prematurity, 81
Blindness, in old age, 187
Blood glucose, age-related changes in,
 166, *167*
Blood pressure, in adolescence, 143
Blood tests, in childhood, 123
Body proportions, in childhood, 113
Bone, aging changes in, 177
"Bone age," 6, *8*
Bone density, adult decrease in, 154, *155*
Brain, growth of, 9, *9, 10*
Brain syndrome, acute vs. chronic, 184
Brain tumors, in childhood, 128
Braxton-Hicks contractions, 60
Breasts, in pregnancy, 53, *56*

Cancer. See also *Malignancies.*
 in middle years, 163, *164*
 in old age, 186, *186*
Cardiovascular changes
 in adolescence, 143
 in pregnancy, 58, *58*
Catch up growth, 15–16
Cellular aging, 21–22
Central nervous system
 in childhood, 116
 in infancy, 89
Cerebral palsy, 133
Cerebrovascular disease, 187
Chadwick's sign, 59
Chemical agents, fetal problems caused
 by, 48, *49*
Child abuse, 103–104
Childhood, 105–137, *105–112*
 accident proneness in, 126
 accidents in, 124–126
 allergies in, 129
 behavior problems in, 134–137
 blood tests in, 123
 body proportions in, 113
 central nervous system in, 116
 cerebral palsy in, 133
 chronic illness in, 134
 circulation in, 116
 common problems in, 124–137
 congenital malformations and, 133
 dental and physical examinations in, 123

Childhood (*Continued*)
  developmental assessment in, 123
  diabetes in, 130
  disobedience in, 135
  emotional development in, behavioral
    view of, 120–121
    social psychological view of, 120
    traditional view of, 119–120
  endocrine system in, 116
  epilepsy in, 133
  face in, 114
  gastrointestinal tract in, 115
  handicapping conditions in, 130–134,
    131
  hearing handicap in, 132
  height and weight measurements in, 122
  hyperactivity in, 136
  immunizations in, 121
  immunologic system in, 115
  infections in, 126–128, *127*
    epidemiologic aspects of, 126
  language development in, 118
  life situation in, 113–125
  lower extremities in, 114
  malignancies in, 128–129
  malnutrition in, 130
  measurements in, percentile charts for,
    192–195
  mental retardation in, 132
  mortality and morbidity during, 124,
    125
  nutritional and metabolic disorders in,
    130
  obesity in, 130
  otitis media in, 127, *127*
  peer adjustment in, 136
  physical development in, 113–115, *113*
  physiologic development in, 115–117,
    117, 118
  posture in, 114
  preventive health measures in, 121–124
  psychosis in, 133
  psychosocial development in, 118–121
    normative data for, 118–119
  reading problems in, 135
  reproductive system in, 116
  respiration in, 116
  screening health procedures for, 122
  sensory organs in, 116, *117, 118*
  sexual development and sex education
    in, 136
  streptococcal infections in, 128
  tuberculosis screening in, 122
  urinary tract in, 115
  urine analysis in, 123
  visual handicap in, 132
Chloasma, in pregnancy, 55
Cholesterol, serum concentration of, age
  and, 166, *167*
Chromosomal abnormalities, 50, *51*
Chronic brain syndrome, 183–184

Cigarette smoking
  hazards of, 159
  maternal, as factor in reproduction, 28
Circulation
  fetal, 42
    late, 70, *71*
  in childhood, 116
Colic, infantile, 99
Colon, diverticula of, in old age, 187
Congenital malformations, 50, 133
Connective tissue, aging changes in, 21
Coronary heart disease, 164, *165*
Counselling, genetic, inheritable disorders
  and, 30
Crying, excessive, in infancy, 99

Death, 188–190. See also *Mortality.*
  aging and, 17
  in old age, common causes of, 188, *189*
Deciduous dentition, *198*
Delivery
  fetal presentation at, 66, *67, 68*
  labor and, 62–69
Dental examinations, in childhood, 123
Dentition
  deciduous, *198*
  development of, 10
  in infancy, 87
  mixed, *199*
  permanent, *199*
Denver Developmental Screening Test,
  200–201
Depression, in old age, 183
Development
  growth and, 4–13
    critical periods in, 2, *3*
  sex differences in, 11
Developmental Screening Test, Denver,
  200–201
Diabetes
  in childhood, 130
  in old age, 184
Diabetogenic effect of pregnancy, 57
Diarrhea, in infancy, 100
Diet
  in old age, 180–181
  in pregnancy, 52
Dietary allowances, recommended, daily,
  202
Digestive tract
  in childhood, 115
  in pregnancy, 52
Disease. See names of specific diseases.
Disobedience, childhood, 135
Diverticula, colonic, in old age, 187
Down's syndrome, maternal age and, 27,
  30
Dreikurs, Rudolf, emotional development
  theories of, 120

Drugs
abuse of, 151–153
maternal, as factor in reproduction, 28
fetal problems caused by, 48, *49*
overdose of, in old age, 184
Dying, 188–190

Ear. See also *Hearing.*
middle, infection of, in childhood, 127,
127
Elderly, 171–190. See also *Old age.*
Emmetropia, 116, *117*
Emotional changes, in pregnancy, 51–52
Emotional problems
in adolescence, 151
in childhood, 134–137
in middle life, 160
in old age, 182–184
Endocrine system
changes in, in pregnancy, 55
growth and, 11, *12*
in childhood, 116
Epilepsy
in adolescence, 149
in childhood, 133
Erikson, Erik, emotional development
theories of, 119
Erythroblastosis fetalis, 49
Exercise, in old age, 179–180
Extremities, lower, in childhood, 114
Eyes. See also *Visual.*
in childhood, 116, *117, 118*
in old age, 187

Face, in childhood, 114
skull and, growth sites in, *197*
Familial small stature, vs. familial slow
maturation, features of, 13, *13*
Fetus, 32–51
amniotic cavity and, 45
asphyxia of, 77–81
behavioral components of, 45
circulation of, 42
late, 70, *71*
development of, 33, *33–44*
electronic monitoring of, for detection
of asphyxia, 77, *79*
growth of, 33–45, *34–43*
maternal size and, 4, *4, 5*
hemostasis of, 43
immune system of, 43
intestine of, 45
life situation of, 33–45
physical, 33, *33–44*
physiologic, 33, 38–45
lung development in, 72
mortality and morbidity of, 46

Fetus (*Continued*)
physiology of, general, 33
placenta and, 38
presentation of, at delivery, 66, *67, 68*
problems of, 46–51
chemical and drug, 48, *49*
chromosomal abnormality, 50, *51*
immunologic, 49
infectious, 46, *48*
malformational, 50
maternal disease causing, 46, *47*, 50
maternal malnutrition causing, 48
placental, 46
sociologic situations relating to, 46, *47*,
50
twinning and, 49
renal system of, 44

Gallbladder, in pregnancy, 53
Gallstones
in middle life, 161
in old age, 184
Gastrointestinal tract
in childhood, 115
in pregnancy, 52
Genetic counselling, inheritable disorders
and, 30
Gerontology, 17–25
Glucose, in blood, age-related changes
in, 166, *167*
Glucosuria, physiologic, in pregnancy, 58
Glue-sniffing, 152
Gonadotrophin values, 11, *12*
Gonorrhea, 148
Growth, 1–16
adipose tissue and, 10
basics of, 1–3
catch up, 15–16
dental, 10
development and, 4–13
critical periods in, 2, *3*
endocrine glands and, 11, *12*
factors in, 13–15, *13, 14*
fetal, 33–45, *34–43, 191*
maternal size and, 4, *4, 5*
in childhood, physical, 113–115, *113*
physiologic, 115–117, *117, 118*
psychosocial, 118–121
in infancy, 4
behavioral, 90–94, *91*
physical, 86–87
physiologic, 87–89
social, 94–96, *95*
linear, rate of, 6, *7*
lymphoid tissue and, 10
maxillary and mandibular sites of, *197*
muscular, 11
of brain, 9, *9, 10*
parental size and, 5, *6*

Growth (*Continued*)
  prenatal deficiency in, vs. prematurity,
    46
  secondary deficiency of, humoral factors
    and, 14, *14*
  secular changes in, 12
  sex differences in, 11
  skeletal, 5, 7, *8*
    manner of, 7, 8
Growth hormone, pituitary, maturation
  and, 15

Haemophilus influenzae infections, in
  infancy, 100
Hallucinogenic drugs, 153
Handicapping conditions, in childhood,
  130–134, *131*
Hands, use of, in infancy, 90, *92*
Head
  circumference of, *196*
    in assessment of brain size, 9, *10*
  growth of, in infancy, 87
Hearing
  in childhood, 117
    handicap of, 132
    screening for, 122
  in old age, 187
Heart, size of, in adolescence, 143
Heart disease, coronary, 164, *165*
Hegar's sign, 59
Height, weight and, measurements of, in
  childhood, 122
Height age, 7
Hematologic adaptation, perinatal, 76
Hemoglobin, perinatal, 76
Hemostasis, fetal, 43
Hepatic detoxification, perinatal, 75–76
Hormonal imbalance theory of aging, 22
Hormones, growth deficiency and, 15
Hyaline membrane disease, 82–83, *82*
Hyperactivity, in childhood, 136
Hyperemesis gravidarum, 52
Hyperopia, 116, *117*
Hypertension, 166, *166*, 168

Immune system
  fetal, 43
  in adulthood, 163
  in childhood, 115
  in infancy, 87
Immunizations
  in childhood, 121
  in infancy, 97
Immunologic problems
  fetal, 49
  in infancy, 100–101
  in old age, 186

Infancy, 85–104
  accidents in, 101–103
  behavioral changes in, 90–94, *91*
  behavioral disorders in, 99–100
  common disorders of, 99–104
  diarrhea in, 100
  growth rate in, 4
  immunizations in, 97
  infectious and immunologic disorders in,
    100–101
  iron deficiency anemia in, 101
  language development in, 93
  life situation in, 85–96
  measurements in, percentile charts for,
    192, 194
  mortality in, causes of, 27, *29*
    drop in, in twentieth century, 26, *27*
  motor development in, 90, *91*
  neoplasia of, 101
  nervous system in, 88
    central, 89
  nutrition in, planning of, 97
  nutritional disorders in, 101
  otitis media in, 101
  physical abuse in, 103–104
  physical changes in, 86–87
  physiologic changes in, 87–89
  social development in, 94–96, *95*
  tuberculosis in, 101
  wellness care in, 96–99
Infantile colic, 99
Infections
  fetal, 46, *48*
  in adolescence, 147–148
  in adulthood, 162–163
  in childhood, 126–128, *127*
    epidemiologic aspects of, 126
    middle ear, 127, *127*
    streptococcal, 128
  in infancy, 100–101
  in old age, 185–186
  maternal, as factor in reproduction, 29
  perinatal, 74
Infectious mononucleosis, 147
Inheritable disorders, genetic counselling
  and, 30
Intestine, fetal, 45
Intrauterine growth, *191*
Iron deficiency anemia, in infancy, 101

Jaundice, physiologic, of newborn, 76
Joint disease, in middle years, 162
Juvenile obesity, 148

Kernicterus, 76
Kidney(s). See also *Renal.*
  in infancy, 87

Kidney(s) (*Continued*)
  in newborn, 74–75, *75*
  in pregnancy, 57, *58*
  Wilms' tumor of, 101

Labor
  delivery and, 62–69
  duration of, 68, *69*
  stages of, 65, *66*
Language, development of, in childhood,
  118
  in infancy, 93
Legs, in childhood, 114
Length, in infancy, 86
Leukemia, in childhood, 128
Life
  first two years of, 85–104. See also
    Infancy.
  middle years of, 154–167. See also
    Adulthood.
  new, preparation for, 26–31. See also
    Reproduction.
  perinatal, 62–83. See also *Perinate.*
  prenatal, 32–51. See also *Fetus.*
Linea nigra, 53, *57*
Linear growth, rate of, 6, *7*
Lipofuscin, cellular aging and, 21
Lordosis of spine, progressive, in
  pregnancy, 52, *53*
Lung, fetal development and perinatal
  adaptation of, 72
Lymphoid tissue, growth and, 10

Malformations, congenital, 50, 133
Malignancies. See also *Cancer.*
  in childhood, 128–129
Malnutrition
  growth deficiency and, 14
  in childhood, 130
  maternal, fetal problems caused by, 48
Mandibular growth sites, *197*
Marijuana, 153
Marriage, stresses on, in middle life, 156
Maternal age, as factor in reproduction, 27,
  30
Maternal alcoholism, as factor in reproduction, 28
Maternal cigarette smoking, as factor
  in reproduction, 28
Maternal drugs
  as factor in reproduction, 28
  fetal problems caused by, 48, *49*
Maternal infectious disease, as factor in
  reproduction, 29
Maternal malnutrition, fetal problems
  caused by, 48

Maternal metabolic or disease problems,
  potential fetal problems from, 46, *47*, 50
Maternal noninfectious diseases or disorders, as factor in reproduction, 29
Maternal nutrition, as factor in repro-
  duction, 27
Maternal size, fetal growth and, 4, *4, 5*
Maturation
  secular changes in, 12
  slow, familial, vs. familial small stature,
    features of, 13, *13*
Maxillary growth sites, *197*
Meconium staining of amniotic fluid, 78
Mental retardation, 132
Metabolic disorders
  in adulthood, 160–161
  in childhood, 130
  in old age, 184–185
  maternal, potential fetal problems
    from, 46, *47*
Middle ear infection, in childhood, 127,
  127
Middle years, 154–169. See also *Adulthood.*
Mitotic rate, growth and, 1, *2*
Molecular aging, 22
Mongolism, maternal age and, 27, *30*
Mononucleosis, infectious, 147
Morbidity
  fetal, 46
  in adolescence, 146
  in adulthood, 168, *169*
  in childhood, 124, *125*
  in old age, common causes of, 187–188
Mortality. See also *Death.*
  fetal, 46
  in adolescence, 146, *146*
  in adulthood, 168, *169*
  in childhood, 124, *125*
  in infancy, causes of, 27, *29*
    drop in, in twentieth century, 26, *27*
Mortality curves, aging and, 17, *18, 19*
Motor development, in infancy, 90, *91*
Muscle
  aging changes in, 177
  development of, 11
Myopia, 116, *117*

Nausea, in pregnancy, 52
Neoplasia
  in infancy, 101
  in old age, *178,* 186
Nervous system
  aging changes in, 177
  central, in childhood, 116
    in infancy, 89
  in infancy, 88
  perinatal, 77
Neuroblastoma, in infancy, 101
Neurologic adaptation, perinatal, 77

Noninfectious diseases, maternal, as factor in reproduction, 29
Nutrition
  disorders of, in adulthood, 160–161
    in childhood, 130
    in infancy, 101
    in old age, 184–185
  growth deficiency and, 14
  in infancy, planning of, 97
  maternal, as factor in reproduction, 27
    fetal problems and, 48
Nutritional adaptation, perinatal, 73

Obesity
  in adolescence, 148
  in childhood, 130
  in middle age, 158, 160
Old age, 171–190
  accident prevention in, 180
  accidents in, 185–186
  acute brain syndrome in, 183
  alcoholism in, 183
  atherosclerosis in, 187
  autoimmune disorders in, 186
  bacterial pneumonitis in, 185
  blindness in, 187
  bone changes in, 177
  "chain reaction" catastrophes in, 171
    prevention of, 181
  chronic disease in, prevalence of, 171, 172
  chronic obstructive pulmonary disease in, 188
  common problems of, 182–188
  deafness in, 187
  death in, 188–190
    common causes of, 188, 189
  degenerative and structural disorders in, 187
  depression in, 183
  diabetes mellitus in, 184
  diet in, 180–181
  diverticula of colon in, 187
  drug overdose in, 184
  exercise in, 179–180
  family and interpersonal relationships in, 178
  gallstones in, 184
  health maintenance in, preventive measures for, 179–182
  homeostatic balance in, 171
  immunologic disorders in, 186
  infectious disorders in, 185–186
  life situation in, 171–179
  maintenance of function in, 181–182
  metabolic and nutritional disorders in, 184–185
  morbidity in, common causes of, 187–188

Old age (Continued)
  multifactorial disorders in, 187
  muscle changes in, 177
  neoplastic disorders in, 178, 186
  nervous system changes in, 177
  osteoporosis in, 187
  physical aspects of, 171–172, 171, 172
  physiologic aspects of, 172–178
    vs. medical changes of disease, 172, 173
  posture in, 178
  schizophrenic disorders in, 183
  sexual behavior in, 179
  social and behavioral components of, 178
  socioeconomic factors in, 179
  suicide in, 185
  trauma in, 185
  tuberculosis in, 185–186
Organs and organ systems, aging process in, 20–21, 20
Osteoarthritis, 158
Osteoporosis, in old age, 187
Otitis media
  in childhood, 127, 127
  in infancy, 101

Palsy, cerebral, 133
Parental size, growth and, 5, 6
Paternal age, as factor in reproduction, 27
Peer adjustment, in childhood, 136
Peptic ulcer, 168
Perinatal life, for mother and baby, 62–83
Perinate, 70–83
  Apgar evaluation of, 80, 80
  cardiopulmonary adaptation of, 70–72, 71
  common problems of, 77–83
  hematologic adaptation of, 76
  hepatic detoxification in, 75–76
  infectious disease and, 74
  neurologic adaptation of, 77
  nutritional adaptation of, 73
  renal adaptation of, 74–75, 75
  temperature regulation in, 73–74
Physiologic aging, 20, 20
Pica, pregnancy and, 52
Pigment, "age," 21
Pituitary growth hormone, maturation and, 15
Placenta
  disorders of, fetal problems from, 46
  fetal growth and, 4
  fetus and, 38
Pneumonitis, bacterial, in old age, 185
Postmaturity syndrome, 32
Posture
  in childhood, 114
  in old age, 178

Pregnancy
  emotional changes in, 51–52
  life situation and common disorders of, 51–61
  physiologic changes in, 52–59
Pregnant uterus, 59–61, *59–61*
Prematurity, 81–82, *81*
  vs. prenatal growth deficiency, 46
Prenatal growth deficiency, vs. prematurity, 46
Prenatal life, 32–51. See also *Fetus.*
Presentation, fetal, 66, *67*
Preventive health measures
  in childhood, 121–124
  in infancy, 96–99
  in old age, 179–182
Progeria, adult, 24
Pseudostrabismus, *105*, 114
Psychogenic underachievement, adolescent, 151
Psychosis, childhood, 133
Psychosocial development, in childhood, 118–121
Puberty, 139. See also *Adolescence.*
  social and behavioral changes of, 143–146
Pulmonary changes, in pregnancy, 59
Pulmonary disease, chronic obstructive, in old age, 188
Pulmonary function, in adolescence, 143
Pulse rate, in adolescence, 143

Reading problems, childhood, 135
Renal. See also *Kidney(s).*
Renal adaptation, perinatal, 74–75, *75*
Renal functional changes, in pregnancy, 57, *58*
Renal pelvis, dilation of, in pregnancy, 52, *54*
Renal system, fetal, 44
Reproduction
  control of, means of, 26, *28*
  preparation for, 26–31
    factors in, 27–30
    practical measures in, 31
Reproductive system, in childhood, 116
Respiration, in childhood, 116
Respiratory changes, in pregnancy, 59
Respiratory distress syndrome, idiopathic, 82–83, *82*
Retardation, mental, 132
Rh factor, fetal problems and, 49
Rh incompatibility, as factor in reproduction, 29
Rubella, fetal disease from, 47

Schizophrenia
  in childhood, 134
  in old age, 183

School underachievement, 150–151
Secular changes in growth and maturation, 12
Seizure disorders
  in adolescence, 149
  in childhood, 133
Senescence, 17
Sensory organs, in childhood, 116, *117*, *118*
Serum cholesterol concentration, age and, 166, *167*
Sex differences in growth and development, 11
Sex education, 136
Sex hormone values, 11, *12*
Sexual behavior, in old age, 179
Sexual development, in childhood, 136
Sexual role, adjustment to, in adolescence, 144
Size
  maternal, fetal growth and, 4, *4*, *5*
  parental, growth and, 5, *6*
Skeleton, growth of, 5, *7*, *8*
  manner of, 7, 8
Skinner, B. F., emotional development theories of, 120
Skull, face and, growth sites in, *197*
Sleep, wakefulness and, in infancy, 88
Small stature, familial, vs. familial slow maturation, features of, 13, *13*
Smoking
  hazards of, 159
  maternal, as factor in reproduction, 28
Social changes, in adolescence, 143–146
Sociologic situations, fetal problems relating to, 46, *47*, 50
Spine, lordosis of, progressive, in pregnancy, 52, *53*
Streptococcal infections, in childhood, 128
Striae gravidarum, 53, *56*
Stroke, 187
Subcellular aging, 22
Suicide, in old age, 185–186
Symbiosis, 134
Syndrome. See names of specific syndromes.
Syphilis, 148

Teeth
  deciduous, *198*
  growth of, 10
  in infancy, 87
  permanent, *199*
Temperature regulation, perinatal, 73–74
Thyroid gland
  in pregnancy, 55
  maturation and, 15
Tissue aging, 21–22

Trauma. See *Accidents.*
Tuberculin tests, in childhood, 122
Tuberculosis
    in childhood, screening for, 122
    in infancy, 101
    in old age, 185–186
Twinning, fetal problems caused by, 49

Ulcer, peptic, 168
Underachievement, school, 150–151
Ureter, dilation of, in pregnancy, 52, *54*
Urinary tract, in childhood, 115
Urine analysis, in childhood, 123
Uterine contractions, 62, *63*
    types of, 64, *64*
Uterine muscle, physiology of, 62
Uteroplacental insufficiency, 78, *79*
Uterus, pregnant, 59–61, *59–61*

Venereal disease, 147, 148
Vision screening, in childhood, 122
Visual. See also *Eyes.*
Visual acuity, 117, *118*
Visual handicap in childhood, 132
Volatile substances, sniffing of, 152
Vomiting, in pregnancy, 52

Wakefulness, sleep and, in infancy, 88
Weight
    changes in, in adulthood, 154, *155*
    gain in, in pregnancy, 48, 52, *54*
    height and, measurements of, in child-
        hood, 122
    in infancy, 86
    low, at birth, vs. prematurity, 81
Wellness care, of infants, 96–99
Werner's syndrome, 24
Wilms' tumor, 101

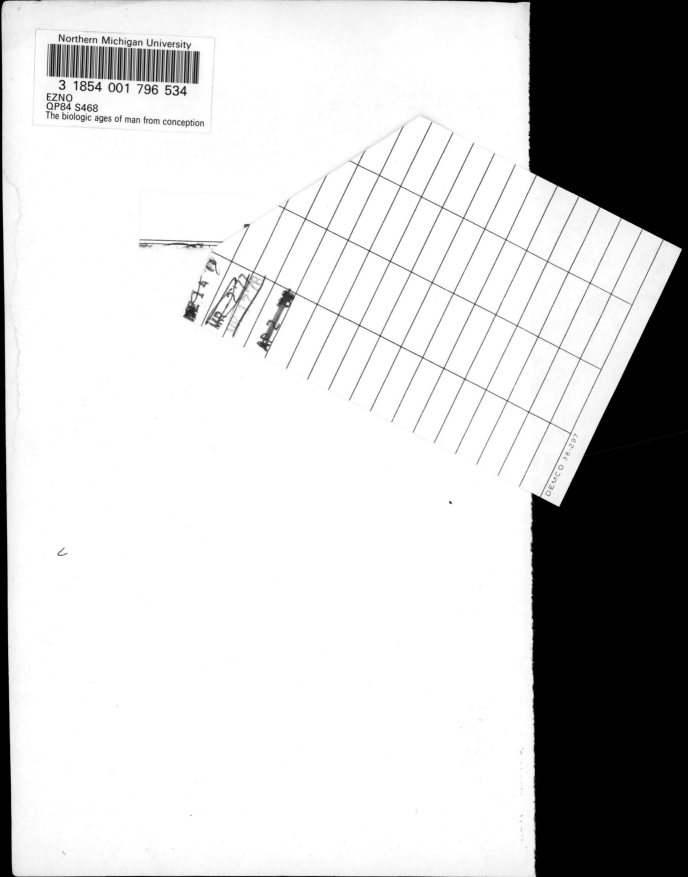